DECISION MAKING IN THE U.S. COURTS OF APPEALS

D1523231

FRANK B. CROSS

Decision Making in the U.S. Courts of Appeals

STANFORD UNIVERSITY PRESS

STANFORD, CALIFORNIA 2007

Stanford University Press
Stanford, California

Printed in the United States of America on
acid-free, archival-quality paper

Library of Congress Cataloging-in-Publication
Data

Cross, Frank B.
    Decision making in the U.S. Courts of Appeals /
Frank B. Cross.
        p.   cm.
    Includes bibliographical references and index.
    ISBN 978-0-8047-5366-1 (cloth : alk. paper) —
ISBN 978-0-8047-5713-3 (pbk. : alk. paper)
    1. Judicial process—United States.   2. Appellate
courts—United States.   3. United States. Supreme
Court.   I. Title.
KF8990.C76 2007
347.73'24—dc22   2006010258

Typeset by Newgen in 10/14 Janson

Contents

DECISION MAKING IN THE U.S. COURTS OF APPEALS

Prologue

This book deals with the decisions rendered by the United States circuit courts of appeals and with the opinions from those decisions. These courts are intermediate, between the trial courts and the Supreme Court, and they resolve appeals from the legal rulings of the trial courts as well as from some administrative agencies. The United States has twelve basic circuits of broad appellate jurisdiction, divided geographically (e.g., the first circuit governs Massachusetts, Maine, New Hampshire, Puerto Rico, and Rhode Island), plus the relatively new federal circuit, which has limited subject matter jurisdiction. When a party appeals a lower court decision, that decision is typically assigned to a panel of three circuit court judges, who will affirm or reverse it. Although cases are sometimes heard en banc, before all the judges of the circuit, this is rare. The overwhelming majority of decisions are rendered by three-judge panels.

While most public reportage and even scholarly research deals with the U.S. Supreme Court, the circuit courts are much more important in setting and enforcing the law of the United States. The Supreme Court now decides only seventy-five cases a year and cannot address, much less resolve, most legal questions facing the nation. By contrast, the circuit courts resolve more than fifty thousand cases a year. Each of those decisions is binding precedent within the geographic bounds of the circuit and typically influences the application of the law even outside those bounds. When the circuit courts agree, they essentially establish the law for the entire nation. When the circuits disagree, they create a circuit split, under which the law is unsettled and geographically variant. In either situation, the circuit courts set the legal ground rules for citizens. They are the court of last resort for most litigants. Fewer than 15% of circuit court decisions are even appealed to the Supreme Court and fewer than 2% of those appeals are taken by the high court.

Thus, in large measure, it is the circuit courts that create U.S. law. They represent the true iceberg, of which the Supreme Court is but the most visible tip. The circuit courts play by far the greatest legal policymaking role in the United States judicial system. The district courts, as trial courts, hear far more disputes than do the circuit courts but district court decisions are heavily fact based and jurisdictionally limited in effect, and they do not set the significant legal precedents that make up the law. By contrast, circuit court decisions are almost always about defining the law, and they set binding precedents for the multistate area that the circuit covers. These decisions are also commonly used as persuasive precedent by courts in states outside the circuit's jurisdiction and even by the Supreme Court. Although an individual Supreme Court decision is more important than a corresponding individual circuit court decision, the very limited docket of the Supreme Court leaves U.S. law largely to the judgment of the circuits.

Despite the great importance of the circuit courts, they have been studied relatively little. Both law school researchers and political scientists have expended far more time and effort on the Supreme Court than on all the circuit courts combined. Although several valuable analyses of circuit courts have been written, no one has studied the topic in anywhere near the detail with which researchers have studied the Supreme Court. This book is a small step toward righting this balance.

Data

In analyzing the decision making of circuit courts, I draw heavily on large, publicly available data sets. This book is grounded centrally in two extremely valuable databases. The first is the United States Courts of Appeals Database (hereafter, the courts of appeals database), produced by Donald Songer of the University of South Carolina under a National Science Foundation (NSF) grant. The second is a database of judicial backgrounds, the Database on the Attributes of United States Appeals Courts Judges (hereafter, the judicial attributes database), prepared by Gary Zuk, Deborah J. Barrow, and Gerard S. Gryski under a separate NSF grant. The two are easily integrated to enable testing of the effects of judicial attributes on decisions. I have supplemented these databases with data from other sources. I am grateful to Micheal Giles of Emory University for providing me more sophisticated coding on judicial ideology and to Barak Richman of Duke Law School for providing me with data on the ideological balance of Congress over time. After combining these sources, I have introduced more data. In some instances I have transformed existing variables through calculations to create new variables that allow the testing of new hypotheses. In other instances I have accumulated additional data for many decisions in the database, such as their subsequent use as precedent.

The courts of appeals database is very large, taking at least fifteen cases per circuit beginning in 1925 and running through 1992, with more than eighteen thousand cases total. The data are organized in two ways: by the vote of each judge and by the decision of the full panel. I use both throughout the book. For each case, the database codes for numerous variables. These include the ideological direction of the decisional outcome (whether liberal or conservative), whether the decision was a reversal or affirmance of the decision below, the type of case being decided (e.g., criminal, civil rights, economic regulation, and so on), the nature of the parties to the action, and some of the legal issues presented in the case. I use many of these variables in this book, as I explain in each of my analyses.

The judicial attributes database provides considerable information about the individual circuit court judges. This information includes factors such as race, gender, religion, the identity of the appointing president, and occupational background before elevation to the circuit court bench. These data enable empirical testing of the effect of these variables on the detailed decisional variables of the courts of appeals database.

The available data inevitably have some limitations, though the courts of appeals database is currently the gold standard for circuit court research. The courts of appeals database provides coding for only the published opinions of the circuit courts and does not cover unpublished opinions (which outnumber those that are officially published). There is dispute over the representativeness of published opinions, and some have found that unpublished decisions tend to be more complex and less legally clear[1] or of lesser practical significance.[2] Whether or not the published decisions are perfectly representative of the full corpus of circuit court decisions, these published opinions are the most crucial ones. Published opinions set the primary judicial precedents that make up U.S. law. The reader should bear in mind, however, that all the studies in this book contain the same caveat; they analyze published circuit court decisions and do not explicitly consider the unpublished opinions.

This book is data rich, containing scores of analyses of circuit court decisions and opinions. My approach is not methodologically complex, and I use standard techniques of basic statistics and regressions. I have sought to present and explain the results of the analyses in a manner accessible to a broad readership, including those without statistical training. I commonly refer to statistical significance, for which I use a .05 standard. This standard means that there is less than a 1 in 20 probability that the association between the variables measured is one of chance. Given the many analyses reported, though, this means that at least a few of them may be ascribed to chance. Consequently, conclusions may be confidently made only when they are supported by multiple analyses, as is the case for my central variables. In addition, the reader should not place undue importance on a finding of statistical significance, because such a finding shows a correlation between variables but by itself does not prove the substantive significance of that correlation. One must also consider the magnitude of the association.

The courts of appeals database is vast and encompasses thousands of cases and individual judge votes. This vastness has some implications for an appreciation of the reported results. With such a large-N database, statistically significant associations are likely to be discerned, even when those associations are very small.[3] Hence, a report of statistical significance, while meaning-ful, may not have great practical significance. Consequently, to understand the true importance of the association in circuit court decision making, the reader of the regressions should attend to the size of the reported coefficient and the R^2 term, which measures the extent of variance explained by the full model, including the role of all the independent variables.

The reader will notice that many of the R^2 terms are relatively small, generally at 0.10 and well below.[4] These small R^2 terms mean that the vari-ables isolated in the particular equations do not appear to explain a high percentage of circuit court decisions. The small R^2 terms are also to some degree a feature of the immense courts of appeals database. Although the database codes for a very large number of discrete variables, it is practically impossible to code highly detailed facts for each of the thousands of cases. It is also not possible to code for the nature of the substantive law analyzed in each case, which potentially limits the explanatory power of any models.

In addition, some relevant factors cannot be objectively measured. For example, the database can characterize outcomes as liberal or conservative but cannot estimate *how* liberal or *how* conservative that decision was. It can-not segregate moderately liberal from extremely liberal results. The coding is also contingent on the facts of the case. For example, a court may reach an outcome classified as liberal only because the alternative position was an extremely conservative one that even conservative judges found unaccept-able. This inevitably creates some inaccuracies in the specification of the variables, a problem discussed in individual chapters. These specification errors typically cause an underestimation of a true relationship. Hence, the association and related R^2 terms might generally be considered an underes-timate or floor of the true relationship between the variables assessed. The reader should also appreciate that a small R^2 term may be of considerable practical significance. The courts of appeals database includes all types of cases, ranging from the mundane to the very important. If a variable ex-plains only 10%, or even 1%, of the outcomes, that small subset of cases can have extremely significant real-world effects. Even small effect sizes can be significant.[5] As we have seen with the Supreme Court ruling in *Bush v. Gore*, one single opinion can have huge consequences in the real world.

The courts of appeals database, combined with the judicial attributes database and other sources of data, provides the essential foundation for all the analyses of this book. I have supplemented the courts of appeals database in several ways for these studies. In some instances I calculated new variables based on the variables already in the database. For example, I calculated a variable for the ideological direction of the decision being reviewed by the circuit court. In other instances I added new variables based on other sources. For example, each judge in the courts of appeals database was assigned an ideological position, the Supreme Court justices were assigned ideological positions, and various congressional representatives were given ideological positions at different times. These ideological scales were not always consistent in direction. To make the scales and reported results easier to understand, I converted them so that higher numbers always mean more liberal and lower numbers (in some instances negative numbers) mean more conservative. Thus, a negative sign for the coefficient on all regressions means a conservative association, whereas a positive association means a liberal association.

The Study of Judicial Decision Making

Researchers have developed a number of theories of circuit court decision making that are evaluated throughout the book. These include theories of ideological decision making, strategic decision making, litigant selection effects, and others. Most of these theories have already been subjected to empirical testing, usually on smaller databases focused on a shorter period of time and a particular class of cases, with the data often developed by the authors. In each chapter I begin with a summary of the rationale underlying the theories of judicial decision making and briefly summarize the existing research on their effect.

Very few of these theories have been fully tested with the broad courts of appeals database. This book provides the first test of many of these theories using this rigorously coded and expansive database. Using quantitative empirical methods to analyze judicial decisions has some inherent limitations because it is simply impossible to control for all the relevant factors underlying a decision. Nonetheless, such analyses provide important information and are valuable as rigorous tests of theories that otherwise rely on anecdotal evidence or simple assumptions. The book tells something of a story, in which I first measure the conventional variables used to predict judicial decisions and then elaborate those analyses by adding other variables or refining the set of cases analyzed.

The book begins by considering ideological, or political, theories of circuit court decision making. This approach is the convention for empirical research on judicial decisions; most of these studies have been conducted by political scientists oriented toward finding political explanations. A considerable body of existing research demonstrates the significance of these ideological determinants, though only a small portion of this research has analyzed the circuit courts. Chapter 1 confirms the previous studies in finding that ideology has a statistically significant effect on decisions. Judges appointed by more conservative presidents consistently produce more conservative decisions on the bench. I find that this effect varies considerably over time and by the type of case under review. Chapter 1 also begins the exploration of the nature of the ideological role, considering the effect of relatively extreme ideologies on judicial decisions.

Chapter 2 introduces the role of the law in appellate decision making. This topic has lacked sufficient attention in the existing research, probably because of the difficulty of capturing a legal variable for a quantitative analysis. I have used legal procedural requirements as a way to test the impact of the law. For example, some judicial review standards are meant to be more deferential to the lower court's decision, and I find that judges are indeed more deferential when confronted with a legal requirement to be that way. Indeed, as a determinant of decisions, the magnitude of the effect of legal deference is much greater than that of judicial ideology (though the ideological effect does not disappear). This important finding has generally been overlooked in previous quantitative analyses. Substantive legal requirements, which are much more difficult to operationalize in quantitative research, might be expected to play a role as well. The finding on legal deference testifies to the need to incorporate such variables in quantitative analyses.

In Chapter 3, I introduce other judicial background variables, such as race, gender, religion, and previous life experiences of the circuit court judges. Existing studies on the effect of these judicial characteristics have generally found that they exercise little impact on outcomes. I study the effects on judicial decisions of race, gender, previous occupational background, American Bar Association (ABA) judicial qualifications ratings, and net wealth, with controls for the effect of judicial ideology as measured by the appointment standard. I find relatively little effect for judicial background, though female and minority judges appear more liberal in criminal cases. One new and interesting finding of these studies is that judges of greater net wealth appear to render more conservative decisions.

Chapter 4 turns to the effect of other institutions on judicial decision making and possible judicial strategy. An extremely large amount of research has been devoted to claims that judges are influenced by these institutions, which may overrule a decision or even punish the judicial branch for decisions with which the other institutions disagree. For circuit court judges, the most obvious external influence would be the Supreme Court, to which circuit court opinions may be appealed. According to this theory, circuit court judges would strategically adapt their decisions to conform to the ideological preferences of the contemporaneous Supreme Court. The most significant finding in Chapter 4 is that the circuit court judges do not so adapt but instead respond to the ideology of the recent past Supreme Court. This result is an independent confirmation of the significance of the legal model, through an admittedly imprecise capture of substantive legal standards. I also consider the prospect of adaptation to the overall composition of the circuit court and find some possibly strategic responsiveness here, as well as responsiveness to the preferences of the recent past circuit court ideology. There is little evidence that the courts respond to the preferences of Congress and the risk of congressional override, though. In general, strategic adaptation is apparently not a significant determinant of circuit court decisions, though conservatives in Congress may exert some small influence.

Chapter 5 turns to the effect of litigants on circuit court decisions. Judges are not perfectly autonomous decision makers, because they can render judgments only on the cases that reach their courts. This leaves open the possibility that strategic litigants can manipulate judicial outcomes by carefully selecting the cases heard on appeal. Such a litigant effect is supported by much theory and some limited empirical evidence. The research in this chapter demonstrates that certain categories of litigants, especially the state and federal governments, are indeed disproportionately successful before the circuit courts. To truly identify a litigant influence, though, one has to control for the other variables known to drive circuit court decision making. Although this is difficult to do with the available data, a study of some limited areas of law finds little litigant effect beyond the ideological and legal effects.

In Chapter 6, I consider the interactive effects, called panel effects, of the three members of the circuit court panel. Under the conventional social scientific theory, decisions would be dictated by the preferences of the median panel member. If ideology is central, the most politically moderate panel member would make the call, and the preferences of the other members would be irrelevant. Psychological research suggests, however, that people may be influenced by others, and some research suggests that circuit court judges are indeed influenced by their colleagues who hear the same appeal. This collegiality effect appears to be at least as powerful as the individual judge's own preferences.

Chapter 7 begins the exploration of legal doctrine. The existing empirical research largely examines judicial characteristics as determinants of decisions and ignores the role of the law. Chapter 2 showed that the law matters in these decisions, and Chapter 7 explains how it matters. A number of legal threshold requirements, such as jurisdiction and standing, must be satisfied before a plaintiff can have his or her case heard on the merits. The analysis of cases involving these threshold rules demonstrates that they have a great effect on judicial outcomes, independent of judicial preferences, and have systematic consequences on the ideological outcomes produced.

Chapter 8 branches into another new field of legal study by examining the precedential effect of particular judicial decisions. Although a decision itself resolves only the outcome of a dispute between two parties, the accompanying opinion sets out the law to govern all future actions in the circuit's jurisdiction and influences other jurisdictions. The significance of that effect lies in the power of the opinion as precedent. This chapter examines the relative power of different precedents. It considers the types of legal rulings that yield the most precedents, ideological effects on precedents, and other factors, such as the length of the published opinion.

The book presents some striking new findings (while confirming other existing findings). The standard conclusion about ideological decision making is supported, but with considerable qualification about its impact. Some other aspects of judicial background matter, the other judges on the panel matter, and the law certainly matters. Legal rules are much better determinants of outcomes than is judicial ideology. Of course, many of the results reported in this book might be considered preliminary or even just exploratory. I hope that they can serve as a foundation for more-detailed analyses of circuit court decisions and opinions.

I am a professor of law, not a degreed political scientist. My interests correspond closely with those social scientists who study judicial politics, though, and I have worked closely with social scientists. Given my background, the statistical analyses presented in this book are not highly sophisticated. I hope that my training and interest can lend some multidisciplinary perspective to the research and facilitate understanding between legal and political scholars.

Political Ideology and Circuit Court Decision Making

This book begins by examining the role of judicial politics in decision making in the circuit courts. Beginning with ideology might seem surprising, because judges are expected to follow the law and eschew politics when making decisions. Philosophers have debated for millennia, however, whether adjudicators such as judges resolve disputes through neutral legal principles or exercise their own political will. A major movement among legal academics, commonly called legal realism, subscribes to the political nature of judicial decision making. Social scientists who have empirically studied judicial decision making have focused on judicial political ideology, which is sometimes called the attitudinal model of judicial decision making. Indeed, in "some corners of the university . . . it is widely considered a settled social scientific fact that law has almost no influence on the justices."[1] Political scientists have even ridiculed the conventional theory that judges decide according to law as "meaningless, . . . acerebral," irrational, or "no more a science than creative writing, necromancy, or finger painting."[2]

Consequently, the analysis of judicial politics provides the starting point for the book's examination of circuit court decisions.

Judges are commissioned to resolve disputes between litigating parties. If there were no law, judicial decisions would presumably be ideological. Without law, the judge would examine the facts of the dispute and reach the result that he or she deemed to be the most equitable. The judge's sense of equity or fairness of outcome would inevitably be contingent on his or her ideological inclinations. Suppose that a case involved a contract between a large corporation and an individual consumer. Judges who ideologically favored a free market and associated bargaining would probably enforce the contract according to its precise terms. Judges who were ideologically inclined to favor the underdog might not enforce terms that seemed terribly unfair. The outcome of a case would depend on which judge heard the dispute. In the contemporary United States, however, judges do not decide in the absence of law. There are statutes, precedents, and other legal materials that apply to such contract disputes. The consideration of ideological judicial decision making therefore must consider the role of these laws.

Judicial politics or ideology is commonly juxtaposed with decision making according to law. As such, it is typically decried. Classic decision making according to law, discussed in detail in the next chapter, presumes that judges will use the recognized appropriate materials of the law to reach a decision. Ideological decision making occurs when judges do not adhere to legal materials but act as if there were no governing law and impose their own ideological preferences in making their decisions. Judges are *supposed* to adhere to the law and should not simply impose their ideologies on the outcome of cases. One cannot blithely rely on the assumption that people will do what they are supposed to do, however. Personal objectives and incentives should be considered. Judges are free from most of the incentives that may influence other jobs. Federal judges cannot get salary increases by working harder or better. Life tenure and other guarantees of judicial independence mean that judges face little risk of losing their jobs or suffering any other adverse consequences of their decision making. Given these circumstances, one could reasonably expect that such judges might choose to use their positions to do justice as filtered through their ideological beliefs.

This chapter considers the meaning of ideological decision making and the previous research on the issue. I conduct new statistical analyses to determine the significance of ideology for the votes of individual circuit court judges, both overall and in particular case areas. I then consider the role of ideology on overall decisions, rather than individual judge votes, and the relative significance of ideological extremes in judicial decisions.

The Meaning of Ideological Judicial Decision Making

Critics commonly ascribe judicial decisions to judicial ideology, a notion often called lawlessness. Before one can capture the ideological role in judicial decision making, the concept of judicial ideology must be defined. Judicial ideology generally does not mean partisan politics. An ideological judicial activist does not have his political party's interests at heart, according to the attitudinal model. Instead, the judge has a personal ideology, on a two-dimensional liberal to conservative scale, that drives his or her rulings. Such judges are presumed not to be involved in political bargaining or lobbying within the court or with members of the other branches of government, but are sincerely voting their personal preferences, conservative or liberal. Thus, the term *ideology* is generally preferable to the term *political* when describing judicial preferences.

Even after ideology is defined, the researcher needs a way to identify and separate ideological decision making from other determinants of judicial outcomes, such as the law itself. The identification of ideologically motivated action is an elusive one, however. Politicians and commentators commonly complain of "activist" or "political" judicial decisions, but these complaints often mean only that the politician or commentator disagrees with the judicial outcome. Such objections may speak only to the ideology of the complainer, not that of the judge. This became quite obvious in the *Bush v. Gore* litigation, during which conservatives claimed that the Florida Supreme Court was activist and ideological, while liberals claimed that it was the U.S. Supreme Court that was activist and ideological.

It is relatively easy to find particular decisions that can be plausibly ascribed to a judge's ideology. It is also relatively easy, however, to find particular decisions that seem contrary to that judge's ideology. Relying on anecdotal examples is not useful, and the tendency to analyze individual decisions as ideological or not cannot resolve the issue. Indeed, it is virtually impossible to definitively ascribe any particular judicial decision to ideology rather than law. No lawyer appears before a judge and argues: "You're a liberal and I'm on the liberal side in this case, so I should win." Instead, the lawyers for both sides cite legal materials, such as precedents, and claim that those materials call for a decision favoring their respective clients. When a judge makes a decision, he or she justifies it by referring to preexisting legal materials, not to his or her ideology. Although critics frequently claim that a particular decision was political, they cannot *prove* that fact; they only assert it. The critic claims that the judge engaged in a biased assessment of the law, but this claim depends on the dubious presumption that the critic can better apply the law to the case than did the judge. Moreover, even if the judge did get the law wrong, he or she might have done so out of error rather than ideology.

Those who believe judicial opinions are ideological often invoke the fact that both sides in a dispute can cite supporting legal material. If both sides have legal arguments, perhaps we are restored to a world without any governing law, where judges are free to exercise their political preferences. This criticism is too facile, though, because not all legal arguments are equally valid. Both sides have legal arguments, but one side's arguments may be better, more logical, or more applicable to the facts of the instant case. Whether the judge is deciding according to the better legal arguments or to his or her ideology is the question.

Quantitative empirical research is suited to help answer this question. The evaluation of any individual case is subjective and cannot distinguish ideology from error. A broad examination of many cases can reveal a systematic pattern of decisions, and statistical analyses add rigor to claims of ideological bias. If a given judge consistently reaches liberal outcomes in his or her decisions, that is a sign that the judge's decisions are ideologically influenced. It is possible, of course, that the law dictated liberal decisions in those cases. But if a different judge consistently reaches conservative outcomes in the same or similar cases, that creates a strong inference of ideological influence for one or both judges. The distribution of outcomes might be a matter of random chance; statistical methods are designed to evaluate this possibility. As a matter of logic, the different outcomes can at best show that one of the two sides, conservative or liberal, is deciding ideologically. One side might be following the law. Absent any reason to think that either conservatives or liberals are more honest than the other side, though, the most likely inference is that both are ideologically influenced in their decisions.

Ideological decision making need not mean that judges are consciously privileging their ideology over the governing law, and empirical evidence cannot demonstrate the truth of any such claim. The leading proponents of the attitudinal model are expressly agnostic about whether the ideological bias is a conscious one. Judges may effect their ideological preferences through what psychologists call "motivated reasoning"—a subconscious process by which people attempt to construct a rational justification for a preset desired conclusion.[3] Those engaged in motivated reasoning may use cognitive shortcuts in processing information, an approach that can skew conclusions. Judge Frank Coffin from the first circuit court of appeals referred to this as a "hidden tilt" for one side of the litigation.[4] Although the consciousness of the judicial bias has not been determined, the existence or nonexistence of such consciousness may be important. If we were to try to combat ideological judicial decision making, choosing the best strategy might depend on whether the bias was conscious or subconscious.

Judges on Ideological Judicial Decision Making

Judges generally do not ascribe their decisions to their ideological preferences, either formally or informally, but they do recognize something akin to an ideological role in their decision making. Although judges are loathe to confess to ideological or political decision making, they have often conceded that the content of the law may not determine decisions and that they may be influenced by factors that are something like ideology. Supreme Court justice Stephen Breyer claims that "politics" do not drive judicial decisions but acknowledges that "personal ideology or philosophy is a different matter."[5] In J. Woodford Howard's survey of judges from three circuit courts, a majority of the responding judges reported that their personal views of justice in the case were "very important" to their decisions.[6] Given anonymity and the right questions, judges were ready to admit to extralegal factors in decision making.

Rarely do judges publicly confess to or openly use ideology as a basis for their decisions. Occasionally, a judge will charge other judges with ideological decision making. A recent dissent by Judge Alex Kozinski of the ninth circuit court of appeals more widely conceded that judges "know very well how to read the Constitution broadly when they are sympathetic to the right being asserted," but "when we're none too keen on a particular constitutional guarantee, we can be equally ingenious in burying language that is incontrovertibly there."[7] Although such open candor is relatively rare, it still hints at the sub rosa role for ideology. Even Kozinski, however, rejects the extreme realist position that all law is merely political, and has referred to this theory as "horse manure."[8]

In some respects, the debate over ideological decision making is a semantic one. Judges do not like to be called ideological or activist, and they shun those labels. Reflective judges, though, realize that their decisions are influenced by some extralegal factors and that their personal background and sense of justice are among those factors. In this book I refer to such decisions as *ideological*, as a convenient shorthand, but I could as easily have used a different term, such as *just*. It seems fair to call the factor ideological, though, because empirical evidence has shown that federal judges' decisions can be correlated with the ideologies of their appointing presidents. Judicial testimony seems to admit to some level of conscious judicial ideological bias, although there may be a subconscious effect as well. Empirical methods can help measure the magnitude of this effect.

Empirical Research on Ideological Judicial Decision Making

An enormous amount of quantitative empirical research has been conducted on the effect of ideology on judicial decision making. Most of this existing empirical research has been conducted by political scientists and involves the Supreme Court. The Supreme Court provides a ready proving ground for assessing judicial ideology because it includes nine different justices with different ideologies deciding exactly the same dispute. The existing research seems conclusive in establishing that the justices of the Supreme

Court are ideologically influenced. Professors Jeffrey Segal and Harold Spaeth have conducted extensive research, using a database of all Supreme Court decisions since 1962. They found that certain liberal justices (such as former justice William Brennan) consistently reach liberal decisions, while other justices (such as Justice Antonin Scalia) consistently reach conservative decisions.[9] Numerous other studies have generally confirmed the Segal and Spaeth results. The evidence is sufficiently strong that researchers have sometimes suggested that *only* ideology influences the votes of Supreme Court justices and that the law plays no role whatsoever. Other research has demonstrated an ideological effect on numerous underlying actions of the Supreme Court, such as the assignment of opinion-writing duties, the formation of coalitions, and decisions on whether to grant certiorari to an appeal.[10]

Some have taken this research and extended it to all judicial decisions, but the research on the Supreme Court cannot necessarily be extrapolated to circuit decision making. The Supreme Court carefully selects the cases it will hear and typically chooses the most controversial and difficult cases. These cases are relatively few (currently fewer than one hundred per year) and not representative of the much larger number of cases heard by other courts. It is plausible to suggest that the Supreme Court chooses to decide those cases, sometimes called "close cases," in which the law is relatively evenly balanced on each side of a dispute. If so, these cases reflect a world without governing law, where some ideological influence is inevitable. The circuit courts, by contrast, hear many more cases and cannot pick and choose the cases they decide. The circuit courts must address every case brought to them by the litigants. This much broader set of cases is unlikely to be so evenly balanced on the law, so circuit court judges may not be forced to consider ideology, as Supreme Court justices are.

There is also a considerable body of empirical research on decision making in circuit courts. A study of environmental law decisions on the D.C. circuit court of appeals found a profound effect of ideology on decision making.[11] A study of circuit court reviews of administrative agency decisions found some significant ideological effect on decisions.[12] Another study of circuit court decisions across the board likewise found a statistically significant association between presumed judicial ideology and decision making.[13] Various other studies have confirmed this association, though the results of the research are not entirely consistent and reveal considerable variation in the power of the judicial ideology effect on decisions.

A meta-analysis of the available comparable research to date found that ideology was a statistically significant determinant of decisions for every level of court, though the power of the ideological effect varied by type of case.[14] The magnitude of the weighted mean effect size was, however, greater for the Supreme Court (+.637) than for the federal circuit courts of appeals (+.242).[15] These findings suggest that ideology is an important determinant of circuit court decisions but also that the extensive Supreme Court findings cannot be directly transferred to the distinct context of circuit courts. Although there is considerable evidence that ideology matters, there is great uncertainty about how much it matters.

The considerable research conducted by social scientists on ideological judicial decision making is important but limited. Such research is only as good as its design and operationalization, and researchers have too often been oblivious to the possible intervening role of apolitical law or have misunderstood the functioning of the law. Strictly legal research offers some confirmation of the quantitative studies by political scientists. The legal realists long ago made similar claims about the effect of ideology on decision making, based on close examination of cases rather than on statistical methods. More recently, a study of hundreds of applications of the traditional "irreparable injury" requirement for equitable relief found that the legal standards were largely irrelevant, as judges ruled according to their intuitive sense of justice.[16]

The Measurement of Ideology

Conducting an empirical test of ideological decision making requires some prior measure of judicial ideologies and the ideological importance of particular case outcomes. Statistical analyses are only as good as the data, methods, and variables they use. To demonstrate an ideological effect on decision making, a researcher must identify particular judges as conservative or liberal, identify particular case outcomes as conservative or liberal, and then match the two together. Only if liberal judges consistently reach liberal outcomes and conservative judges consistently reach conservative

TABLE I.I
Presidential judicial appointments

Administration	Same party	Activist
Reagan	96.2%	65.4%
Carter	82.1%	73.2%
Nixon/Ford	93.0%	59.7%
JFK/LBJ	95.1%	70.5%
Eisenhower	93.3%	68.9%
Truman	88.5%	61.5%
FDR	96.0%	66.0%

SOURCE: Sheldon Goldman, *Picking Federal Judges* 355 (1997).

outcomes can one show the effect of ideology in decisions. Consequently, the researcher requires a measure for the ideology of judges and outcomes.

Political scientists have devised various methods to capture the ideology of particular judges. Historically, researchers used the party of the president who appointed the judge as a guide to the judge's own ideology. Considerable research shows the association between party affiliation and ideology. Ample evidence indicates that presidents tend to choose like-minded judges in their court appointments. Federal judicial appointees consistently come from the president's own political party and were frequently political activists before the appointment.[17] Table 1.1 breaks down this tendency by administration for the second half of the twentieth century.

Given this historic pattern of appointments, researchers have presumed that judges appointed by Democrats are ideologically liberal whereas those appointed by Republicans are ideologically conservative. This method of assigning judicial ideologies has been criticized, however, because not all presidents of the same party are equal in their ideologies. (President Reagan was more conservative than President Eisenhower, for example.) Also, all presidents do not have the same level of party activist appointments. Simply lumping all Republicans together misses many distinctions of relative judicial ideology. The ideological measure has been improved by assigning relative levels of ideological preferences to particular presidents and to the judges that those presidents appointed. This measure has been refined further by considering the ideological preferences of the senators who are typically consulted in such appointments. Micheal Giles has constructed the best currently available measure for circuit court judicial ideology; this measure incorporates both the presidential and senatorial preferences.[18]

Political scientists have also devised rules for assessing the ideological direction of judicial outcomes. We know that certain kinds of disputes are ideologically colored, with liberals tending to favor one set of parties or decisions and conservatives opposed. Thus, in a labor dispute, we expect liberals to favor the union side and conservatives to favor the employing business. In an abortion case, liberals will favor the right to an abortion, while conservatives will not. In prosecutions, liberals will be more sympathetic to the constitutional rights of criminal defendants, while conservatives will more typically side with the government. Political science researchers have developed a consistent system of coding judicial decisions for whether they were liberal or conservative. The accuracy of this system surely varies by type of case, as some technical disputes have no clear ideological significance.

The available methods for measuring the ideology of judges and decisions are rough and imperfect. Translating something so amorphous as ideology into a numerical measure for quantitative analysis will inevitably be imperfect. Moreover, rarely does one have the same ideological perspective on all subjects. It is relatively common for an individual to be liberal on social issues and conservative on economic issues, for example. In such a case, a simple single-point measure will miss much of the individual's ideological preference pattern.

The operationalization of a quantitative ideology score for judicial preferences faces other practical problems. Presidents and senators do not choose judges who perfectly replicate their own ideologies. Instead, presidents and senators have imperfect knowledge about their appointees' preferences and may be influenced in their choices by nonideological factors, such as patronage or judicial aptitude. There is no flawlessly accurate tool for measuring judicial ideology. Likewise, the measurement of decisions cannot perfectly capture ideological positions. Although liberals may be sympathetic to the rights of criminal defendants, they will not always rule for such defendants. Conservatives may favor the prosecution but are not oblivious to the rights of criminal defendants. Some cases may raise arguments that are too liberal even for liberal judges or too conservative for conservatives.

The imperfect operationalization of judicial and decisional ideology does not doom the empirical research project. An empirical researcher does not need a perfect measure of variables to reach conclusions. Imperfections in measurement tend to obscure results rather than produce spurious positive results. If research with imperfect measurements nevertheless produces a statistically and substantively significant finding, that research probably understates the true result. If a judge designated as conservative reaches a liberal outcome, that judge might still be deciding ideologically; the arguments presented in the case were simply too conservative for the conservative judge. Hence, the inability to precisely capture ideology may well mean that its effect is understated in the empirical analyses.

Political History of the Circuit Courts

The significance of the legal impact of ideological judicial decision making depends on the ideological composition of the circuit courts. If the courts contain a relatively even balance of Republicans and Democrats, an ideological effect on individual decisions would not necessarily alter the overall path of the law. But, for example, if conservatives predominated on the court for a certain time period, that could cause a systematic pattern of relatively conservative circuit court decisions. If liberals predominated on the court, the pattern would reverse, thus yielding considerable fluctuation in the path of the law over time. Figure 1.1 displays the overall partisan makeup of the circuit courts over the twentieth century.

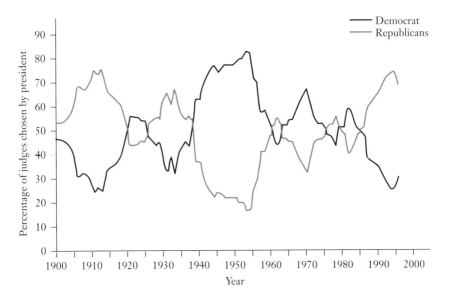

Figure 1.1   Partisan Make-Up of the Federal Circuit Courts, 1900–1994

The ideological makeup of the circuit courts obviously changed considerably during the twentieth century. Republicans dominated the early years of the century, until the Franklin D. Roosevelt cohort of judges ushered in a period of overwhelming Democratic dominance during the middle of the century. After a period of approximate equality, the century ended with considerable Republican dominance again. If judicial decision making is centrally ideological, one would expect these partisan differences in circuit court composition to show up in changing ideological patterns of decisions.

Ideological Effects of Presidential Cohorts

The premise of the empirical analysis of ideology in judicial decision making is that a judge's ideology can be measured, at least roughly, in accord with the ideology of the appointing president. Although there is sound theoretical reason to believe this is so, some empirical testing is warranted. Using the courts of appeals database, I measured the relative ideology of the decisions reached by appointees of post–World War II presidents for all the cases. The following list reports the mean ideology of appointment outcomes by presidential cohort, with 1.0 for conservative and 3.0 for liberal, so that smaller numbers represent more conservatism:

Truman	1.9470
Eisenhower	1.7772
Kennedy	1.8676
Johnson	1.8523
Nixon	1.8000
Carter	1.8669
Reagan	1.6317
Bush	1.5682

The pattern of these results is consistent with a finding that presidential ideologies are reflected in the ideologies of their judicial appointees. The Republican appointees were consistently more conservative, on average, than the Democratic appointees. This evidence does not directly prove that presidents consciously appoint judges that agree with their ideology who then intentionally decide cases in accord with that ideology. It does show, however, that judges appointed by certain presidents tend to render decisions that are relatively consistent with the preferences of those presidents. The finding is suggestive of the expected association.

The preceding list of presidential appointment outcomes shows that there was not always a dramatic difference associated with party of appointing president, and this analysis omitted many variables that might influence the outcome, including the preferences of the senators associated with the appointment, the type of case presented to the court, the legal posture of the appeal, the identity of other judges on the panel, and numerous other factors. At this early stage of the investigation, though, there appears to be some correspondence between appointer ideology and the decision making of the appointee, which enables us in analyses of decision making to begin with the appointing president's ideology as a proxy for that of the judge.

But reliance merely on party of appointing president clearly misses some important intraparty differences in ideology: Nixon appointees were ideologically closer to Johnson appointees (−.0523) than they were to Reagan appointees (+.2683). The traditional scale, then, on which judges were merely categorized by appointing party, is a limited guide to ideology, given the intraparty differences. The data on judicial votes in the earlier list also appear to capture the intraparty ideological difference to some degree. The next list presents a rank ordering of the ideology of judicial decisions by appointees of particular presidents and the ideology of the those presidents (using Poole-Rosenthal NOMINATE scores), from conservative at the top of the list to liberal at the bottom:

Judicial Decisions	*Presidential Ideology*
Bush	Reagan
Reagan	Bush
Eisenhower	Nixon
Nixon	Eisenhower
Johnson	Carter
Carter	Johnson
Kennedy	Kennedy
Truman	Truman

The correspondence is not perfect, but it is relatively close. Within each party, the more conservative presidents generally tended to appoint more conservative judges, applying our initial but limited preliminary test for judicial voting. The use of appointing president thus seems a reasonable proxy for judicial ideology. The rest of this chapter elaborates on the ideological measure of judicial decision making, adding refinements to the analysis.

Preliminary Regression Analysis of Judicial Decision Making

The next study of the ideological effect of judicial decision making uses the added rigor of regression analysis. My first analysis simply regresses a measure of judicial ideology against a measure of outcome ideology. The independent variable of judicial ideology is the Giles measure, which incorporates both presidential and senatorial preferences (labeled Ideology).[19] The dependent variable is the ideological direction of each judicial vote. Each vote was recoded as a binary variable where liberal = 1 and conservative = 0, and a logit analysis was used for the regression.[20] Table 1.2 reports the outcome of the analysis.

Table 1.2 demonstrates that my measure of judicial ideology is correlated with ideological outcomes with a high degree of statistical significance (.000), enabling a rejection of the hypothesis that judicial ideology did not matter. The study incorporated 27,024 individual judge votes for which the necessary data on ideology were available. The correlation coefficient is .061, which suggests that a unitary change in the judicial ideology measure will produce a 6% change in associated ideological decisions. There is a 95% confidence that the true change lies somewhere between 4.4% and 7.8%. This unitary difference is just slightly less than the difference between the most liberal and most conservative circuit court judges. Thus,

TABLE 1.2
Regression of ideology on judge votes

Variable	Coefficient	P-value	N	R^2
Ideology	.061	.000	27,024	.002

replacing one of the most conservative judges with one of the most liberal judges would change 6% of the resulting votes. Up until now, there has been strong evidence that ideology matters for judge votes, but that evidence does not suggest that it matters a great deal.

Ideological Decision Making by Issue Area

Circuit courts address virtually all legal disputes that arise under federal law and a good number of disputes arising under state law, due to federal diversity jurisdiction. These cases range from appeals of criminal convictions to actions enforcing constitutional rights to ordinary economic disputes among private parties. The makeup of the civil court docket changed substantially over the course of the twentieth century.[21] For example, civil rights and criminal cases are far more common today than they were in 1925, and ordinary economic disputes are less common. Since World War II, the case distribution has been relatively stable, save for a significant increase in civil rights claims in the wake of the federal antidiscrimination legislation of the 1960s.

The role of ideology in judicial decisions may be affected by the type of case before the courts. Past researchers have often studied a subset of cases in a particular topical case type but have not emphasized the significance of that fact. It may be that findings for a particular type of case cannot be reliably generalized to the full corpus of cases. Ideology may have a case type–specific role and be overwhelmed by other factors in other types of cases. If so, this would demonstrate that ideology is not the sole driver of circuit court opinions.

The cases in the courts of appeals database are broken down into eight broad categories: criminal, civil rights, First Amendment, due process, privacy, labor relations, economic activity and regulation, and miscellaneous cases that were unclassifiable. Each of these categories is further subdivided by more-detailed case type characterization. Most of the cases in the database fit into only one of these eight broad categories. The different types of cases presumably have different ideological importance. Some cases may have no ideological importance at all. For example, a boundary dispute between two states would not seem to involve ideology.

Some topical case types might conduce to particularly liberal or conservative results, for a variety of possible reasons entirely independent of the judicial ideology. In criminal actions, for example, the prosecution side might have much better representation or have a generally favorable law, so one would expect the prosecution to prevail more often, which would appear to produce a relatively conservative mean outcome. In other cases, the opposite might be true. The next list reports the mean ideological outcome by case type, with higher numbers being more liberal, on the scale that ranges from 1.0 to 3.0. Perfect ideological neutrality would show up as a mean ideology of 2.0. The results are as follows:

Case Type	Mean Ideology
Criminal	1.4155
Civil rights	1.8190
First Amendment	2.0728
Due process	1.6765
Privacy	1.7600
Labor relations	2.2262
Economic activity and regulation	2.0130
Miscellaneous	2.1601

Clearly, different case types have different degrees of conservatism or liberalism in outcomes. Whereas criminal cases are overwhelmingly conservative (pro-prosecution), cases involving First Amendment issues, economic activity and regulation, or labor relations issues are plainly more liberal in their mean outcomes. Although this may be attributable to different judges hearing different types of cases, the large sample size makes this unlikely. Instead, it appears that the type of case may be more important to the direction of the outcome than is the ideology of the particular judge (though this finding could also reflect a specification error regarding the ideology of the judicial preferences or the case outcomes). Moreover, the different mean ideology by case area tells us nothing about the relative significance of judicial ideology by case area; it merely establishes the starting point around which ideological variation occurs. Research on the Supreme Court has similarly identified different patterns of ideological voting, depending on the case topic.[22]

One wouldn't necessarily expect ideology to play the same role in all types

TABLE 1.3
Regression of ideology by case type

Case type	Coefficient	P-value	N	R^2
Criminal	.041	.001	9,158	.001
Civil rights	.060	.019	3,134	.001
First Amendment	.058	.321	509	.000
Due process	.228	.000	395	.031
Privacy	−.115	.427	71	.009
Labor relations	.184	.000	2,327	.016
Economic	.043	.002	10,829	.001
Miscellaneous	.000	.991	593	.000

of cases. Some cases may simply be more salient or ideologically charged, and preliminary empirical evidence shows that the nature of circuit court ideological decision making varies by case type.[23] It is also possible that the general Ideology score better reflects ideological positions for some case types. Determining the impact of ideology by case type requires a regression of the sort reported in Table 1.2. The next analysis involves the same simple regression of Ideology and ideology of case outcome on individual judicial votes for each of the eight broad case types provided by the courts of appeals database. The goal was to ascertain the relative significance of judicial ideology for each of the categories. Table 1.3 reports the results.

Clearly, the relative significance of judicial ideology differs by type of case, with due process cases showing the greatest effect. Judicial ideology had a statistically significant association with votes for five of the eight case categories. The lack of significance for privacy and First Amendment issues may simply be a specification error in coding the ideology of at least some of the case outcomes (especially because the direction of the relationship for privacy was negative, with conservative judges rendering more opinions coded as liberal). The miscellaneous cases may represent those technical legal issues that lack an ideological association. The power of ideology also varies greatly among those case types for which it is significant, as evidenced by the considerable difference in coefficients and R^2 terms by case type. All of the R^2 terms still remain low, which means that the substantive significance of ideology is still unproven.

The different results by case type have several possible interpretations. Under a strict political interpretation, one might claim that some case types

TABLE 1.4
Regression of ideology by case categories

Case type	Coefficient	P-value	N	R²
Constitutional	.009	.159	5,747	.000
Federal statute	.028	.000	7,922	.003
Amicus	.044	.005	1,016	.008
Class action	−.035	.126	482	.005
Criminal procedure	.034	.004	1,733	.005
Civil procedure	.020	.032	2,942	.002
Diversity	.032	.629	59	.004

have greater ideological charge or more accurate specifications for ideology of outcomes. An alternative explanation would go beyond politics, however. In some case types, the governing law may be clearer, leaving less room for judicial ideological discretion. The greatest ideological effect appeared in *due process* and labor relations cases. The meaning of the term due process is notoriously vague, enabling more room for ideology than in other types of cases. Yet another possibility is that, for some case types more than others, the judges are being influenced by public opinion, the preferences of other governmental institutions, or some other external factor. Ideology appears to be a factor in judicial decision making, but the available evidence can demonstrate only that it is a relatively small factor.

The data may be broken down by factors other than topical case type. The courts of appeals database also provides coding for some general categories of cases, including some that are orthogonal to topical case type. One might expect to see more ideological judging in constitutional and federal statutory cases that are politically charged. The presence of amici participation may signal the societal importance of a case and thus trigger more ideological judging. Class actions might be similarly important. One might expect criminal procedure cases, which involve contested issues of defendants' rights, to be more ideological than civil procedure disputes. Cases that come to the courts under diversity jurisdiction involve state law issues that might be less ideologically charged, so less ideological judging might be expected. Table 1.4 reports a sequence of regressions using Ideology and ideological direction of judge vote for each of these categories.

The results do not paint a clear picture of changing ideological importance. Federal statutory actions and amicus actions are significantly ideological, but constitutional cases are not as ideological. The regression for class actions has a negative sign. Criminal procedure is more ideological than civil procedure, and diversity decisions show little ideological significance. In none of these areas is the effect great. The role of ideological judging seems to vary by category of case, but the difference doesn't appear to be great or systematic in some obvious way.

Ideological Decision Making over Time

Some argue that in recent years the judiciary has become increasingly ideological in its decisions. In this view, the courts in the past were neutral arbiters of disputes, but judges in recent times have become more political in their decisions. Others claim that the judiciary has always been ideological, and they can point to the earliest days of our republic and that era's partisan struggle over the judiciary. The legal realist movement that ascribes judicial decisions to extralegal factors, such as ideology, arose in the first half of the twentieth century. Complaints of ideological judging are not new. Much of the existing research on judicial decision making has not accounted for changes over time.

To test the ideological variation in judicial decisions over time, I measured the mean ideology of judicial decisions for each decade of the second half of the twentieth century. The results are reported in the following list (data for the 1990s capture only the beginning years of the decade, after which courts of appeals database coding stopped). This list uses the scale with 2.0 as the ideologically neutral result:

Decade	Mean Ideology
1950s	1.8897
1960s	1.7917
1970s	1.8708
1980s	1.8151
1990s	1.6556

The mean ideology of circuit court decisions has fluctuated over the decades, though not too dramatically. The courts of the 1990s clearly appear

TABLE 1.5
Regression of ideology over time

Decade	Coefficient	P-value	N	R²
1950s	−.088	.391	806	.001
1960s	.011	.079	6,908	.000
1970s	.008	.187	8,120	.000
1980s	.029	.000	8,198	.003
1990s	.016	.020	5,255	.001

to be the most conservative, though this finding is only tentative. It is possible that the mean ideology findings do not reflect any real ideological change but instead reflect a change in the composition of case types brought before the court. Some types of cases tend to produce a certain ideological pattern, as shown in the list on page 26. The ideological difference by decade could be real, though, and explained by the changing ideological makeup of the circuit courts. The results seem to confirm the hypothesis that judicial outcomes follow political outcomes with a lag of about ten years. The relatively liberal opinions of the 1950s may be due to Roosevelt appointees, the more-conservative opinions of the 1960s attributable to an influx of Eisenhower appointees, and the more-liberal opinions of the 1970s ascribed to Kennedy/Johnson appointees. Then we see a slight shift to conservatism in the 1980s with Nixon/Ford/Carter appointees and a dramatic shift to conservatism in the 1990s as Reagan-appointed judges took the bench. These data do not suggest that the judiciary's ideological nature has changed radically over the time period studied.

The preceding list reported only the mean ideological outcome by decade and not the relative significance of judicial ideology for case outcomes. Examining this relative significance requires a regression analysis, broken down by decades, of the effect of Ideology on the ideology of judicial votes. Table 1.5 reports the findings of these regressions on the outcome of individual judge votes.

The regressions suggest that recently the judiciary has indeed become somewhat more ideological. There was no clear statistically significant association between judicial ideology and judicial votes until the 1980s. In the 1950s, the directionality of the relationship was even negative. Assessing this finding of greater ideological judging in recent years requires a measure of caution. It is possible that the significance of judicial ideology remained constant over time but that our measure of judicial ideology, Ideology, became more accurate. The apparent increase in ideological decision making might also be due to the different composition of cases that came before the court in different decades and the degree to which those cases were ideologically important, rather than because of the ideological effect on judging.

Analysis of Decisions

The above discussion has all been based on the votes of individual judges. Circuit court panels typically have three judges, though, and en banc reviews may encompass all the judges on the circuit court. The vote of an individual judge does not produce a decision; a case outcome requires two or more judges to agree. If a judge is ideological when writing a dissenting opinion, that has no real effect on the decision and thus relatively little effect on the composition of the law. Therefore, it is valuable to analyze the ultimate decisions of the circuit court panels, not just the votes of individual judges.

The analysis of individual judge votes might actually understate the ideological effect of judging. Consider a panel with two conservatives and one liberal. On hearing a case, each judge reacts ideologically. The liberal realizes that he or she is outvoted and the case outcome will be conservative. The liberal judge might well go along with the conservative decision rather than make the effort to write a liberal dissenting opinion that could have no practical effect. In this scenario, the liberal judge would cast a conservative vote, but this vote is misleading. Had there been another liberal on the panel, the liberal judge probably would have exercised his or her ideological interests and voted for the liberal position. Looking at individual judge votes alone would understate the true power of ideological decision making by one-third. It is theoretically possible that ideological voting would explain 67% of the individual judge votes and still explain 100% of the opinions. Hence, it is important to analyze decisions rather than just votes.

The analysis of decisions is also important in considering panel effects. Individual judge votes might be influenced by the ideology or other features of the other judges on the panel. The significance of panel effects will be addressed in detail in Chapter 6 but it bears some attention here. Studies have shown that judge votes are influenced by the ideology of other panel members. One study found that circuit court panels containing both Republicans and Democrats were far more moderate in their decisions than panels composed entirely of appointees from a single party.[24] These findings must be addressed when measuring the ideological decisions of full circuit court panels.

The methods for measuring the ideology of individual judges using the variable Ideology have been addressed. There remains the question of how to transfer this measurement to find the ideology of a panel. One might simply cumulate the total ideological scores of all the panel judges to get a measure of panel ideology. The use of the median panel member, though, is probably a better tool for capturing the ideology that is relevant to a judicial decision. The total panel ideology could be dramatically influenced by a single outlier judge with such an extreme ideology that his or her vote would not drive the case decision. When analyzing voting, political scientists typically rely on the median voter theorem.[25] This widely accepted theory (analyzed in much greater detail later in this chapter and in Chapter 6) holds that when individuals are arrayed along a two-dimensional ideological continuum, it is the median voter who is at the fulcrum and who determines the decision.

Take a hypothetical panel with three judges of varying degrees of liberalness. If a litigating party's position is too liberal for even the most liberal judge, the entire panel will unanimously cast their votes in a conservative direction, for the other litigating party. If the position is too liberal for two of the three judges, the decision will again be conservative, if only by majority vote. If the position is too liberal for only one of the judges, though, the decision will be for the party supporting the relatively liberal position. Hence, it is the "middle liberal" in this arrangement, or median ideological voter, who ultimately determines whether the decision itself is liberal or conservative.

Regression Analysis of Panel Decision Making

The first analysis is a simple regression analysis of ideology on the ultimate case decision. The most obvious variable is set at the median Ideology rating on the panel and is called MedianIdeology. Another variable is the cumula-

TABLE I.6
Regression of ideology by case outcome

Variable	Coefficient	P-value	N	R^2
MedianIdeology	.504	.000	9,851	.009
TotalIdeology	.290	.000	10,019	.006
PartyRatio	.369	.000	13,947	.005

tive Ideology ratings of all the judges on a three-judge circuit court panel and is called TotalIdeology. A third variable disregards the individualized Giles scores and relies on the research on split versus unified panels by political party. This variable simply takes the ratio of Democrat to Republican appointees on the panel and is called PartyRatio. Such a ratio has been commonly used in past research on circuit court decision making. Each of these measures is a different approach to capturing the ideological effect on judicial decisions. Table 1.6 presents the results of the three separate simple regressions. The analysis was limited to panels of only three judges so that the cumulative rating was not distorted by different numbers of judges on the panel.

All three measures of panel ideology produce statistically significant results on judicial decisions. The median voter theorem suggests that MedianIdeology should best predict outcomes, and the data are consistent with this hypothesis. Although the correlation coefficient for MedianIdeology is the highest, TotalIdeology is also relatively significant. All three measures for ideology are better predictors of panel decisions than the individual Ideology measure was as a predictor of judicial vote, demonstrating the importance of considering decisions in addition to analyzing individual judicial votes. These results confirm the statistical significance of ideological voting, but they leave the magnitude of the effect uncertain. Although a substantial, one-unit change in the score of MedianIdeology is associated with a fairly substantial change in decision outcome, the actual differences in MedianIdeology between the cases appear to explain less than 1% of the variation in case outcomes. The results suggest that ideology does matter but perhaps not very much. We must consider many other variables, however. For example, these results do not take into account the ideological direction of the district court decision being reviewed. Consideration of additional factors might evidence greater or lesser effect for circuit court ideology.

Effect of Ideological Extremes

The analysis heretofore has assumed a linear model of ideology, that is, that all changes in ideological level are equally important for judicial decisions. The analysis has presumed that a given quantitative change in ideology is the same, regardless of whether that change reflects the difference between a moderate liberal and a moderate conservative or the difference between a moderate liberal and an extreme liberal. This assumption is obviously not correct, and the importance of ideological considerations may vary, depending on whether the judge is relatively moderate or relatively extreme.

The precise effect of ideological extremity is not clear, however. It might be that the power of ideology grows proportionately greater at the extreme. The linear model presumes that a judge with twice the Ideology score of another judge is twice as conservative. Another possibility is that the judge with twice the Ideology score was a true ideologue who was less influenced by the law and perhaps four times as conservative. If so, one would see a greater ideological effect at the extremes. This appears to be the view of the Senate, which has confirmed most presidential judicial selections for the circuit courts but has refused confirmation for a few judges perceived to be too ideologically extreme. Senators seem to screen out the ideological extremes but accept some more-moderate ideological bias. There is reason to believe that ideological extremity could increase ideological decision making in a supralinear manner. Some evidence of this effect comes from research showing that unified panels with appointees of just one party are dramatically more ideological than split panels, with one representative of the other party.[26]

If other nonideological variables come into play, however, one might actually see a somewhat muted ideological effect at the extremes. If the law were important in judicial decisions, it might constrain the absolute number of decisions that could be ideologically determined. If only a limited percentage of cases were "close cases" that enabled ideological considerations to determine outcomes, the relative power of ideology might actually decline at the extremes. The moderate ideologues would vote ideologically in the truly close cases and the extreme ideologues could not be much more

TABLE I.7
Effect of ideological extremity

Variable	Coefficient	P-value
MedianIdeology	.507	.000
MedianIdeology^2	.129	.574

ideological in the remaining cases, which were not close enough on the law for ideology to play a determining role.

Table 1.7 tests the effects of having a relatively more ideologically extreme median voter on judicial panels. It uses two independent variables, MedianIdeology and MedianIdeology^2. The second variable, MedianIdeology^2, has the effect of exaggerating extreme scores using a quadratic equation rather than a linear equation. If MedianIdeology^2 is positive and significant, it would indicate that the extremes are disproportionately more ideological. If the variable is negative, it would indicate that the extremes are relatively less ideological than those judges closer to the ideological median.

These results confirm neither hypothesis about the effect of ideological extremity. The MedianIdeology^2 association is positive but not statistically or substantively significant. There is no suggestion that ideological extremity either exacerbates or mutes the effect of ideology in judicial decision making. To the extent that judicial ideology matters, its relationship to decision making appears to be a linear one that affects all ideological positions with approximate equality. By studying only the median panel member, however, this analysis inevitably ignores the true extreme ideologues, who will not be medians. The effect of ideological outliers who are not median voters is discussed further in Chapter 6.

Ideology and Opinions

Arguably, the most important part of a circuit court decision is found in the opinion rendered rather than the mere case decision. Although the outcome resolves the dispute between the two parties, the opinion sets a precedent for future court decisions (assuming that the law is not perfectly ideological, so the content of opinions matters). Perhaps more importantly, the content of judicial opinions may dictate extrajudicial behavior. Once a given opinion is written declaring the state of the law, private and government actors aware of that opinion may adjust their behavior accordingly, to correspond to the law's dictates. The content of opinions may also cast a shadow over litigation decisions. Parties may be more or less likely to bring future cases and more or less likely to settle those cases, depending on the content of opinions written in prior cases. Hence, opinion content, which is commonly neglected by empirical research, can be an important subject for study.

Unfortunately, the courts of appeals database can tell us little about the opinions rendered by the circuit court. Coding for details of the opinion's content would be complex and possibly very subjective. The database does permit coding for one aspect of the opinion, though: its length in pages. The mere length of the opinion does not inform much, however. An opinion might be longer than average for several reasons. A longer opinion might evidence more legal analysis and possibly indicate greater potential precedential importance. Opinion length has been used as a proxy for the relative importance of an opinion,[27] although longer opinions may alternatively have the effect of limiting the clear importance of a ruling. A judge might write a longer opinion specifically to narrow the significance of a precedent, by hedging it about with conditions and qualifications and dwelling on the unique factual circumstances of the case. Although the significance of length is relatively opaque, the length of an opinion probably correlates with some sort of quantity of legal analysis. The length proxy for opinion analysis is very rough but worth some exploration.

The mean majority opinion length for the cases in the courts of appeals database (once a few obviously erroneous page counts were excluded) is 4.61 pages.[28] This brief length indicates that most cases receive relatively little detailed legal or factual analysis from the circuit courts. Table 1.8 shows the first analysis on this variable—the effect of ideological outcome on opinion length for the case outcomes in the database.

TABLE 1.8
Ideology and opinion length

Variable	Coefficient	P-value	N	R^2
Outcome ideology	.056	.000	13,400	.003

TABLE 1.9
Judicial Panel ideology and opinion length

Variable	Coefficient	Significance	N	R^2
MedianIdeology	.029	.005	9,507	.001
TotalIdeology	.029	.004	9,668	.001
PartyRatio	−.079	.000	13,225	.006

The regression shows that liberal opinions are longer than conservative opinions. The difference is small but statistically significant. This finding could have many meanings, including that (a) liberal judges tend to write longer opinions, (b) liberal opinions require more extensive legal justification, or (c) liberal opinions are written to have greater precedential importance. The question is worth further exploration.

The next analysis focuses not on the direction of the opinion but on the makeup of the panel. Table 1.9 reports the effects of different ideological panel makeups on opinion length.

The Ideology results confirm that more liberal judicial panels tend to write slightly longer opinions. But panels with more Republicans wrote longer opinions, a very curious combination of findings. If this means anything, it suggests that panels composed of ideologically moderate Republicans and relatively extreme Democrats tend to produce longer opinions. Another explanation for these findings would simply be historical. The PartyRatio data cover more cases from the first half of the twentieth century, and it may be that ideological associations with opinion length shifted over the course of that century.

Future researchers might explore this further to discern the reasons for this phenomenon. Perhaps some types of judges tend to use more precedents in support of their rulings, which could be readily and objectively measured. Alternatively, opinion length might have nothing to do with the law but might instead be fact based. Although most circuit court opinions do not resolve factual issues, they do typically summarize the facts of the case before embarking on legal analysis. Judges might for some reason choose to discuss the case facts in more detail before legal analysis, another possibility that is amenable to testing and might inform us of the nature of ideological decision making on circuit courts of appeals.

Conclusion

The large courts of appeals database enables various approaches to testing the effects of ideology in judicial decision making across different case types and over time. The results are fairly consistent in showing some effect of ideology that is typically a statistically significant association. The results do not suggest, however, that ideology is the only factor influencing judicial decisions. The significance of ideology varies by type of case and over time. Moreover, the measured effect size for ideology is always a fairly small one. The data to this point do not support expansive claims about the role of ideology in judicial decision making. The small size of the effect may be due to the difficulties of specifying particular judicial ideologies or in specifying case outcome implications. The crude directional coding for outcomes may not precisely capture whether a ruling is liberal or conservative.

Examining the effect of ideology is just the first step in studying circuit court decision making. Additional variables, including legal considerations, need also be assessed. When these additional variables are considered, the ideological effect might disappear, or it might be heightened. The rest of the book builds on the findings in this chapter and elaborates the model of judicial decision making. The following chapters consider various factors in circuit decisions: the role of the law, the effect of the Supreme Court and other institutions, the influence of the litigants, and others.

The Law and Circuit Court Decision Making

Having considered in Chapter 1 the research on the role of judicial ideology in decision making, it is important to turn to the examination of law
as a determinant of those decisions. The law is the formally expressed basis of circuit court decisions, as explained in judicial opinions. One of the
shortcomings of much empirical research on political decision making is
the failure to use any variable to capture the potential effects of the law on
decision making. Judges are *supposed* to use the law to render decisions, and
they *claim* to rely on the law in making decisions, so surely the possibility
of law-based decision making should be directly assessed. The parties in an
action present their arguments to the judges in legal form. References to the
law pervade the judicial decision-making process. Yet some social scientists
have been too quick to dismiss the possibility of a role for the law.

Most circuit court decisions are accompanied by an opinion that explains
and justifies the decision in terms of accepted legal materials. The case's
outcome is attributed to the force of the law. Judges never use explicitly

ideological language to explain their decisions and only rarely rely on any extralegal justifications whatsoever for their decisions. Using Ockham's Razor, law would therefore seem to explain judicial decision making. Yet Judge Richard Posner has cautioned that we not "be so naïve as to infer the nature of the judicial process from the rhetoric of judicial opinions."[1] And Oliver Wendell Holmes reputedly declared that lawyers spend a great deal of time "shoveling smoke." Perhaps judicial language is merely a beard for the judges' true decision basis, ideological or otherwise. Hence, closer scrutiny of the legal model of decision making is necessary. Chapter 1 demonstrated that judicial ideology plays at least some determinative role in decision making, even though it arguably should not do so under a strict legal model. Like many other studies on judicial ideology, however, that chapter is flawed because it fails to include any model for legal factors or other case details. Some have suggested that as studies have more closely focused on comparable cases, "political affiliation as a predictor declines."[2] This chapter tests the effect of some legal variables on decisions.

The Meaning of Legal Judicial Decision Making

Everyone has a general but also typically vague sense of what it means to decide according to the law. Legal decision making at its most abstract is simply logically reasoned decision making based on certain materials deemed legitimate for judicial consideration. When a judge is deciding a constitutional question, the law clearly calls for the judge to consider the text of the constitutional provision at issue. But the judge may also consider existing precedents interpreting that text. The judge might also consider the intent of James Madison and the other authors of the relevant constitutional text, as well as the contemporary understanding of the text and its purposes and how this understanding might be best advanced in the future. All these factors play an important role and all are considered legally legitimate considerations, especially when interpreting very general constitutional terms such as *due process*. The legitimate legal materials are then applied to the ascertained facts of the case to reach a ruling. Synthesizing these relevant factors under the legal model is a matter of "reasoned response to reasoned argument."[3] Through this process, one obtains "legal reasoning that can generate outcomes in controversial disputes independent of the political or economic ideology of the judge."[4] Central to this legal model is the basing of decisions on some neutral legal principles, free from any political contamination. By its very nature, the identity of the judge should not determine the judicial outcome, if the law rules.

If all the legally legitimate source materials point in the same direction, the judicial outcome under law is clear. When the legally legitimate sources call for contradictory results, as they often do, the correct legal answer is much less clear. Ideally, the reasoned judgment in such a case explains how the sources are not truly contradictory and integrates them into a coherent synthesis, in which all the contrasting concerns are satisfied. In many cases, this synthesis is unavailable, and a choice must be made among the legal theories. It is not rare for a party to argue that a given precedent was wrongly decided, according to other legal sources, such as the constitutional text. In the hierarchy of legally legitimate sources, correct textual interpretation may trump precedent, so such an overruling is theoretically an appropriate legal decision. This decision, however, involves considerable judicial discretion and is not a formulaic, purely legal determination.

Given such discretion in the application of reasoned judgment to legally legitimate sources, ideology or other factors can obviously intrude and even dictate the legal outcome. Many judges concede that the law underdetermines some decisions and that extralegal factors may enter into their choices. The extralegal factors, which might include political ideology, are to enter the decision-making equation only when inevitable, though, and are to remain subordinate to the law. The contemporary model of judicial legal decision making does not claim that it is purely formalistic but maintains that judges use "good faith" to render decisions in accord with the law, insofar as reasonably possible.[5] The theory of good-faith legal decision making actually admits to some role for differences between individual judges and even possibly for judicial ideology. Good-faith decision making, however, could never allow the ideological impact to be transcendent. Values and individualized judgment are to play a role only in interstitial matters in which the legal materials do not provide the necessary guidance. Legal decision making does not and cannot admit to a major role for political ideology. The evidence in Chapter 1 of some ideological role may seem contrary to legal decision making, but the relatively small explanatory power of that evidence is potentially consistent with a regime of good-faith judicial decisions that neutrally apply the rule of law in most decisions.

One important aspect of legal decision making is the role that procedural rules play. The paramount model of legal decision making in the last half century was the legal process school, which not only set forth the reasoned decision-making approach but also stressed the centrality of procedure to legal decision making. Although judges must grapple with substantive rules, this objective is arguably secondary to their establishment and enforcement of procedural rules. Thus, cases are resolved on procedural grounds, such as lack of jurisdiction or standing or under the statute of limitations, without regard to the substantive merits of the action. This crucial aspect of the legal model has been overlooked too often by social scientists and other empirical researchers. Examining procedural rules provides an opportunity to compare the effects of law and of ideology in circuit court decisions.

Judges on Legal Judicial Decision Making

Judges consistently claim to be relying on the law in their decisions, and they may be adamant in this claim. The famous supreme court justice, John Marshall, declared in an opinion that courts were the "mere instruments of the law and can will nothing," so that judicial power "is never exercised for the purpose of giving effect to the will of the judge; always for the purpose of giving effect . . . to the will of the law."[6] Judge Harry Edwards of the D.C. circuit court of appeals has taken issue with those who argue that judging is ideological; he stressed that "it is the law—and not the personal politics of individual judges—that controls judicial decision making in most cases resolved by the court of appeals."[7] The public pronouncements of the judiciary consistently profess that decisions are governed by applicable law.

J. Woodford Howard's survey of circuit courts found judges reporting that the vast majority of cases were readily resolved by settled legal rules, and he concluded that adherence to precedent was the "everyday, working rule of American law."[8] David Klein's more recent survey found that judges continue to place paramount importance on reaching "legally correct" decisions.[9] Although Judge Richard Posner warned against taking such professions at face value, the judicial testimony is surely some evidence of the role of law in judicial decision making. Judges appear to be sincere in their aim of legal model decision making and not actively misleading the public. But given the ready availability of precedents and arguments for each side of a dispute and the relative vagueness of the legal model itself, the determinative power of that model cannot simply be assumed. Judges may be ideologically driven, even if that drive is only a subconscious one, and they may therefore render decisions that are contrary to the best interpretation of the law. Friedrich Nietzsche suggested that "at our foundation, there is clearly something that will not learn . . . of predetermined decisions and answers to selected, predetermined questions."[10] Even judges determined to rely on the law may be influenced by their attitudinal predispositions. Today's psychologists call this motivated reasoning, or the confirmation bias, and they have demonstrated its effect.[11] It is surely plausible to suggest that judges are influenced by the tendency.

The Reason for Legal Judicial Decision Making

Some are skeptical of the claims of judges that they follow the law; these skeptics ask why judges would choose to decide according to law. For those who adhere to a traditional legal approach, the question is foolish and the answer is obvious—because judges are supposed to adhere to the law. For those of a more social scientific bent, this answer is foolish because we know that people regularly do not do what they are supposed to do. Although such duty-bound behavior is not unheard of, self-interest is generally a better determinant of human behavior. So we are still left with the question of why judges would decide according to the law.

One reason why judges might do their duty is the threat of enforcement against them if they do not (the enforcement theory). Perhaps ideological judicial decision making will incur the wrath of some other societal institution on the judges in question. This possibility is the subject of Chapter 4, and the evidence there shows that the threat of enforcement does not explain consistent duty-bound behavior by judges. Moreover, if judges are adhering to the legal model only because of the threat of enforcement, then that behavior is not truly legal decision making but is better characterized as strategic action, possibly in pursuit of some illegitimate extralegal end. If enforcement is the key to legal judicial decision making, judges will not decide according to law when they can evade detection or punishment.

Another reason for legal judicial decision making could be an instilled sense of duty (the duty theory). According to this view, judges suppress their ideological preferences to fulfill their oath to decide according to law. This is a form of altruism, of which economists are skeptical. We know, however, that altruism does sometimes occur. Role theory suggests that a person's institutional role comes with responsibilities that the person will follow. Those who occupy an institutional role are subject to role expectations that make them inclined to adhere to role behavior.[12] People are socialized into conforming to expectations, and judges are expected to conform to the law in their decision making. A judge who is trained in the law and appreciates the gravity of his or her position might have his or her ideological attitudes modified by the role. J. Woodford Howard has shown that different judges have different interpretations of their role and that these interact with their ideological preferences in a two-dimensional model of judicial decision making.[13]

A recent elaboration of the duty-based role theory is the notion that judging is like playing a game. In this vision, judges want to "win" (give effect to their ideological preferences) but only insofar as they can do so within the rules (the law). This theory has been advanced by Richard Posner and Allan Hutchinson, among others. The game theory suggests that judges will exercise their facilities to logically rationalize their preferred outcome but that they cannot always do so because the accepted legal materials do not permit such an outcome. In this case, the judges would rather "lose" than violate the rules of the game. The judicial process need not be one of conscious manipulation of legal rules, as judges may simply engage in "a good faith attempt to interpret and apply a rule so as to produce a satisfactory result."[14] The amorphous and possibly ideological "satisfactory result" objective of the judge may be entirely subconscious, but it still explains some portion of judicial decision making under this theory. Of course, for some judges the advancement of ideological objectives may be a conscious one, in which the legal game is a challenge for the production of desirable outcomes.

A less commonly invoked reason for legal judicial decision making is that of judicial self-interest (the preference theory), which simply elaborates the theories of ideological decision making. This theory may be the most plausible integration of law and ideology. Judges may have an intrinsic or instrumental preference for adhering to law because the law is the fundamental source of judicial power. Social scientists too blithely dismiss the possibility that judges might *desire* to enforce the law. If judges place value on the law, its advancement is not altruistic but selfish, as is the advancement of ideological ends. Just as economists may too readily assume that people care only about financial wealth, political scientists can too quickly presume that people care only about politics or ideology. There is no intrinsic reason, however, that judges would care more about the ideology than the legality of their rulings. Given the judicial background of training in the law, judges might indeed care about the law itself, which could motivate them to render decisions according to the directives of that law, even when the decision would be contrary to what they might prefer ideologically. Under the preference theory, the law is not so much a limiting factor as another element of the judicial utility function, to be balanced and integrated with ideological preferences. The preference theory is also potentially consistent with the role theory discussed above, as role expectations may form part of the basis for judges' legal preferences.

These explanations are purely theoretical, of course, and do not prove that judges abide or do not abide by the law. The previous explanations do explain why judges *might* choose to abide by the law. They answer the "why" question in that it is not inherently implausible that judges might choose to decide according to the law rather than according to their personal ideological preferences. Law is a plausible variable to explain judicial decisions. Whether this possibility is a reality will require more rigorous empirical examination of actual judicial decision making.

Quantitative Empirical Research on Legal Judicial Decision Making

Designing an empirical test of the legal model is quite challenging, and some have suggested its impossibility. An early prominent test of the role of law examined Supreme Court cases involving the death penalty but used case facts as proxies for the legal model.[15] The study found an effect for its factual and legal variables, but those facts might have captured merely an ideological effect. Facts are certainly relevant when one is making an ideological decision, just as they are for a legal decision. Jeffrey Segal and Harold Spaeth more recently designed a study to test the effect of legal precedents at the Supreme Court level. They examined whether justices who preferred a particular outcome would reverse their rulings once the contrary outcome had prevailed in Court precedent. The study found that justices who dissented in an initial seminal Court decision continued to dissent when the legal issue reappeared before the Court, rather than accepting the earlier case as precedentially binding.[16] Although this research established that precedent had limited power in controversial Supreme Court rulings, it did not truly address the power of the broader legal model.

There is other material research on the effect of the law. Studies have shown that circuit court decisions are responsive to changes in Supreme Court precedent, as the law directs they should be.[17] This does not unambiguously demonstrate the effect of the law, because the change may be due to a simultaneous change in the ideological composition of the circuit courts or to other factors, but the findings suggest the legal role. Some studies of precedent from courts below the Supreme Court also found that it exerts an effect on subsequent decisions. A study of seminal circuit court decisions in the areas of antitrust, environmental law, and search and seizure found that they appeared to influence subsequent rulings, independent of ideology.[18] A study of gay rights decisions at all levels of federal and state courts found that a clear precedent had an extremely strong influence on judges, who subordinated their ideological preferences to conform to the precedent.[19] This empirical research has given new credibility to the legal model of decision making. There is some rigorous evidence that the law matters. The research to date, however, has generally been limited to one measure of the legal model, the effect of a precedent, in some discrete areas of the law. The broader impact of the law has not been studied, probably because of the difficulties associated with measuring and applying truly legal variables in quantitative empirical research.

The Measurement of Law

Although accurately capturing an empirical variable for ideological decision making was a challenging task, measuring legal decision making is far more daunting. As discussed in Chapter 1, there are typically nonfrivolous legal arguments for each side in circuit court cases, so it is impossible to code certain cases as being legally correct (or incorrect) without the researcher second-guessing and effectively overriding the judge. Such an approach offers an unreliable tool for evaluating judicial decisions because it probably reflects more about the researcher than about the judges being evaluated. Research requires a more objective tool for evaluating the law.

Some quantitative measure for a legal variable is essential, though, if we are to evaluate the role of the law in decision making. Failure to use a legal variable also seriously undermines efforts to measure other determinants of judicial decision making. The law is an obvious possible explanation for decisions, and the failure to control for its effect calls the findings on other measures into question. It is distinctly possible that, on at least some issues, a legal variable could be collinear with an ideological variable or some other explanatory variable, which would mean that a finding of significance for ideology or another variable might capture a legal effect.

Although it is difficult to capture a variable for the "correct" decision on the substantive law applied in the case, the legal importance of procedural rulings does enable the researcher to separate out some effect for the law. The consideration of these procedural standards is central to the legal process model and the operation of the law as an adjudicatory system; thus, the evaluation of procedural variables is particularly well designed to capture an effect of the law on judicial decision making. A number of procedures are considered in the courts of appeals database. These include whether the lower court decision was affirmed or reversed and the presence of various threshold legal issues, such as jurisdiction.

In the empirical testing for an ideological decision-making effect, I noted that there was no reason why a judiciary that was purely legal would produce results in which some judges systematically made liberal or conservative political decisions. The presence of such a pattern was persuasive evidence that ideology had some influence on the judiciary. Consideration of procedures enables us to test the converse proposition. If judging were perfectly ideological, the presence of a legal procedural rule should not show any effect on decisions. The ideological judiciary would be able to render the politically preferable decision, using a substantive or procedural rule as they chose. The procedural issues do not intrinsically favor the liberal or conservative side in the dispute (though some types of procedural issues may tend to produce ideological results in some types of cases). Although one cannot test for whether a given court correctly applied a procedural rule, it is possible to test for whether a procedural rule has an effect on the role of judicial ideology on votes or on case outcomes. If the presence of the procedural rule has such an effect, that would be persuasive evidence that the law mattered to judges, either as a constraint or as an objective.

Procedure, therefore, offers a promising variable for testing the effects of law on judicial decision making. A variety of procedures might be used in such a test. The most obvious procedural consideration is the circuit court decision whether to affirm or reverse the judicial or administrative decision that was appealed. Circuit courts are to defer to the lower court's findings on the facts of the case, and review is largely confined to legal disputes. Given the standard of some deference to the lower court, the legal procedural requirement creates a bias in favor of affirmance. Judge Frank Coffin referred to these legal rules of deference as constraining the effect of judicial values on decisions,[20] but the claim needs empirical testing.

The requirement of some measure of deference suggests that, under the legal model, the appellee defending the lower decision should prevail more often than does the appellant who challenges that decision. The ideological model would not predict this result, because there is no reason to think that the ideology of appellees would align with that of the judges. Using the courts of appeals database enables a test of this hypothesis. Although the database codes decisions for many judicial outcomes, I have reduced the codes to a simple binary value reflecting whether the lower court decision was at least in part affirmed or reversed. The following list shows the proportion of affirmances among judge votes, broken down by decade for the second half of the twentieth century:

Decade	Percent Affirmed
1950s	73.2%
1960s	73.8%
1970s	65.2%
1980s	62.5%
1990s	64.4%

Plainly, the majority of circuit court votes are affirmances, as the legal model would predict. The percentage of affirmances dropped by about 10%

after the 1960s, which might be considered evidence of a dwindling effect of the law over time. Because there is no objective standard for the "correct" number of affirmances, though, this conclusion is unclear. Even in more recent decades, nearly two-thirds of the lower court decisions were affirmed.

The presence of this affirmance bias must be integrated into the models of political decision making. The high affirmance rate might be explained by the ideological alignment of the lower court and the circuit court, in which case the rate would not be evidence of legal considerations. The courts of appeals database does not directly code for the ideological composition of the judge being reviewed or ideological direction of the decision below. The database does, however, enable the rough construction of a variable for the ideological direction of the decision below, using the data on the ideological direction of the circuit court decision and whether that decision was an affirmance or a reversal. For future purposes, this measure of the ideological direction of the decision being reviewed is called LowerCourt. Examining this variable shows that for 63.6% of the judge votes in the database, Lower-Court was conservative. The preponderance of conservative lower court decisions means that the affirmance bias might merely be a conservative bias at the circuit court level rather than a legal model effect. Subsequent regressions attempt to isolate a distinct nonideological affirmance bias. First, though, I consider the specific legal requirements and contexts that could influence the affirmance rate.

Legal Context of Appellate Review

The circuit courts hear cases that arrive in various procedural contexts. As a general rule, circuit courts review only final decisions, but those decisions may have been rendered after a full trial on the merits or simply after a judgment on the pleadings before any case facts have been developed. A judgment on the pleadings is commonly called a dismissal and is rendered because the plaintiff lacks a legally valid claim, even after the court assumes the plaintiff's factual allegations are true. A summary judgment is another pretrial decision, made after many facts have been identified; it is rendered because no genuine dispute remains over the material facts of the case, so no trial is necessary to ascertain those facts. Consequently, the decision is a purely legal one. Other appeals are from the results of a full trial before the judge or a jury. Still other appeals relate to postjudgment orders. The most prominent of these is known as the J.N.O.V., a ruling in which the lower court judge overrules a jury verdict as unreasonable and enters a judgment for the party that lost the jury verdict. The following list provides a breakdown of the procedural context of cases in the courts of appeals database:

Posttrial	39.4%
Summary judgment	7.5%
Dismissal	16.6%
Postjudgment (J.N.O.V.)	1.6%

The remaining cases in the database were either unclassifiable or involved some standard that is not procedurally comparable (such as a ruling on injunctive relief, an appeal of a nonfinal judgment, rulings on pretrial orders, and so on).

Although there is no legally objective standard for the correct affirmance rate for the different categories of rulings, there are legal rules that call for a greater or lesser degree of deference in different legal contexts. The standard of appellate review may not perfectly align with the nature of the decision being reviewed, but the association is a close one. For example, when a district court dismisses a complaint at the outset of a case, that lower court is due little or no deference because its decision is purely law-based on given facts alleged in the complaint. If a court grants a pretrial summary judgment motion, the decision may be due some deference because it rests in part on the court's findings of undisputed facts. The coding doesn't perfectly capture the variables, because it also covers appeals in which a motion to dismiss or for summary judgment was denied; more deference would be expected for these types of denials. In most cases, however, the denial of a pretrial motion cannot be appealed because it is interlocutory and not final. Presumably, most cases coded as dismissal or summary judgment contexts were cases in which the motion was granted and less deference was due that judgment.

When a posttrial determination is reviewed, the lower court decision is due the greatest deference because the decision is based on a determination of the facts after they have been fully ventilated. But if a judge has reversed a jury's decision posttrial in a J.N.O.V., that decision receives the least deference because the jury was assigned the fact-finding responsibilities. If the legal model is operating, one would expect the affirmance rates to vary by the degree of deference due the lower court decision in light of its legal context. Under the legal model, one would expect the standard of review to be "critical to the outcome" of circuit court decisions.[21] The courts of appeals database does not precisely code for all the procedural context variables discussed earlier, but provides for some variables directly and allows some measure for others. The following list reports for the full database the affirmance rates using individual judge votes by the procedural legal context in which the circuit court heard the issue:

Procedural Context	Percent Affirmed
Trial judgment	68.0%
Summary judgment	61.1%
Dismissal	61.1%
J.N.O.V.	55.1%

These results are generally consistent with what the legal model would dictate. The highest affirmance rates are associated with the trial judgment context in which the greatest deference is due the lower court ruling, and the lowest affirmance rate is associated with the J.N.O.V., which is subject to closest appellate scrutiny. The identical results for pretrial rulings on summary judgment and dismissal are not exactly as predicted, but the results for these contexts are consistent when compared with trial judgments and J.N.O.V. ruling appeals.

The analysis of the preceding list can be refined further by considering which party brought the appeal. Plaintiffs generally bear the burden of proof on factual issues. This is not universally true, as defendants have the burden of proof on some types of legal issues, such as affirmative defenses, but it is fair to say that the burden of proof usually lies with plaintiffs. Consequently, a ruling for plaintiffs will generally be subject to more scrutiny at the circuit court level. So far as this hypothesis is true, one would expect rulings for plaintiffs to be reversed more often than rulings for defendants.

In the following investigation I strengthened the analysis by adding significance testing to the descriptive statistics. Table 2.1 shows a regression

TABLE 2.1
Reversal probability by procedural context and party

Procedural context	Coefficient	P-value
Summary judgment for plaintiff	.063	.000
Summary judgment for defendant	.006	.344
Trial judgment for plaintiff	.061	.000
Trial judgment for defendant	.017	.005
Dismissal	.005	.425
N	30,029	
R^2	.007	

on the probability of reversal in different contexts and whether the difference is statistically significant from the norm. It considers the difference in summary judgments for plaintiffs, summary judgments for defendants, trial judgments for plaintiffs, trial judgments for defendants, and dismissal judgments (virtually all of these are for defendants). The regression is limited to civil cases among private parties.

These results lend mild support to the legal model hypothesis. Courts are more likely to reverse decisions that favor the plaintiff, who bears the burden of proof, and this difference is statistically significant. The explanatory power of this effect is not very great, however.

The preceding results were limited to the standards for civil cases heard in district court. A second group of legal rules applies to circuit court reviews of executive agency decisions. Congress has chosen to apply different review standards to different types of administrative decisions, according to the statutory basis for the decision or the type of agency action. The most deferential of these review standards is the arbitrary and capricious standard adopted as the default rule by the Administrative Procedure Act. Under this standard, the agency is due great deference and should be reversed only if its determination was arbitrary or capricious or clearly contrary to the governing statute. The least deferential standard is called de novo review, which requires no particular deference to the agency. In between these standards of deference are several other standards, called the substantial evidence test, the clearly erroneous test, and the abuse of discretion test. All call for a measure of deference by the appellate court, though the precise degree of deference associated with such tests is not clear. The courts of appeals database codes directly for the particular review standard used by the circuit court. The following list reports the rates of affirmance of administrative decisions, according to the review standard applied by the court:

Review Standard	Percent Affirmed
Arbitrary and capricious	75%
Clearly erroneous	73%
Abuse of discretion	72%
Substantial evidence	70%
De novo	67%

Again, the affirmance rate is roughly as predicted by the legal implications of the review standard. These findings are strongly suggestive of power for the legal model but the findings are not conclusive. One problem with drawing conclusions from these findings is the possibility that the judge may have some discretion in choosing a review standard and may select the standard that best suits the judge's preferred ideological outcome. If so, the association might not demonstrate the constraining power of the review standard but only the judge's use of a deferential standard when his or her extralegal preferences are for deference. Moreover, the difference in affirmance rates is small and suggests that the power of the legal deference rules may not be great.

The tables and lists in this chapter so far all present evidence of legal judicial decision making. The legal model suggests that more decisions should be affirmed than reversed and that the affirmance rate should vary according to the degree of deference commanded by particular legal review standards. The results conform reasonably well to the predictions of the legal model for decisions. Up until now, however, I have not considered the possible intervening effects of other variables, such as judicial ideology. Such additional variables require investigation to effectively test for the legal model.

Regression of Deference and Ideological Variables

Assessing the relative importance of general legal deference to lower courts and judicial ideology requires that both variables be incorporated in a

T A B L E   2 . 2
Regression of deference and ideological variables

Variable	Coefficient	P-value
Ideology	.040	.000
LowerCourt	.149	.000
N	27,023	
R²	.091	

single equation. Doing so requires some manipulation of the variables in the courts of appeals database. The variables on affirmance/reversal and ideology of the circuit court outcome were used to interpolate the ideological direction of the lower court's outcome (the variable LowerCourt). Then, the ideology of the lower court can be used as an independent variable, with the ideology of the circuit court as the dependent variable. Thus, I could measure the effect of affirmance deference, even when the lower court ruling is contrary to the circuit court's preferred ideology.

The next analysis uses individual judge votes as the unit of analysis. The independent variables are the judge's ideological measure, Ideology (described in Chapter 1), and the lower court ideology (LowerCourt). If the judge's vote is to affirm, there will be an association between LowerCourt and the ideological direction of the vote, so LowerCourt serves as a proxy for affirmance deference by the circuit court. Table 2.2 reports the results of this regression.

Both affirmance deference and ideology are statistically significant in this equation, and the deference variable seems to demonstrate the significance of procedural law in judicial decision making. The R^2 term is much larger, by an order of magnitude, once legal model deference is incorporated in the basic model described in Chapter 1, and the LowerCourt coefficient for legal deference is substantial when compared to the ideological variable (even after accounting for different scales). The affirmance deference variable is a statistically significant determinant, and the introduction of this legal procedural variable clearly improves the accuracy of the model, suggesting a significant role for the law in circuit court decision making.

The relative roles of the law and ideology can be measured by another approach that also considers the procedural legal context of the decision. For this test, the dependent variable is affirmance of the lower court. The independent variable, designed to capture ideology, is whether the lower court decision was ideologically aligned with judicial preference (Align). This variable was created using LowerCourt and Ideology, and each judge and lower court decision was characterized as liberal or conservative.[22] The following list reports affirmance rates for when the lower court was ideologically aligned with the judge and when it was not:

Aligned	70.7%
Unaligned	64.5%

This list gives some proportion to the relative ideological and deference effects. Judges are more likely to affirm ideologically aligned decisions (by 6.2%), showing some effect of ideology. But judges affirm most of even those decisions that are not aligned with their ideology, demonstrating the considerable power of the legal deference effect.

Using this analytical structure, one can measure the effects of differing legal standards for deference. The following list reports the results of a regression that considers ideological alignment with the lower court along with the different review standards for a dismissal motion, summary judgment motion, trial verdict, or J.N.O.V. A test for each of these review standards demonstrates which are most likely to result in an affirmance. P-values are reported in parentheses following the coefficient:

Legal context	Affirmance
Align	.304 (.000)
Dismissal	.058 (.079)
Summary judgment	−.324 (.000)
Trial	−.030 (.240)
J.N.O.V.	−.497 (.000)
N	42,582
R^2	.011

The results offer mixed support for the legal model. The statistically significant and relatively high reversal rate for J.N.O.V. reviews is consistent with the model. The high affirmance rate for dismissals may seem inconsistent with the legal model, though this result is readily explicable. District courts use dismissals to screen out the easy cases, and it may be that the district court decisions in these actions were not difficult ones. Ideology (here expressed as Align) remains a statistically significant determinant, even with controls for review standard, showing that the ideological effect of judging survives the introduction of legal variables.

Effect of Presidential Cohorts

The effects of law and ideology may vary across judges and over time. The next analysis breaks down different cohorts of presidential appointees. I grouped the judicial appointees into five sets of judges appointed by presidents of roughly comparable ideology (Reagan/Bush, Nixon/Ford, Eisenhower, Johnson/Truman, and Carter). Then I considered each group's affirmance rate for both liberal and conservative lower court decisions. From the difference between the two affirmance rates, I could calculate the relative significance of ideology and affirmance deference for each of the sets (by taking the overall average affirmance rate and the relative difference in affirmance rates by the ideology of the lower court outcome). Table 2.3 reports the results of this comparison for all cases and also for noncriminal cases (because criminal cases produced significantly different results than other actions).

Obviously, different groups of judges show very different patterns of importance for affirmance deference and for ideology. As noted above, affirmances have declined over time, and the more recent presidential cohorts show lower affirmance rates. The earlier judges—appointees of Truman, Eisenhower, and Johnson—were less ideological and more inclined to affirm. The judges appointed by Presidents Reagan and G. H. W. Bush appear to be particularly ideological. Carter judges were not particularly liberal and were distinctly conservative in criminal cases.

These results contradict the conventional stereotype of the activist liberal judiciary. In general, the appointees of conservative presidents were more ideological in a conservative direction than were the appointees of liberal presidents in a liberal direction. The conservatives showed less deference to lower court rulings. This result might be explained by timing. The Republican appointees joined the circuit courts after decades of dominance by Roosevelt and Truman and then Kennedy and Johnson judges.

TABLE 2.3
Affirmance and ideology by appointee groups

President	ALL CASES		NONCRIMINAL CASES	
	Affirmance	Ideology	Affirmance	Ideology
Reagan/Bush	5.6%	19.4%	5.6%	11.1%
Nixon/Ford	5.2%	14.4%	6.1%	2.2%
Eisenhower	17.8%	7.4%	16.0%	3.3%
Johnson/Truman	18.9%	0.7%	14.3%	5.1%
Carter	5.0%	−7.8%	0.7%	−0.1%

This dominance may have produced a set of relatively liberal precedents, so that the conservatives had to be more ideologically aggressive to avoid producing their own pattern of liberal decisions. The results should at least dispel the fears sometimes expressed by conservatives that their judges are too passive and bound by the law and that they therefore create a pro-liberal ratchet effect in the courts. The Republican judges appear quite capable of effecting their ideologies.

Deference and Ideology on Panel Decisions

As shown in Chapter 1, it is important to investigate the decisions of full panels, rather than just individual judge votes. It is the panel decisions that make law, and individual judges may simply go along with a majority rather than expressing their true feelings in a dissent that lacks any direct consequences for the law. One would expect an analysis of panels to better demonstrate the effect of ideology (or legal variables) on the course of the law. Table 2.4 shows analysis incorporating both affirmance deference and ideology on panel decisions. It reports three independent multiple regressions; each regression uses one of the ideology measures (median judge ideological rating, total panel ideological rating, and the ratio of Democrat to Republican appointees on the panel) considered in Chapter 1. For each regression, Table 2.4 reports the correlation coefficient and the statistical significance level in parentheses.

The results make clear that both legal deference and judicial ideology matter for judges' votes. All variables are highly significant in all equations, though their relative weight varies considerably. The results for panel

TABLE 2.4
Panel regression of deference and ideological variables

Variable	(1)	(2)	(3)
LowerCourt	.150 (.000)	.150 (.000)	.163 (.000)
MedianIdeology	.072 (.000)		
TotalIdeology		.080 (.000)	
PartyRatio			.053 (.000)
N	9,906	9,906	14,017
R^2	.10	.10	.11

ideology are again stronger than for those of individual judge votes. Although the R^2 terms remain relatively small, they have grown as we have considered the role of the law and the decisions of full circuit court panels.

Some caution is required when interpreting the magnitude of the relative effects displayed in Table 2.4. The correlation coefficient represents the significance of a one-unit change in the independent variable. For the PartyRatio variable, a unit change would be the difference between a 3–0 Republican panel and a 3–0 Democrat panel, that is, from extreme conservative to extreme liberal on this scale. For the MedianIdeology variable, a unit change represents about half this difference, and for the TotalIdeology variable, a unit change is even less. Consequently, the contrasting unit changes and correlation coefficients suggest that the MedianIdeology and TotalIdeology variables capture ideology better than the more traditional PartyRatio variable. Indeed, TotalIdeology appears to be every bit as important as MedianIdeology.

Chapter 1 reported that ideology appeared to play a different role in different types of cases. To compare the relative significance of ideology and affirmance deference, I report in Table 2.5 the same regressions as in Table 2.4, with the criminal cases excluded.

Once affirmance deference is factored in, the determinants of decisions in civil cases do not appear to differ greatly from those in the full sample, which includes criminal cases. Affirmance deference appears to be slightly lower in civil cases than in criminal actions. Civil cases cover a wide range of actions, though. Chapter 1 showed that due process cases demonstrated the greatest ideological effect on decision making. Table 2.6 conducts the aforementioned three regressions, combined with the affirmance deference variable, for the due process cases in the courts of appeals database.

TABLE 2.5
Panel regression of deference and ideological variables in noncriminal cases

Variable	(1)	(2)	(3)
LowerCourt	.132 (.000)	.132 (.000)	.146 (.000)
MedianIdeology	.067 (.000)		
TotalIdeology		.080 (.000)	
PartyRatio			.050 (.000)
N	6,543	6,657	9,899
R^2	.07	.08	.09

TABLE 2.6
Panel regression of deference and ideological variables in due process cases

Variable	(1)	(2)	(3)
LowerCourt	.016 (.705)	.020 (.634)	.019 (.638)
MedianIdeology	.226 (.007)		
TotalIdeology		.237 (.004)	
PartyRatio			.154 (.051)
N	140	145	161
R^2	.05	.06	.03

Here we have dramatically different results. Affirmance deference lacks statistical significance in due process actions in all the equations, whereas ideology plays a much greater role. This may be attributed to the ideological salience of the due process actions, though the much smaller sample size for due process cases cautions against conclusive claims in this regard.

The above regressions also provide some information on how best to capture judicial preferences in panel decisions. Surprisingly, some evidence from all these regressions suggests that the TotalIdeology variable may be an equal or better determinant of outcomes than is the MedianIdeology variable, which is contrary to traditional median voter theory. This finding will be explored further in Chapter 6.

The above results demonstrate that the introduction of a legal model variable matters when analyzing judicial decision making. Affirmance deference, and different standards for affirmance deference, is a statistically significant determinant that can considerably improve the model's ability to predict judicial outcomes in most but not all categories of cases. The next questions are why, how, and when the legal model variables matter. The rest of this chapter models theories of the law's importance and tentatively tests those theories.

Modeling Theories of the Law's Importance

As discussed earlier, various theories suggest why judges might abide by the law, even at the expense of their ideological preferences. These include the enforcement theory, the duty theory, and the preference theory. Understanding the basis for legal compliance is of practical importance, because the role of the law will have different significance under different theories. For example, under the enforcement theory, the law will not matter if the hierarchical enforcers share an ideology with the circuit court panel, which would be free to ignore the law. This section provides some tentative modeling to enable testing of the theories. The enforcement theory is by far the most complex, and it will be addressed in Chapter 4.

Under the duty theory, one might speculate that ideology should not matter at all, and that evidence of any ideological decision making undermines this theory. This is not necessarily true, however. The governing power of the law depends on language, and language is inherently indeterminate to some degree. Even legal positivists, such as H. L. A. Hart, have recognized the inherent indeterminacy of legal language. Attempts to bind future judges using language are inherently imperfect and enable some discretion. The indeterminacy of language may be exacerbated by legal rules that provide conflicting guidance. Karl Llewellyn famously analyzed the canons of statutory construction and showed that they could be used to support different conclusions.

Some radical critics of law have used the concept of linguistic indeterminacy to argue that the law is therefore meaningless, but this carries indeterminacy too far. Words do have some meaning, at least within common linguistic communities. Words have both a core meaning that is determinate and a penumbral meaning that is indeterminate.[23] Classical Langdellian formalists and their heirs are sometimes called Foundationalists. Their radical critics, such as those of the Critical Legal Studies movement, have been characterized as Anti-Foundationalists, because they reject all claims of linguistic constraint on the law. The answer to this debate need not be found at either extreme. It is both possible and intuitively likely that the law as expressed in the language of statutes and opinions exercises some influence on the judiciary but does not totally control judicial decisions.

Even the legal realists did not totally disclaim a role for law in judicial decision making. Llewellyn conceded *"some* relation between *any* accepted rule and judicial behavior," but demanded that the nature of this relationship be examined empirically rather than be merely assumed.[24] This empirical examination of the law's role is the object of this chapter. The analysis discussed earlier demonstrates that the law, or at least certain legal procedures, plays a significant role in circuit court outcomes. This research did not address which of the theories of law's relevance was most likely operating in the courts. Understanding which theory is most accurate can help us understand when and how the law matters.

Figure 2.1 depicts how the effects of the duty theory might operate. The line is a two-dimensional expression of ideological position from liberal to conservative. The current state of the law is at ideological position A. Because of the inescapable indeterminacy of the expression of this legal position, however, courts have some degree of flexibility in its application, within the ideological range expressed by the brackets. Suppose a judge with ideological position C has to apply the law. The judge would prefer to reach a decision at ideological point C and would do so if unconstrained. But if the judge feels a duty to apply the law, the judge will be constrained. The judge would render a decision at point B, which is as close to C's ideologically conservative position as the constraint of the law allows. If penumbral language has a limited space beyond which it cannot plausibly be stretched, there would be boundaries on how far ideology can control decisions. Under the duty theory, the legal rules, as applied in good faith, do not compel just one outcome but determine a range of permissible outcomes.

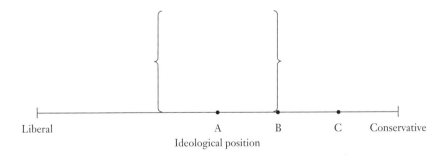

Figure 2.1   Duty Theory Constraints

Figure 2.1 shows how the law and ideology could interact in a way in which both matter in judicial decision making. If the decision of the judge with ideological position C were purely ideological, the result would be at point C; if the decision were purely legal, the result would be at point A. The combination of the two factors results in an intermediate result at point B.

The duty theory is but one possible way in which the law and ideology might interact. The preference theory requires a different display, that of Figure 2.2. Although it is more difficult to reduce legal preferences to a single two-dimensional scale, this reduction might be conceived of as a degree of devotion to a particular legal interpretive theory, such as textualism. In this figure, point A is the judge's preferred point, both ideologically and legally. The judge is then confronted with a particular case. The judge could decide this case at point B, in accord with his or her ideological preference. To reach this ideologically desirable position, however, the judge would have to depart considerably from his or her legal preference (the ver-

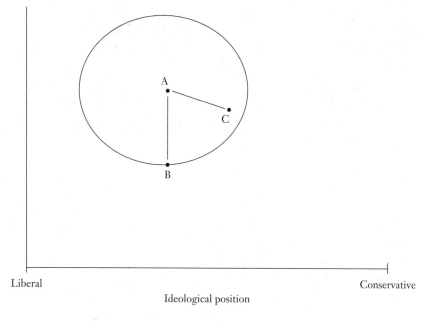

Liberal   Conservative

Ideological position

Figure 2.2   Preference Theory Application

tical distance between A and B). The judge might alternatively decide at point C. Although C is more ideologically (horizontally) remote from A than is B, C is inside the radius of the circle, which means its total (combined ideological/legal) distance from A is less than the distance of B from A. If the judge placed equal importance on law and ideology, the judge would prefer point C to point B.

Figure 2.2 shows how, under the dual preference theory, a judge might prefer an ideologically more distant point to an ideologically equivalent point, given the existence of legal preferences. Under the preference theory, the judge would sometimes defer to the law and would other times rely on ideological preferences, depending on which approach maximized his or her combined legal and ideological preferences.

Ideological Extremes and the Law

There is no clear and direct means of testing the duty theory and preference theory of judicial decisions. One might argue that the due process results discussed earlier refute the duty theory of circuit court decision making. Due process is a constitutional issue of significant ideological importance, and the judicial panels appeared wholly unconstrained by affirmance deference, contrary to what the duty theory would suggest. Although this is a plausible inference, the results are not necessarily contrary to the duty theory. Due process is a notoriously amorphous concept, and it might simply be that the binds of law in this area are especially loose, giving ideology freer rein.

Consideration of ideological extremes is a better tool for analysis of the theories. If judges adhere to the law according to the duty theory, the extent of their ideology has a limit. They can decide ideologically only within the bracketed region shown in Figure 2.1, which should constrain the overall effect of ideology. Consequently, the most ideologically extreme judges should have their ideological effect muted under the duty theory because there are bounds on the degree to which ideology can be implemented in judicial decisions. By contrast, under preference theory, one would not expect the more ideologically extreme judge to be muted; no brackets limit the degree to which ideology may be involved in decision making. Under the preference theory, we would expect ideological extremity to have an equal or possibly even greater effect on decision making than would more moderate ideological preferences.

The next analysis shows the overall regression for ideological extremity and includes the effect of this variable in the context of affirmance deference. The dependent variable is the ideological direction of the circuit court panel decision, and the independent variables are Lower-Court, MedianIdeology, and MedianIdeology^2. The last variable, Median-Ideology^2, captures the relative effect of the more extreme ideological preferences among the judges. There should be a negative association between Median-Ideology^2 and outcomes under my hypothesis about the duty theory, whereas a positive association would be expected under the preference theory. The following list gives the results of the regression:

LowerCourt	.15 (.000)
MedianIdeology	.07 (.000)
MedianIdeology^2	.01 (.158)
N	9,906
R^2	.10

As I reported in Chapter 1, with no legal variable, judicial ideological extremity has a positive though not statistically significant effect on outcomes. These results are more consistent with the preference theory of legal decision making than with the duty theory. More ideologically extreme positions are not muted by affirmance deference. The results indicate that the determinative effect of judicial ideology is essentially linear or perhaps even a little more powerful at the extremes. MedianIdeology^2 is not a powerful variable in the preceding list but it is positive and approaches the more liberal tests for statistical significance, which suggests that ideological extremes are not especially constrained by legal rules. Although these results do not entirely disprove the duty theory of legal decision making, they suggest that it does not create a powerful constraint, because the results indicate that the brackets imposed by duty are so broad that they can accommodate some effect for even the most ideologically extreme judicial panels. The law still matters, though, in a manner that is statistically significant and apparently more substantively significant than the measures for judicial ideology. Thus, it appears that legal preferences are significant in the circuit courts.

Law and Opinion Length

One would expect that certain legal variables, such as affirmance versus reversal, could influence opinion length. Because of the legal presumptions favoring affirmance, reversals might be expected to require lengthier opinions, at least to the degree that the law matters in opinion writing. The following list reports the results of a study of opinion length that incorporates Reversal as a separate independent variable along with the ratio of Republican to Democratic judges:

Reversal	.132 (.000)
Party ratio	−.08 (.000)
N	13,225
R^2	.024

These results confirm the hypothesis that reversals produce longer opinions. The absolute difference in opinion length is small but could be pragmatically meaningful. The median opinion length for an affirmance among all the cases was three pages. The median opinion length for a reversal was four pages. Although the one-page difference for reversals might seem insignificant, it represents a 33% increase in opinion length. Such an increase could have material legal importance and possibly give reversals greater precedential power.

The preceding list did not fully capture the intersection of ideology and opinion deference with opinion length because my analysis did not distinguish between ideological and anti-ideological reversals and affirmances. Perhaps judges write longer opinions when they ideologically prefer the case outcome. The regression in Table 2.7 breaks down the effect of ideological alignment on opinion length. For an independent variable, the study uses the effect on opinion length of judicial ideology alignment or nonalignment with the district court opinion, for cases of reversal and of affirmance of the rulings shown in the table.

TABLE 2.7
Alignment, affirmance, and opinion length

	Reversal	Affirmance
Aligned	−.008 (.623)	−.072 (.000)
N	4,066	8,114
R^2	.000	.005

When the circuit court reverses, its ideological alignment has no effect on opinion length. When the court affirms, by contrast, unaligned panels will write longer opinions than aligned panels. One could hypothesize that the longer opinions in this circumstance are meant to limit the scope of the holding and its precedential effect because the outcome apparently does not align with judicial ideological preferences. One might expect to see a similar effect for unaligned reversals, though such reversals are much less common and the results may sometimes reflect specification errors.

Another analysis considers the effect of the judgment under review on opinion length. Under the legal model, one would expect summary judgment reviews to require the lengthiest analysis, because a key issue on review is whether the material facts were subject to genuine dispute. A review of a dismissal should require shorter length because less factual explication is needed. A review of a trial judgment might be of intermediate length because the facts were at issue, but the factual findings of the court below were entitled to great deference by the circuit court. Table 2.8 incorporates these variables into a multiple regression analysis on opinion length, with and without control variables for affirmance versus reversal and ideological direction of the outcome.

These results are consistent with the prediction of the legal model. Reviews of summary judgments require longer opinions than reviews of dismissals, when I controlled for affirmance. Reversals require significantly longer opinions, as the legal model would suggest. Some ideological effect remains, though, because liberal outcomes have slightly longer opinions than do conservative holdings.

The opinion length analyses cannot tell us much with clarity, but they do add some additional heft to the findings that the law matters, at least in the context of affirmance deference. The greater length of reversal opinions, as opposed to affirmance opinions, is what the legal model would predict,

THE LAW AND CIRCUIT COURTS **67**

TABLE 2.8
Opinion length by procedural context

Procedural context	(1)	(2)
Trial judgment	−.021 (.027)	−.018 (.066)
Summary judgment	.052 (.000)	.049 (.000)
Dismissal	−.068 (.000)	−.064 (.000)
Reversal		.123 (.000)
Ideology		.022 (.014)
N	13,400	13,400
R²	.008	.025

because of affirmance deference. The greater effort required to write a longer opinion may also provide a pragmatic explanation for the effect of affirmance deference on the circuit courts, beyond what the legal model commands. Reversing a decision apparently requires greater judicial effort.

Conclusion

There is ample empirical evidence in this chapter that legal rules matter in determining judicial outcomes. The evidence does not support strong Foundationalist claims because it leaves room for the influence of ideology. But the evidence does refute contrary claims, because it demonstrates that, beyond ideological influences, legal rules of procedure matter greatly in determining outcomes. Consideration of such rules significantly improves the pure ideological model when explaining circuit court outcomes.

This chapter has tested only one small slice of the legal model, the procedural rules of deference. The role of the law identified in the earlier results is by no means the limit of the law's influence, because substantive rules of law were not even measured. As discussed previously, it can be very difficult to construct a test for such substantive legal standards. If procedural legal rules demonstrably matter in case outcomes, however, it seems reasonable to assume that substantive rules also matter, even if they cannot be readily measured with available coding.

The findings thus have major specification limitations. The variable for the law has captured only a small number of the legal issues before the circuit court and has captured that only imprecisely. Such specification weaknesses are inevitable in such a complex area as circuit court decision making and in such a large database sample. The results probably capture only the tip of the iceberg but are nevertheless informative about the nature of circuit court decision making. Because the law has a more pronounced effect than does ideology and because the specification for law is probably much worse than that for ideology, it seems clear that the law is a major determinant of circuit court outcomes. As I elaborate on the basic law and ideology models in subsequent chapters, more detail about such decision making will be understood.

THREE

Judicial Background and Circuit Court Decision Making

Much of the quantitative empirical research on extralegal factors in judicial decision making has focused on the political party of the appointing president as a proxy for judicial ideology. Although people have many background factors that might influence their opinions, such as race, religion, gender, and occupational background and wealth, many political scientists have suggested that these factors are unimportant. The original legal realists, though, placed great importance on a judge's background. One could plausibly suggest that background helps us understand the extralegal ideological component of judicial decision making. The so-called country club Republicans differ in their views from the religious right, for example.

Although there is some obvious reason to think that judicial background might matter, the situation is unclear. Candidates for the judiciary are screened by presidents and the Senate before they assume the bench; they are not randomly selected from others of the same background. Consequently, circuit court judges that share one background trait do not necessarily share other traits common to that background. For example, blacks are more liberal on average on at least some issues, but such blacks as Clarence Thomas, appointed by Republican presidents, may not be liberal. If presidents screen for ideological preferences, that effect may wash out the effect of any general background traits, which may be why past research has often dismissed those traits. The judicial attributes database contains a wealth of information on the backgrounds of the circuit court judges, which enables testing for whether the generalized features of personal background have a surviving influence on judicial decision making.

Judicial Background and Decision Making

Although judges are generally loathe to explain their decisions with ideology, they have been quite open about conceding that some aspect of their personal background influences their decisions. Supreme Court justice Stephen Breyer conceded that a judge's background and values inevitably play a role in judgments. Judge Patricia Wald, while downplaying the role of ideology in decisions, observed that judges "cannot help but be influenced by their life experiences."[1] Judges who disclaim the importance of party affiliation are much more willing to concede a background effect.

Nothing about the influence of personal background is any more theoretically legitimate than reliance on ideological or political factors, though. The rule of law does not suggest that it is acceptable for the law's application to vary depending on the judge's background. If a judge is more likely to vote for a litigant of his or her own race, for example, that must be bad. Thus, it is somewhat surprising that judges have been so willing to concede the influence of background while resisting claims of ideological influence. Perhaps the reason for the distinction is that one's background is immutable and inescapable and no judge can overcome it. If this is so, one might expect background to play a distinct role in judicial decision making.

If the role of background is indeed inevitable, that does not make background more legitimate in judicial decision making but does suggest that our policies need to acknowledge and adapt to the role of background. For Judge Frank Coffin, this meant the use of an "antidote" in the form of "the variety of backgrounds usually represented on a multi-judge court" to "offset or at least minimize particular predispositions."[2] A finding that judicial background is significant could support claims of the importance of diversity on the bench. No one has demonstrated, though, that life background is an inevitably important determinant of judicial decisions. The rest of this chapter examines the possible association.

Personal Life Background

Various personal factors might influence judicial decision making. Gender and race are obvious examples of individual characteristics that may affect a person's outlook. Age might be another influential factor, as might sexual orientation. One can imagine any number of such influential background factors, including even birth order, that might sway decisions, but this chapter focuses on those that intuitively seem most consequential and for which there is available data.

Gender is certainly a fundamental feature of an individual's life. Regardless of whether gender is considered innate or socially constructed, it plays a significant role in the nature of one's experiences. Some theorists have postulated that men and women have fundamentally different views, arguing that women focus on caring while men focus on rights and rules.[3] Such a difference in perspective, if true, would obviously play a significant role in judging. Given this hypothesized difference, one would expect male judges to be harsher toward criminal defendants than would female judges. There is also evidence that men and women have different political voting patterns, commonly called the gender gap; such voting differences might show up on the bench as well.

Race is an undeniably sensitive topic in contemporary America. People are loathe to assign particular characteristics or views to anyone based on their race. As with gender, however, a person's race may play a part in forming his or her attitudes, if only because of the social construction of racial differences. There is a vast racial gulf in political voting, with blacks overwhelmingly favoring Democratic candidates. Minorities in general tend to identify more with underdogs than does the majority group. This tendency could appear in patterns of judicial decision making.

Religion is another personal factor that might be expected to influence judicial decision making. Religion, sincerely believed, should logically play a substantial role in one's value choices, including those that judges must inevitably make. Religion is also analogous to political ideology because religion involves a deliberate individual value choice and thus captures something fundamental about an individual's belief system. Consequently, one has good reason to expect that religion would matter in judicial decision making. Of course, any effect of religion or any other personal trait could be washed out by the preappointment screening process.

Personal Experience Background

In addition to innate features, such as gender, and life decisions, such as religion, one's attitudes can be shaped by personal experiences. It is said that a conservative is a liberal who has been mugged, and surely being a victim of crime could influence a person's attitudes about the criminal justice system. Justice Breyer lost much money in an investment in Lloyd's of London as a consequence of that company's asbestos litigation, and this might have influenced his views of the liability system.

The most salient personal experiences may come from the occupational background of judges. Most judges have considerable experience within the justice system. Some have been prosecutors, and so might be expected to identify and side with the prosecution. But former prosecutors might also be more aware of possible prosecutorial abuses. The same could be true of those who were former plaintiffs' attorneys or defense attorneys in civil actions. Many circuit court judges have been elevated from the district courts. They might be inclined to grant more deference to their former brethren than would a former law professor or former prosecutor.

Nonoccupational life experiences might also have some effect on judicial decisions. A judge who has been mugged might be stricter on criminal defendants than one who has never been a crime victim. A wealthy judge might have greater interest in protecting property rights than one of meager means. Everyday experience informs us that such life situations and experiences influence people's political opinions, so we should not be surprised if judges are likewise affected. Of course, the general probabilistic differences associated with different life experiences might also be washed out by the preappointment screening process. Even if this were so, some reasons remain to favor diverse backgrounds on the judiciary.[4]

Empirical Research on the Effect of Judicial Background

Some of the earliest quantitative studies of judicial decision making conducted by political scientists focused on the background of judges. The pioneers of this analysis suggested that background was a leading determinant of decisions. Empirical testing of the theory followed. One major study of Supreme Court decision making could correctly predict 70–90% of the decisions based on background variables.[5] But the study used party of appointing president as one of the background variables, and that variable proved to be the most powerful of all those studied. The research did not establish that background, other than party, was a major factor (though it did find past prosecutorial experience to be relatively significant in the civil liberties cases studied). Jeffrey Segal and Harold Spaeth concluded that the empirical evidence provides little support for the relationship between social background factors and judicial attitudes.[6] Studies of race and gender have generally shown little power in explaining judicial decisions. J. Woodford Howard observed that his study of past judicial experience had no significant effect, except for in civil rights cases.[7] For some time, quantitative studies did not use any independent variable to test for either personal or occupational background effects.

More-recent studies have renewed interest in the consideration of background effects. A large and detailed study of decisions on the constitutionality of federal sentencing guidelines examined several background characteristics.[8] It found that gender did not appear to play a role in judicial decisions, that there were some racial differences but not statistically significant ones, and that some aspects of occupational background, such as past prosecutorial experience, seemed to play a role in judicial decisions. Many other studies have generally found little background effect. A study of President Carter's circuit court appointees found no real difference between men and women and a difference between black and white judges that was confined to criminal cases.[9] Another study, however, found no difference between black and white judges in their criminal sentencing.[10]

The significance of particular background factors may vary considerably by case type. Some recent studies have found that a judge's race and gender have a significant effect in some types of civil rights actions. The best recent study of background effects examined judicial decisions on gay rights.[11] The results showed a dramatic effect for several background factors, with minority race and female gender producing significantly more decisions in favor of gay rights. Religion was a very significant variable, with Judaism producing decisions for gay rights and Catholicism producing contrary results. Age also played an important role, with younger judges favoring gay rights. But this study included all types of courts, including courts of last resort and state courts, the latter to which judges are often elected. Party affiliation played a greater role in federal courts and background a lesser role, findings consistent with the theory that appointment screening mutes the effects of background differences. The significance of judicial background characteristics on circuit decisions is still generally undemonstrated.

Implications of Background Effect

Although judges have often characterized the role of background as an innocuous factor, when compared with judicial ideology the implications of background analysis are actually more troublesome. Circuit court judges are selected by the president, with the advice and consent of the Senate. It is uncontroversial for the president to choose judges who are ideologically amenable and for the Senate to use ideology as a screen for approving those judges. This practice recognizes the role of ideology in judging. It would be more controversial, however, for the president and Senate to use at least some of the background variables in judicial selection. If a president declined to appoint, say, women or Jews, based on their expected decision making, such a conclusion would surely create a political firestorm and possibly be unconstitutional. When the Democrats in the Senate declined to confirm several Bush nominees who happened to be Catholic, the Republican party took the offensive and charged that the Democrats were engaged in religious discrimination. The appearance of direct consideration of background factors can be politically sensitive.

Some have directly made the case for consideration of background factors in arguing for a more diverse judiciary. The case for diversity need not rely on a finding of background effects in decision making. Diversity might be supported by its potential contribution to public confidence in the judiciary, or by its provision of likely role models, or by its contributions to panel analysis. If judicial background *is* an important determinant of decisions, though, the case for diversity on the bench could seem more compelling. One might prefer a judiciary that "looks like America."

Unlike the legal and ideological variables, many background variables are easy to precisely operationalize in statistical analysis of judicial decision making. The courts of appeals database, when integrated with the judicial attributes database, which has tremendous detail on judicial background, enables direct testing for the influence of factors such as race, gender, wealth, and employment history. The judicial attributes database is missing some potentially interesting variables, such as sexual orientation, but contains coding for most of the relevant background variables.

By adding background variables, we can also better understand the effect of the ideological variables. Maybe what appears to be an ideological effect is truly a background effect, or maybe ideology carries different degrees of significance in the context of certain personal backgrounds. Also, certain backgrounds may counteract the ideological effect in some circumstances.

Personal Background Variables

This section of the chapter presents regressions of the effect of personal background variables on decisions, beginning with the effect of race. The overwhelming majority of judge votes in the database (more than 96%) are characterized as by whites. I created a new variable, Minority, to determine whether the voting patterns of blacks and Hispanics differ from those of the overwhelming majority of white judges. Table 3.1 reports a simple regression of race on ideological voting, and a second regression, with Ideology as another variable, to control for the effect of appointment screening.

Minority status has a statistically significant effect in this analysis and produces more liberal decisions. Controlling for ideological appointment screening does not explain away this result; consideration of this variable actually strengthens the minority effect. The consequences of Minority, in the R^2 term, are vanishingly small, but there is some effect to the background variable. Table 3.2 conducts the same analyses but with affirmance deference as the dependent variable. Although there is no particular theoretical reason why background should play a significant role in the level of affirmance deference, the analysis is included for exploratory reasons.

Minorities on the bench show less affirmance deference, even after controlling for Ideology. This interesting finding might suggest that minorities are more ideologically motivated or it might simply indicate that minorities have less faith in the district court judges whose decisions are under review. As noted in Chapter 1, the type of case influences decision making, so this too should be considered. The identified minority effect may be attributable to a particular set of cases, so Table 3.3 conducts regressions on ideology and affirmance with criminal cases excluded.

The ideological effect of minority status disappears in this analysis, showing that the effect is entirely attributable to criminal cases. Given the large percentage of minorities arrested for crimes, perhaps it is unsurprising

TABLE 3.1
Race and ideological votes

Variable	(1)	(2)
Minority	.012 (.013)	.018 (.005)
Ideology		.038 (.000)
N	41,627	27,002
R^2	.000	.002

TABLE 3.2
Race and affirmance deference

Variable	(1)	(2)
Minority	−.016 (.001)	−.029 (.000)
Ideology		−.003 (.680)
N	41,627	27,002
R^2	.000	.001

TABLE 3.3
Race in noncriminal actions

Variable	Ideology	Affirmance
Minority	−.002 (.784)	−.015 (.052)
Ideology	.045 (.000)	−.000 (.999)
N	17,846	17,846
R^2	.002	.000

TABLE 3.4
Gender and ideological votes

Variable	(1)	(2)
Female	.018 (.000)	.020 (.001)
Ideology		.040 (.000)
N	41,627	27,002
R^2	.000	.002

TABLE 3.5
Gender and affirmance deference

Variable	(1)	(2)
Female	−.004 (.403)	.011 (.065)
Ideology		−.003 (.676)
N	41,627	27,002
R^2	.000	.000

that minority judges are more sympathetic to their claims than are white judges. But the effect of minority status remains nearly significant in the affirmance equation for noncriminal cases. This finding shows that the lack of affirmance deference for minorities is not primarily a matter of ideology but more due to minority skepticism about lower court decisions.

Gender is another background variable worthy of consideration. The judges in the database are also overwhelmingly (more than 97%) male. The same analyses run to assess the effect of race were used to test gender, with Female as the independent variable. Table 3.4 displays the results.

As with race, gender has a statistically significant effect, with women more likely to cast liberal votes than men. At this point, it appears that judicial background, or at least being minority and female, has a liberalizing effect on votes, even beyond measures of judicial ideology. Like minorities, female circuit court judges might be more dubious of lower courts. Table 3.5 reports the effect of gender on affirmance deference.

Female judges do not show the same pattern as minority judges on affirmance deference, though a hint of this effect appears in the second regression with the control for Ideology. Female judges do not appear significantly skeptical of lower court outcomes. The minority effect was confined to criminal cases, and Table 3.6 reports the regressions for female judges, with criminal cases excluded.

As with minorities, the female ideological effect is confined to criminal

TABLE 3.6
Gender in noncriminal actions

Variable	Ideology	Affirmance
Female	.000 (.953)	−.003 (.700)
Ideology	.045 (.000)	−.004 (.589)
N	17,846	17,846
R^2	.002	.000

cases, with no ideological difference in noncriminal matters. Women, like minorities, are more sympathetic to criminal defendants. The normative significance of this finding depends on the reference point. Perhaps white males have an antidefendant bias and so are the biased ones in criminal matters. The regression results cannot tell us which group, if any, is the more ideological in criminal actions, but the results demonstrate some significance for background.

The next variable to be tested is religion. Early research found a significant effect for judicial religious affiliation in certain types of cases, such as civil liberties and criminal procedure disputes.[12] Religion cannot be captured in the same binary manner as race or gender because the database codes for more than twenty religious affiliations, and even this level of detail might be too simplistic (e.g., for failing to differentiate between branches of Judaism). I have created new religion variables for Catholic, Jewish, and Protestant affiliation of the judges. The Protestant variable includes members of many mainstream Protestant affiliations, including those judges characterized in the database as Baptist, Christian, Congregationalist, Episcopalian, Lutheran, Methodist, Presbyterian, or simply Protestant. In contrast with race or gender, the religious background of circuit court judges is reasonably diverse. The following list sets out the relative frequency of judicial votes in the database by the judge's religion, for all faiths that had more than 5% of the judge votes:

Episcopalian	18.6%
Catholic	18.4%
Presbyterian	13.3%
Jewish	11.8%
Methodist	10.1%
Protestant	8.9%

Unitarian	6.4%
Baptist	5.1%

Although the largest number of votes come from judges affiliated with some form of Protestantism, there is considerable theological difference between even some of the Protestant faiths. A much smaller percentage of judge votes were associated with faiths such as the United Church of Christ, Universalists, Congregationalists, and other denominations. No judges characterized themselves as agnostic or atheist, though no religious affiliation was coded for 3.8% of the judge votes, so these judges might possibly fall into those categories.

Each of the primary religions is introduced as a separate variable for the effect of religion on ideological outcome of the judge's vote. Simple regressions were run for each religious grouping alone, and then with the Ideology variable as a control. The results are reported in Table 3.7.

Religion does not appear to play much role, though there is some association between being Jewish and voting more conservatively. The effect is very small, however. Neither being Catholic nor being Protestant shows any material effect on judicial voting. The effect of ideology seems to clearly trump any effect from religious background.

Another personal variable that could affect decision making is age. Winston Churchill allegedly declared that if you're not a liberal at age twenty, you have no heart, and if you're not a conservative at age forty, you have no brain. Some early research found that older judges were more conservative, though the effect was small.[13] The study on gay rights decisions found a more pronounced association between age and conservatism. If Churchill's aphorism is indeed true, one might expect to see an ideological impact

TABLE 3.7
Religion and ideological votes

Religion	(1)	(2)	(3)	(4)	(5)	(6)
Catholic	−.035 (.212)	.308 (.670)				
Jewish			−.009 (.007)	−.097 (.116)		
Protestant					.014 (.542)	−.006 (.420)
Ideology		.014 (.000)		.319 (.000)		.047 (.000)
N	34,347	22,001	34,347	22,001	34,347	22,001
R^2	.000	.002	.000	.003	.001	.002

from the age of judges (though there were no twenty-year-old circuit court judges to be tested). The variable Age was computed from the database by subtracting the judge's year of birth from the year of the judicial vote. The following list reports the age distribution of judicial votes in the database:

Younger than 40	0.6%
40s	9.4%
50s	32.1%
60s	39.6%
70 and older	18.3%

Circuit court judges are relatively mature, with most votes cast by judges in their fifties and sixties. The database contained a few coding errors, including six votes reportedly cast by a 138-year-old judge. These were excluded, and the few other errors should not matter much among the tens of thousands of judge votes. The first evaluation is the effect of judicial age on ideological case outcome. Table 3.8 reports the association of age and ideology of judicial vote.

There is no meaningful association of age and ideology for judge votes. Older judges actually cast more liberal votes than did younger judges, but the difference was not statistically significant. Again, any effect of age is overwhelmed by the effect of ideology, and even combined they explain relatively little variance in the judge votes.

Age might also be expected to have an association with the level of affirmance deference. An affirmance might take less effort than a reversal because a reversal could require more explanation in the opinion, given the legal standards of deference. If older judges are less able or less interested in working hard, there might be some association between advancing age and increased affirmance deference. Table 3.9 reports the results of a regression of judge age and votes to affirm, by age and by the judicial Ideology measure.

TABLE 3.8
Age and ideological votes

Variable	(1)	(2)
Age	.003 (.518)	.008 (.210)
Ideology		.042 (.000)
N	34,347	22,001
R^2	.000	.002

TABLE 3.9
Age and affirmance deference

Variable	(1)	(2)
Age	.007 (.147)	−.012 (.058)
Ideology		.004 (.471)
N	35,681	23,002
R^2	.000	.000

The hypothesized association of age and affirmance deference is not supported by the analyses. With controls for ideology, older judges show less affirmance deference than younger judges. Older judges are apparently willing to make the extra effort necessary to reverse. Age does not appear to play a role in either judicial ideology or the degree of deference granted to lower court decisions.

Combination of Personal Background Variables

Until now, the studies have considered only the personal background variables in isolation. Such an approach may produce misleading results because of the possible correlations among such variables. For example, if most minority judges were also female, the liberal outcomes associated with minority votes might actually be due to gender. Only by controlling for all the variables in the same equation can we separate out the effects of each aspect of personal background. Table 3.10 reports the multiple regression on ideological outcome for all judge votes, with all the personal background characteristics included as independent variables, plus Ideology, to control for appointment ideology, and LowerCourt, to control for the level of affirmance deference. The same logistic regression results are reported separately for noncriminal cases because they seem to produce different associations than those for criminal cases.

The incorporation of all variables into a single model increases our understanding of the role played by personal background variables. For all cases, female status is obviously more associated with liberal voting than is minority status. Religion begins to show a distinct influence. Once other background and control variables are introduced, Judaism and Protestantism are significant determinants, with both having a conservative effect, especially in criminal cases. Age remains an insignificant determinant. But the significance of these background variables is overwhelmed by the effect of affirmance deference to LowerCourt and, to a lesser degree, appointment ideology as measured by Ideology. For noncriminal cases, however, none of the background variables is significant. The background variables appear to play a statistically significant role in determining outcomes in criminal appeals, but not in the broad category of civil appeals.

The noncriminal cases covered a wide range of distinct topics. One might expect some effect from the background variables in subsets of civil appeals. For example, one might expect minority or female status to be significant in civil rights actions. The same regression model from Table 3.10 was run for each major group of cases (as described in the list on page 26 of Chapter 1) in the database. Reporting each of these analyses would require too much space in light of the limited results, but Table 3.11 displays by ideological direction and case type the results that were statistically significant at the .05 level.

Few variables are significant, regardless of the case type breakdown. Fe-

TABLE 3.10
Personal background and ideological votes

Variable	All cases	Noncriminal cases
Minority	−.025 (.767)	−.096 (.347)
Female	.187 (.106)	.049 (.719)
Catholic	−.059 (.354)	.014 (.854)
Jewish	−.154 (.026)	−.119 (.155)
Protestant	−.131 (.027)	−.069 (.337)
Age	−.002 (.313)	−.003 (.179)
Ideology	.324 (.000)	.337 (.000)
LowerCourt	1.326 (.000)	1.107 (.000)
N	35,681	24,966
R^2	.119	.096

TABLE 3.11
Significant associations of background by case type

Group	Direction	Case type
Minority	Liberal	Privacy
Minority	Liberal	Labor relations
Age	Liberal	Economic regulation
Jewish	Conservative	First Amendment

male status is not significant for any noncriminal group, but minority status appears to have some liberal effect on limited categories of decisions. The only association for any religious variable was a conservative effect for Judaism in First Amendment cases. The primary case categories in the database are still broad groups, though; a greater effect might be found in smaller and more discrete case areas, such as abortion rights.

Personal Experience Variables

Judges may be influenced not only by fundamental attributes of their personal backgrounds but also by their life experiences. One significant personal experience is occupation. The combined courts of appeals and judicial attributes databases have information on the occupational background of judges that enables us to test for an effect. Some of the backgrounds categorized are previous service as a U.S. attorney; in the solicitor general's office; as a special prosecutor; as a professor of law; in private practice; in the state or federal government's legislature; in the state or federal executive branch, including service as governor, mayor, and in a cabinet-level appointment; as state district attorney; and as a judge. Although the available data enable one to track a judge's entire background experience, this analysis is limited to consideration of the position that the judge held immediately before his or her appointment to the circuit court. There are few obvious theories about how such previous experience should affect ideological outcomes (beyond the individual's own ideology).

To eliminate any possible effect of judicial filtration of occupational background effects, I limited the first analyses to those who were not judges before joining the circuit courts. The effect of background variables on the ideological direction of judge votes was initially tested for all votes. Ideology was used as a control variable, to capture the perceived ideology of the judge and enable some measurement of whether occupational background has some effect beyond this baseline ideological estimate. LowerCourt was also included as a control variable for the effect of affirmance deference. Given the very large number of previous occupations coded, the following list reports only those previous occupations that showed a statistically significant effect (at the .05 level) on ideological outcome and the magnitude of the coefficient for these variables with ideological direction:

LowerCourt	.148
Ideology	.049
State Senate	.030 (conservative)
State governor	.043 (conservative)
District attorney	.018 (liberal)
Other federal	.019 (conservative)
Mayor	.018 (conservative)
Special prosecutor	.024 (conservative)
N	26,840
R^2	.095

Previous occupation seems to have some effect on votes but does not appear to play a major role in the ideological direction of decisions. Although several occupations were statistically significant, the overall effect on the R^2 term was small, increasing it only from .091 to .095 (when compared with the regression using only LowerCourt and Ideology). The coefficients for the occupations were quite small. Moreover, no unambiguous conclusions can be drawn about the small residual effect, but it appears that prior service in state and local government generally leads to slightly more conservative decisions among circuit court judges. This was not true of all such categories (e.g., previous state house service), but it was a common association. Surprisingly, previous district attorney service has a liberal effect.

Perhaps the most likely ideological effect of previous occupation might be seen in criminal cases. One would hypothesize that those who came to the bench with experience in criminal prosecution would favor the government in criminal cases and therefore produce more conservative decisions. The following list uses the same multiple regression as in the preceding list but limited to criminal cases. The statistically significant results are displayed:

LowerCourt	.022
Ideology	.045
Private practice	.032 (liberal)
U.S. Senate	.028 (liberal)
Assistant district attorney	.037 (conservative)

Other federal	.031 (conservative)
Mayor	.030 (conservative)
N	9,125
R^2	.018

The results are not as hypothesized. Although prior service as an assistant district attorney was significantly associated with conservative voting, this was not true for service as a district attorney, U.S. attorney, assistant U.S. attorney, or special prosecutor. This personal experience variable is not an important determinant of judicial decision making. The relatively liberal results for those coming to the bench from private practice may suggest an affinity for defendants, but the overall substantive impact of the associations remains quite low when compared with the ideology baseline and affirmance deference and in light of the small R^2 term.

The preceding analyses excluded those who were judges in other courts before assuming the circuit court position. Many circuit court judges have been elevated from the federal district courts and have that judicial experience in their background. The overall rate of elevation from district court has historically hovered around 40% but has varied considerably by president. Only 26.8% of Carter appointees were such elevations, whereas a majority of G. H. W. Bush and Ford appointments to the circuit courts were elevations.[14]

The significance of prior judicial experience is not perfectly clear. There is no particular reason why such service should produce ideologically different outcomes. One might hypothesize, however, that previous judicial experience might have an effect on legal variables. Thus, a circuit court judge who came from another judicial position might show a greater willingness to defer to the lower court's ruling, even when that ruling is ideologically disagreeable. One good measure for the degree of such deference is the frequency with which ideologically unaligned decisions are affirmed. The overall rate for unaligned affirmance for the full database of judge votes is 64.5%, as reported in Chapter 2. The following list reports these rates for various judicial backgrounds:

Federal district court	65.7%
Other federal judge	63.2%

State supreme court   64.4%
State lower court   64.7%
Municipal court   68.4%

Here we see evidence of a slight effect. Those elevated to the circuit court from the federal district courts were 1.2% more likely to affirm unaligned district court decisions. The small difference is nonetheless statistically significant. Those appointed from municipal courts have a much higher unaligned affirmance rate, but those appointed from other federal courts have a slightly lower rate. Prior judicial experience does appear to exert a modest effect on affirmance deference.

Occupation is not the only personal experience variable of potential interest. One's financial status may also influence decision making. Wealthier judges might be expected to be more conservative, because the wealthy are more likely to be at least somewhat politically conservative and vote Republican. This variable has gone unexamined in the existing research. The supplemented database has information on the assets and liabilities of some of the judges, from which I constructed a variable, Net, determined by simply subtracting liabilities from assets. The calculations yield a range of wealth from $0 to more than $10 million. The mean measure of Net was $923,599 and the median was $313,378. Very little information was available on judicial wealth, so the sample size available to test this variable is much smaller than for previous tests.

To test the effect of judicial wealth, I then regressed the Net variable against the ideological direction of the judge vote. Table 3.12 reports the results for all judge votes and for those in criminal actions, in which the relatively wealthy might be expected to be especially conservative.

These results show a small but statistically significant effect of wealth on conservative ideological voting. The effect is more pronounced for criminal cases. Wealth may be merely a proxy for ideology, though, because conser-

TABLE 3.12
Wealth and ideological votes

Variable	All votes	Criminal votes
Net	−.04 (.014)	−.08 (.007)
N	3,207	1,069
R^2	.003	.015

TABLE 3.13
Wealth and affirmance deference

Variable	All votes	Criminal votes
Net	−.06 (.000)	−.04 (.204)
N	4,064	1,256
R^2	.004	.001

TABLE 3.14
*Wealth, ideology, and affirmance deference and
ideological votes*

Variable	All votes	Criminal votes
Net	−.06 (.003)	−.10 (.007)
Ideology	.50 (.000)	.27 (.242)
LowerCourt	.90 (.000)	.92 (.000)
N	3,077	1,027
R^2	.065	.049

vative presidents may be more likely to appoint wealthy conservatives to the bench.

There is no clear theoretical reason to assume that wealth would be associated with affirmance deference, but the possibility is still worth exploring. If wealthy judges are more ideological, they might be expected to show less legal affirmance deference. Table 3.13 reports the results of the simple regression of wealth on affirmance deference for all votes and for those cast in criminal cases.

Greater judicial wealth is associated with a lower level of affirmance deference. Although the association is not statistically significant in criminal cases, it has considerable significance for all votes.

The apparently significant effect of wealth may simply be attributable to party affiliation. If Republicans selected wealthier judges, then the conservative effect may be just an ideological one. To check for the interacting effects of wealth, baseline ideology, and affirmances, I introduce in Table 3.14 the baseline ideological variable of Ideology and a check for affirmance deference in LowerCourt into a multiple regression to see whether wealth has some effect beyond that of those variables.

The small wealth effect is clearly independent of the baseline Ideology variable. Indeed, in this much smaller sample, the Ideology variable is not significant for criminal cases. The effect of wealth is enhanced, not diminished, after controlling for ideology and affirmance deference. The magnitude of the wealth effect is not great, but the significance of the association survives control variables. Because of the limited data on assets and liabilities, the overall sample is very different and much smaller than that of the earlier regressions, but the consistent significance in the smaller sample lends credence to the effect of wealth.

Wealth and Personal Background Combined

The consideration of wealth has proceeded independently of consideration of any of the other personal background variables. The possibility of collinearity between wealth and minority status or wealth and age might distort the true effect for wealth. To determine if wealth retains its effect, I incorporated the personal background variables into the regressions using wealth, baseline ideology, and affirmance deference. Table 3.15 reports the results of this analysis for all types of cases and for criminal cases.

These results give us interesting information about the effect of background variables. Wealth remains an important determinant of outcomes even after controlling for other aspects of personal background. Once one controls for wealth and the other variables, though, minority judges become more conservative than their white counterparts, a surprising finding. Women, by contrast, continue to be more liberal, even after controlling for wealth. Ideology loses its independent significance. These results may be an artifact of the more limited sample (though the sample remains relatively

TABLE 3.15
Wealth, personal background, and ideological outcome

Variable	All votes	Criminal votes
Net	−.06 (.002)	−.09 (.004)
Minority	−.18 (.139)	−.59 (.030)
Female	.08 (.536)	.53 (.035)
Age	.01 (.184)	.01 (.251)
LowerCourt	.91 (.000)	.97 (.000)
Ideology	.50 (.000)	.28 (.219)
N	3,077	1,027
R^2	.067	.064

large). Unfortunately, the smaller sample for which wealth information is available happens to be a sample in which our other variables of Ideology and LowerCourt are less predictive (as illustrated by the smaller R^2 terms). Given the significance of Net in the findings discussed in this section, research into the effect of judicial background should consider the inclusion of wealth as a variable before trying to draw conclusions about other aspects of background or other determinants of judicial decisions.

Judicial Qualifications

There is no objective, reliable measure to assess the qualifications of circuit court judges. Presidents have for some years, however, submitted their nominees to a panel, chosen by the ABA, for review and rating on a scale that includes exceptionally well qualified, well qualified, qualified, or not qualified. The ABA ratings were introduced as a public check on presidential appointees, in hopes of identifying the introduction of improper considerations, such as patronage and partisanship, into the federal judicial election process.

These ratings have periodically become controversial, when some politicians have charged that the ABA committee had its own ideological bias that it was inappropriately introducing into its rating of nominees. The ABA ratings at their inception may have been intended to make Truman's appointees more conservative and help him select white males.[15] Today, the more common complaint is that the raters have a liberal bias. A conservative fifth circuit judge has made this claim,[16] and the G. W. Bush administration has eliminated the practice of ABA appointee clearance. The ABA disclaims any ideological effect, though, stating that the only criteria for its ratings are the nominee's character and general reputation in the legal community as well as his or her industry and diligence.

The potential ideological bias has been subject to fairly extensive testing. One study found that the ABA apparently gave higher ratings to Clinton appointees than it did to similarly qualified G. H. W. Bush appointees.[17] A reanalysis of the study, though, found the conclusions to be "thin, unstable, and contradictory."[18] In any event, these findings do not involve judicial votes, just associations between the president and ratings.

TABLE 3.16
ABA qualifications and vote ideology

	(1)	(2)	(3)
ABA	−.03 (.130)	.01 (.971)	.01 (.671)
SELPREF		.325 (.000)	.35 (.000)
LDIRECT			1.33 (.000)
N	35,681	35,681	35,681
R^2	.004	.004	.119

The supplemented database uses the ratings, which are incorporated as an ordinal ranking ranging from not qualified to exceptionally well qualified. Table 3.16 reports, in a simple regression and after incorporating controls for the judge's ideology and affirmance deference, the effect of the ABA ratings on the ideology of the judge vote.

ABA qualifications do not appear to play a major role in ideological case outcomes. There is no statistically or substantially significant association of vote outcome with ABA qualifications. These ratings are historical, of course, and cannot resolve the issue of whether the ABA ratings were biased at any point. As a separate matter, the ABA screening process does not appear to produce "better" judges, if better is defined as less ideological and more devoted to the legal model. Higher-rated judges are no less ideological than lower-rated ones. But this test for quality is rough, and the virtues associated with higher ABA rankings might appear in other dimensions that are less amenable to quantitative analysis.

Judicial Background and Opinion Length

The effect of judicial background, like other variables, could appear in opinion content as well as in outcome determination. But, for some backgrounds, no obvious hypotheses suggest themselves on this issue. One might expect that judges would write shorter opinions as they grow older, so age might have a negative association with opinion length. Table 3.17 reports the results of simple regressions of the background variables of minority status, gender, and age on opinion length.

There is no association of judges reducing their opinion-writing effort with age, which contradicts some theories. There is a clear association of

TABLE 3.17
Personal background and opinion length

Variable	Coefficient	N	R^2
Minority	.055 (.000)	13,089	.055
Female	.010 (.264)	13,089	.000
Age	.004 (.635)	13,089	.000

minority status with longer opinions. Minority judges are apparently putting more effort into their opinion writing, though this might be explained by their higher tendency to reverse.

One might also expect to see a greater difference in opinion length based on the personal experience backgrounds of the circuit court judiciary. One feature of opinion length could be the clarity of the resulting precedent. A shorter opinion would be associated with more ambiguity. Those who have been law professors might be expected to produce longer opinions to better direct future cases and because of their affinity for lengthy explication (as evidenced in law review articles). Those with experience on lower levels of the federal judiciary might produce shorter opinions if they sought to leave more discretion for lower court judges (or longer opinions, if they thought that discretion could be misused). Those with experience in private practice might produce longer opinions to better enable practitioners to predict the state of the law and to order their actions accordingly. Those with higher net wealth might produce longer opinions for a similar reason. Judges with a higher ABA rating, if they are indeed of higher quality, might produce longer opinions. Table 3.18 reports a series of multiple regressions using these personal experiences as independent variables, with different combinations and control variables for Ideology and LowerCourt affirmance deference, which have been shown to affect opinion length.

The first analysis confirms the hypotheses about former law professors and private practitioners. The other analyses do not support their hypotheses, but they involve a much smaller sample size because of the limited data and much smaller sample for analyses, including Net. Higher ABA ratings do not produce lengthier opinions. The clearest result is the statistically significant finding that former lower court judges produce shorter opinions. The data discussed earlier suggested that circuit court judges who were formerly on a lower court were slightly more deferential to lower courts in

TABLE 3.18
Experience background and opinion length

Variable	(1)	(2)	(3)
Law professor	.043 (.000)	−.005 (.882)	.000 (.987)
Private practice	.032 (.000)	−.011 (.716)	−.013 (.664)
Federal judge	−.027 (.003)	−.070 (.015)	−.062 (.031)
Net		.040 (.159)	.049 (.081)
ABA		−.043 (.115)	−.042 (.124)
Reversal	.124 (.000)		.086 (.003)
Ideology	.028 (.002)		.053 (.062)
N	13,089	1,331	1,331
R²	.021	.009	.022

outcome; the results in the list on page 26 show similar respect for lower courts, because shorter opinions should leave more discretion for the rulings of future lower court judges.

Conclusion

The results of the analysis in this chapter generally support the commonly held position among political scientists that background variables matter relatively little. Although a number of background variables had some statistical significance on ideological outcome beyond the independent ideology measure for each judge, the effect of the variables was small. The greatest effect was shown for the background variable that has been least considered by existing research—judicial wealth.

There is one obvious reason why such background variables have relatively little effect—selection screening. Even if the average person would be significantly influenced by his or her background (e.g., minorities being more liberal), circuit court appointments are not random selections but carefully chosen by presidents and evaluated by the Senate. Thus, a conservative president might wish to appoint minorities to the bench but limit those appointments to minorities sharing his conservative philosophies. Given this screening process, any effect whatsoever of background might be surprising. The small but significant associations reported in this chapter (e.g., race and gender with ideology in criminal judge votes, race and less affirmance deference) are thus somewhat telling and the greater association with wealth is likewise significant. The attempts to overcome biases through ABA qualification ratings does not appear to have much effect.

Some background variables might still possibly have a substantively and statistically significant effect in a small subset of cases, but even this effect is uncertain. The research on gay rights decisions showed a substantial effect of such personal background variables as religion on decisions, so religion would seem to be a good proxy for background influence. Even in this context, though, the effect in federal courts was relatively small, which could logically be ascribed to the different judicial selection systems used in state and federal courts. Instead of the carefully screened selection process for federal circuit courts, many states have elected judiciaries that might better reflect the median view of people of a certain background. Even with such screening, though, there is a modest effect of personal and experiential background on judicial decisions and the length of the opinions that judges write.

Other Institutions and Circuit Court Decision Making

The previous chapters addressed only what motivated individual judges in their decision-making choices. Implicit in the analysis found in Chapters 1–3 was the assumption that those judges were independent and unconstrained by other institutions and free to make and enforce whatever decisions they thought best. The circuit courts do not exist in a vacuum, though; they operate within a complex institutional structure that involves other circuit court judges, a judicial hierarchy, and the legislative and executive branches of government. All these other institutional actors have some authority to influence the implementation and practical significance of particular circuit court decisions. Under the conventional social scientific rational choice model, wise judges consider the powers and preferences of these other institutions when rendering their decisions. Judge Alex Kozinski has declared that the constraints imposed on the judiciary by the political system are "often overlooked but awesome nonetheless."[1]

Judicial adaptation to these other institutions is the thrust of the strategic model of judicial decision making. The strategic concern for other institutions should function regardless of whether judges are maximizing their personal ideologies or have some other objective. Although most strategic accounts assume that judges are ideological, judges' concern for the actions of other institutions would also be rational if they were seeking other ends, such as legal ones. Whatever their goals, strategic judges might attend to the interests of other powerful governmental actors so that those goals are not undermined by those other actors.

The analysis of judicial strategic concern for other institutions is increasingly popular among political science researchers. Lee Epstein and Jack Knight have produced a seminal analysis of how such institutional concerns operate at the Supreme Court level.[2] Others have focused on the operation of the judicial hierarchy and how lower courts should strategically consider the preferences of higher courts and possibly Congress. One central issue in these analyses is the degree to which a purportedly independent judiciary should and does strategically attend to the preferences of other government institutions, such as Congress. This chapter empirically analyzes the effect of other government institutions on circuit court decision making.

Strategic Theories of Circuit Court Decision Making

Perhaps the most common topic of political science public law research today involves strategic theories of judicial decision making. The strategic theories begin with the premise that judges are not unconstrained but must adapt their decisions to suit their institutional environment. The theories derive from the basic rational choice theory popular in the social sciences and commonly applied to all individual decisions. If a judge has a given set of preferences, he or she will seek to maximize them consequentially; this implies the possible need to strategize to ensure those preferences are effected.

The strategic theories generally presume that the judges' concerns are ideological, as reflected in the policy outputs of their decisions. This ideological value will be lost if the judicial decision is literally or functionally vacated by another government institution. Hence, the theory suggests that judges will to some degree conform their decisions and sacrifice their

personal preferences to satisfy the external constituencies that could somehow invalidate the decisions. If the circuit court does not strategize, the theory goes, its decisions will be reversed and the court will lose all the ideological benefit it would otherwise derive from its preferred ideological outcome.
Strategic judges would modify their outcomes to avert such invalidation.

Some of the strategic theories seem contrary to America's tradition of judicial independence, but this is not intrinsically a serious reason to question
them. Circuit court adherence to the Supreme Court or to the full circuit
is largely consistent with judicial independence because the judicial branch
still retains independent control over judicial outcomes. Compliance with
the preferences of other institutions, such as Congress, is somewhat inconsistent with judicial independence, but the United States has never had absolute judicial independence. Our constitutional system has always admit-
ted to some controls on the judiciary, which has to be checked and balanced
just like any other government institution. Strategy does not imply total
surrender, so some measure of judicial independence would survive even if
the judiciary were attentive to the interests of the legislature.

But the strategic theories, even the theories regarding strategic compliance with higher judicial authorities, are somewhat inconsistent with the
basic rule of law. The rule of law does not admit to strategizing. It directs
that judges be "backward looking" at the established materials possessing
legal authority (such as precedential opinions and passed statutes) and not
"forward looking" at the expected reaction of higher judicial authorities
and other institutions. If a judge renders a decision based on the anticipated
reactions of others, rather than on legal materials, that approach is inconsistent with the rule of law. Of course, any ideological basis for decision
making also sits uneasily with rule of law values. The presence of strategy
does not render the rule of law meaningless, but strategy does undermine
that principle to some degree.

The Circuit Courts and the Supreme Court

The Supreme Court seems the most likely external institution to have
an effect on circuit courts. Circuit court decisions may be reviewed and
altered by the Supreme Court, and circuit courts are supposed to follow

the precedents set by the Supreme Court. The strategic theory typically contends that circuit courts are constrained by the preferences of the Supreme Court because the Supreme Court has the power to reverse the circuit court decision and eliminate any utility that the circuit court judges would obtain from a decision. As a result, researchers have suggested that the circuit courts will conform to the preferences of the Supreme Court, rather than their own preferences, to limit the reversals of their preferred decisions.[3] The prominent exponents of ideology as a determinant of Supreme Court voting, Jeffrey Segal and Harold Spaeth, have suggested that the fear of reversal prevents circuit courts from similar ideological voting.[4]

The strategic theory of circuit court decision making is distinct from legal adherence to Supreme Court precedents. The legal model is retrospective and calls on circuit courts to adhere to the previous rulings of the Supreme Court. The strategic model is prospective and expects that circuit courts will respond to the anticipated future holdings of the Court. Consider the scenario in which the governing precedents for a case are relatively old and conservative in direction but the current Supreme Court is liberal and activist. The legal model would dictate a conservative decision in the case, whereas the strategic model would suggest a liberal decision. A liberal decision in such a scenario is an example of a phenomenon sometimes called anticipatory overruling of past precedents: the circuit court would ignore and functionally overrule the past precedents in the expectation that the precedents no longer find favor with the Supreme Court.

The strategic adaptation to Supreme Court preferences could occur in various ways. The classic strategy is reflected in Figure 4.1. This figure portrays a two-dimensional ideological scale, where point C is the circuit court's ideal outcome and S is the Supreme Court's ideal outcome. Unconstrained, the circuit court would decide at point C. But point C is disfavored by the Supreme Court, which could vacate the circuit court decision and dictate outcome S. The strategic circuit court could avoid the risk of reversal by deciding at point S in the first place. Alternatively, the circuit court might decide its case at ideological position C′. In this strategy, the circuit court captures some of its preferred position (vis-à-vis S) and possibly avoids reversal, because its approximation of S could cause the Supreme Court to overlook the ruling and seek other cases to reverse.

Figure 4.1   Circuit Court Acquiescence Strategy

The two alternatives presented in Figure 4.1 have each been embraced by different branches of political science research, which anticipates different degrees of circuit court responsiveness to Supreme Court preferences. Nearly all the models assume that judges, at both the circuit court and Supreme Court level, care only for political ideology and disregard the law. Figure 4.2 displays one relatively simple depiction of a possible strategy based on this assumption.

Figure 4.2 retains the simple two-dimensional ideological model but incorporates the existing law. Suppose that the existing law, such as might be reflected in recent Supreme Court precedent, dictates a decision at point L. The circuit court's ideologically preferred decision is at point C, however, and the current Supreme Court's ideologically preferred decision is at point S. Although the circuit court might ordinarily be drawn to decide at point L, as part of its legal obligation, the position of the Supreme Court invites an ideologically strategic alternative. The circuit court can decide at C, secure that it will not be reversed for its departure from the law, because the Supreme Court prefers C to L. If the circuit court decision is appealed and certiorari is taken, the circuit court can have some confidence that its departure from L will be affirmed by the Supreme Court. Even if the Supreme Court shifts from point C to point S, the circuit court still has a relatively desirable ideological outcome, one it would prefer to point L.

In both these strategic models, even with some effect from the law, the circuit court is presumed to focus on its ideological preferences, as is the common presumption in much of the preexisting social scientific literature. Neither model recognizes the possibility that the circuit court might have legal preferences as powerful as its ideological preferences, although the second model does incorporate some legal effect as part of the circuit court's strategizing. All the models of hierarchical judicial strategy presume that the preferences of the Supreme Court exert a sort of gravitational pull on, and thus noticeable influence on, circuit court decision making. Although the amount of this influence is in theoretical question,

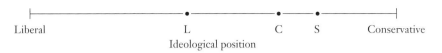

Figure 4.2   Circuit Court Anticipatory Overruling Strategy

there should be some association between Supreme Court preferences and circuit court outcomes. As Supreme Court preferences shift, one should see a corresponding shift, to a greater or lesser degree, in circuit court decisions.

The extremely low rate of Supreme Court review of circuit court decisions gives us reason to doubt the strategic supposition that the risk of Supreme Court reversal would exert such a gravitational pull and materially influence circuit court decisions. At its recent peak, the Supreme Court was issuing about one hundred fifty rulings per year but now the number is well under one hundred rulings. A substantial minority of those rulings are affirmances that leave the circuit court decision effective, and the number of reversals per year is now only around fifty. Given the capacity of the Supreme Court, this number might increase, but not dramatically. The circuit courts terminate more than fifty thousand cases annually. Thus, around 99.9% of circuit court decisions are left undisturbed by the Supreme Court. Moreover, as the number of circuit court decisions has steadily increased over time, the number of Supreme Court decisions has decreased, resulting in less hierarchical supervision of the circuit courts. For example, the ninth circuit in recent years has been distinctly more liberal than the Supreme Court; its ideological inclinations have often reflected its decisions, and it has correspondingly been reversed by the Supreme Court at a rate much higher than that for other circuits. Nonetheless, the Supreme Court has still let stand more than 99% of the ninth circuit's opinions. Judge Stephen Reinhardt of that circuit has declared that judges should not change their view of the law "in order to please the Supreme Court,"[5] perhaps because he is aware of the relatively low rate of reversal that the circuit courts face.

The low rate of Supreme Court review does not inherently disprove a lack of Supreme Court control. J. Woodford Howard noted that "appellate judges no more need to review every decision below than a teacher must admonish every child to maintain order on a playground."[6] It is the threat, not the actuality, of review that can control agents. But there surely must be some credible threat of admonishment to maintain control on the playground. It is doubtful that nine teachers (the Supreme Court justices), who are capable of admonishing at most around one hundred students a year, could effectively keep order on a playground populated by more than fifty thousand students. It seems extremely unlikely that the Supreme Court reverses only 0.1% of circuit court opinions because all the other decisions conform exactly to the Court's preferences. It is far more likely that the Supreme Court has significant resource constraints that severely limit its ability to monitor the lower courts and correct opinions of which it disapproves. Indeed, because the degree of Supreme Court review is "vanishingly small," the Court does not generally engage in "error correction" for lower courts but instead seeks only to set a uniform national law.[7]

The basic strategic theory also ignores the ability of lower courts to insulate their decisions from higher court reversal. Higher courts must find a *legal* error in order to reverse, and clever lower court judges can make it difficult and time-consuming to find such a reversible error. Lower court judges can characterize the facts of a case in a way that may make higher court reversal difficult. By using different legal instruments, lower courts can force higher courts to expend many resources to reverse. Joe Smith and Emerson Tiller have analyzed administrative law rulings and found that circuit court judges protect themselves from Supreme Court reversal by choosing certain procedural bases for decision rather than relying on statutory interpretation.[8] The ability of lower courts to discourage review and reversal goes against the strategic theories of compliance.

The theory that circuit courts must conform to the Supreme Court to avoid reversal suffers another theoretical problem—the lack of affirmative sanctions for any circuit court misbehavior. When teachers seek to control the playground, their tools are not limited to simply halting misbehavior; they also have various tools to punish miscreants, including expulsion from the playground. The Supreme Court generally lacks such tools. The Court may reverse the outcome of the decision, but this causes no unique pain for the reversed circuit court panel. In the event of such a reversal, the circuit court is no worse off than if it had simply conformed to the Court's preferences in the first place. Consequently, there is no ideological policy reason for a lower court to fear reversal. The Supreme Court cannot "expel" the circuit court from its jurisdiction or financially punish the court, the sort of tools that might encourage compliance.

If a reversal by the Supreme Court stigmatized the circuit court judges, that might provide the requisite punishment to induce strategic compliance, but the evidence of such stigma is absent. J. Woodford Howard noted that circuit court judge "reputations appear to be independent of Supreme Court support," and some judges have even worn such reversals as "badges of honor."[9] Judge Alex Kozinski declared that if a circuit court judge was never reversed, that judge was "probably cheating."[10] A bold and risky departure from precedent may even enhance a judge's reputation. Reversal also does not appear to obstruct promotion potential. When Judge Robert Bork was nominated to the Supreme Court, his advocates made much of the fact that he was never reversed while sitting on the D.C. circuit, yet he was functionally rejected by the U.S. Senate. Justice Ruth Bader Ginsburg, by contrast, was elevated to the Supreme Court very shortly after being reversed in a major decision. The survey responses of circuit court judges disclaim any concern for anticipated Supreme Court reversal.[11]

Despite the theoretical problems with the risk of reversal theories, these theories are still widely accepted as possible explanations for circuit court behavior. Research shows that circuit courts are at least somewhat responsive to Supreme Court decisions. Lower courts do generally heed the legal commands of higher courts. Political scientists have argued that the research indicates that "judges on the courts of appeal appear to be relatively faithful agents of their principal, the Supreme Court."[12] This may be the case, though it has not been conclusively proven. Moreover, such adherence, if it exists, to past decisions of the Supreme Court does not demonstrate the existence of strategic behavior by circuit courts. The faithfulness could simply be a product of conventional legal model decision making, as discussed in Chapter 2.

Empirical Research on Strategic Compliance with the Supreme Court

The theory of strategic conformance to Supreme Court preferences has not been tested as thoroughly as has the political model, though recent years have seen increased interest in testing this hypothesis. Much of the research on strategic judicial decision making has addressed the Supreme Court's possible need to obey the preferences of the U.S. Congress. But some studies have examined the hierarchical control of the Supreme Court over the circuit courts, and this research has produced relatively little evidence of a powerful strategic effect.

David Klein tested the strategic model on cases in which he expected it would be most powerful.[13] He identified groups of cases that were both substantively important and in which the law was in flux. He anticipated that these cases would likely be appealed to the Supreme Court and that the Court would be relatively likely to take certiorari in them, both of which were true. Consequently, his analysis isolated the cases in which the strategic model was most likely to apply. But he found no evidence of strategic decision making, even when the ideological composition of the Supreme Court changed dramatically. A subsequent analysis of search and seizure cases, for which Supreme Court review is demonstrably likely, found a weak effect of Supreme Court review probability on lower court deference to Supreme Court preferences.[14]

An article by Tracey George also considered strategic decision making on circuit courts.[15] She controlled for the ideological preferences of the circuit court judges themselves and found that those preferences were the most powerful determinants of their decisions. She identified a few judges, however, who appeared to vote strategically and sometimes represented swing votes. Although this result offers evidence of some strategic impact at the circuit court level, George found that her effect was weak. Another study on the admissibility of confessions in criminal law also found a weak association,[16] and a study on abortion decisions also found a strategic effect, though it was smaller than the effect of the circuit court judges' own ideology.[17]

One recent article identified a set of state law tort cases that the circuit courts heard under diversity jurisdiction, in which the risk of Supreme Court reversal would be unusually low.[18] The authors found that judging in these cases was somewhat ideological but that the judges also seemed highly constrained by law and precedent. Yet another recent article examined the dissenting behavior of circuit court judges.[19] This research tested the theory that such judges would dissent to highlight majority opinions for reversal by the full circuit court, acting en banc. The research found no evidence of such a strategic effect. Dissents could be explained by ideology, case significance, and other factors, but the signaling of decisions for review and reversal was not significant. Thus, the studies to date have shown only very limited evidence of hierarchical strategic decision making by circuit courts.

Investigation of Strategic Compliance with Supreme Court

This section investigates the degree to which Supreme Court preferences influence circuit court decisions. When attempting to measure the degree to which circuit court judges conform to the preferences of the Supreme Court, a researcher requires a measure for the preferences of the Supreme Court justices. The use of the Supreme Court's ideological preferences is a good tool for this measure because of the extensive research demonstrating the ideological grounding of Supreme Court decision making, as discussed in Chapter 1. Considerable research has gone into identifying the ideological preferences of the Supreme Court, and the most widely used measure is commonly known as the Segal-Cover (S-C) score. To test for a strategic effect, I calculated for each year since 1925 the S-C score of the median Supreme Court justice, on the assumption that this ideological measure was the key constraint on the free exercise of circuit court preferences. This measure is expressed as the variable SupremeCourt.

The possibility of legal model decision making somewhat complicates any test of the strategic model. Even if the Supreme Court justices themselves decide cases ideologically, those decisions then become the law that subsequent circuit court decisions are supposed to follow. Suppose that a given conservative Supreme Court issues a series of conservative decisions. Ensuing circuit court decisions are then relatively conservative in nature. Although the circuit court decisions might be an attempt to strategically conform to the Supreme Court's expressed preferences, they might also be attributable to the legal precedential effect of the recent conservative Court rulings. Testing for the strategic model requires that these theories be isolated and separately tested. Most of the previous studies on strategic decision making have not segregated the theories because the researchers did not consider the possible separate effects of legal model precedent on decision making. Although there is no sure quantitative way to capture substantive precedent—a problem discussed in Chapter 2—I created a proxy for following the precedents of previous Supreme Courts by taking the median S-C score for the Court for the five years before the decision; this variable is expressed as OldSupremeCourt.

The SupremeCourt and OldSupremeCourt variables were then integrated into the basic model that includes the circuit judge's own ideology (Ideology) and the effect of affirmance deference, which was identified by the ideology of the decision reviewed by the circuit court judge (LowerCourt). The following list reports the results of the multiple regression of these variables on the ideological outcome of the individual judge vote:

Variable	All Votes
SupremeCourt	−.069 (.000)
OldSupremeCourt	.076 (.000)
Ideology	.046 (.000)
LowerCourt	1.36 (.000)
N	24,623
R^2	.121

The results are striking and directly opposite of what the strategic theories of compliance with the Supreme Court would suggest. The association of circuit court judging with current ideological preferences is statistically significant and *negative*, though the preferences of recent past Courts is a statistically significant positive determinant. Circuit court judicial ideology and affirmance deference remain significant. These results indicate that the circuit court is consistently ruling contrary to the current Supreme Court's preferences.

The negative association with current Supreme Court preferences is surely curious because no apparent theory would suggest that circuit court judges have reason to affirmatively contravene the current Court's ideology. The results do not prove the intentionality of opposing the Supreme Court's preferences, though, and the best explanation may be seen in the results for OldSupremeCourt. It appears that circuit court judges do not anticipatorily

repudiate old precedents but instead aggressively follow old precedents that
are presumptively unattractive to the current Supreme Court. The next list
shows the analyses with OldSupremeCourt but without the measure of the
current Supreme Court's preferences:

Variable	All Votes
OldSupremeCourt	.25 (.000)
Ideology	.40 (.000)
LowerCourt	1.58 (.000)
N	26,855
R^2	.090

The most significant thing about these results is that OldSupremeCourt
remains statistically significant but loses much of its predictive power when
the current SupremeCourt preferences are not part of the model. Thus, the
circuit court judges are following old precedents most reliably when they
are contrary to the Court's current preferences, but circuit court judges
appear somewhat less likely to follow old precedents when those precedents
seem to be aligned with current Supreme Court preferences. Ideology and
LowerCourt affirmance deference remain statistically significant with Supreme Court preferences incorporated into the model.

Although these results could also seem curious, they might be explained
with the theory that circuit courts may be engaged in a different and more
complicated sort of strategy, in which the circuit court judges attempt to use
the Supreme Court in the service of their own personal ideological preferences. Under this strategy, the circuit courts are first engaged in testing
the contemporary Supreme Court to ascertain its true preferences about
particular precedents. The circuit courts may be using Supreme Court decisions to explore the strength of the current Court's ideological attitudes
on specific issues and then manipulating the current Court to further the
circuit court ideology by taking cases for review and reversal.

Consider the following scenario. Assume there is a conservative Supreme
Court succeeding a relatively liberal Court that established a pattern of
relatively liberal precedents. The strategy for the liberal circuit judge is
not to conform to the current Supreme Court preferences but to follow
the liberal precedents of the recent more liberal Courts, essentially calling

the bluff of the current Court. Rather than acquiescing to the current preferences, the liberal judges follow the previous Court's liberal precedents and compel the current Court to expend its resources and declare its preferences through a reversal. Because Supreme Courts are relatively loathe to overturn their own recent precedents, the liberal circuit court judges may see an opportunity to further institutionalize the recent liberal precedents.

Ironically, conservative circuit judges might display some of the same behavior, though in pursuit of a different strategy. Assume that the legal model exerts some tug on these judges, perhaps because they have independent preferences for following that model. In this circumstance, conservative circuit court judges might be more likely to favor law over ideology in those situations in which the Supreme Court was ideologically favorable. Such a conservative court could hold out hope that the Supreme Court would reverse the circuit court's liberal decision, enabling the circuit court to see both its legal and ideological preferences fulfilled. Indeed, since the Supreme Court is more likely to take certiorari in cases that it plans to reverse rather than affirm, the then-current Supreme Court would be more likely to review a liberal decision and reverse it; the conservatives on the circuit court would thus enhance their chances of creating a new conservative Supreme Court precedent when they issue a liberal ruling. This is the opposite of the conventional strategy displayed in Figure 4.2. Circuit courts are not defensively seeking the shelter of the current Supreme Court's preferences but are aggressively pushing the current Supreme Court to render decisions in accord with those current preferences and in the process change the nation's governing legal principles.

Conservative circuit court judges would not consistently render liberal decisions under this strategy—such a decision would surely be counterproductive given the Supreme Court's limited resources. The judges would be producing numerous liberal results with little probability of reversal. Indeed, Ideology remains a significant determinant, showing that conservative circuit court judges tend to render conservative decisions. At the margin, however, there is evidence of some liberal decisions as part of this strategy (note that the coefficient for Ideology is somewhat smaller in the first list of this chapter than in most other regressions). This suggests that conservative circuit courts could be carefully and strategically adopting the

TABLE 4.1

Supreme Court preferences and criminal votes

Variable	(1)	(2)
SupremeCourt	−.42 (.004)	
OldSupremeCourt	.65 (.001)	.46 (.001)
Ideology	.40 (.000)	.40 (.000)
LowerCourt	.65 (.000)	.67 (.000)
Minority	.25 (.116)	.27 (.068)
Female	.59 (.006)	.74 (.000)
N	10,713	10,713
R²	.021	.022

refined strategy for a small fraction of their cases, which is logical given the Supreme Court's limited resources.

Under this theory, the highly counterintuitive findings about the effect of current and past Supreme Court preferences are evidence of rational and strategic behavior by the circuit court. The theory allows both liberal and conservative judges to explore the actual preferences of the Supreme Court on particular legal issues, to adhere to their legal model preferences, and to use strategy in hopes of advancing their respective ideological preferences. Liberal circuit court judges are cautiously clinging to recent precedents and hoping to preserve them, without much hope of help from the high court. Conservative circuit judges, however, are selectively aggressive in their efforts to drive future Supreme Court decisions and establish conservative precedents from that Court.

Previous chapters have demonstrated that the results in criminal appeals differ from the full sample of cases in the courts of appeals database. The multiple regressions use the same independent variables plus minority and female variables, and the dependent variable is the ideological direction of the judge's vote. Table 4.1 reports results of the analyses both with and without current Supreme Court preference measures.

The results of this analysis are roughly the same as for the full set of cases. The R^2 term is much smaller, probably because LowerCourt affirmance deference is weaker in criminal cases. The associations of minority and female judges with more liberal criminal decisions are stronger once the other variables are introduced into the equation. The ideological preferences of the current Supreme Court are apparently negatively associated with circuit court votes, though the preferences of recent Courts have a statistically significant positive association.

Strategy and the Full Circuit Court

The Supreme Court is not the only entity that can review and reverse the decision of a circuit court panel. Each of the thirteen circuits provides an opportunity for a litigant to appeal a three-judge panel decision to the full circuit, which may then review the decision of the three-judge panel. In most cases, if the appeal is accepted, all judges of the full circuit vote on it, though this is no longer the case for the unusually large ninth circuit. This process is called en banc review. After a three-judge panel reaches a decision, the losing party can seek an en banc review of that decision before taking any appeal to the Supreme Court. Consequently, a panel need worry not only that the Supreme Court will reverse but also that the panel's decision will be reviewed and reversed en banc. With random assignment to three-judge panels, one would expect a certain number of those panels to be ideologically divergent from the average for the full circuit court and therefore potentially vulnerable to ideological en banc reversal.

The theory of strategic compliance with full circuit preferences has not been extensively examined. En banc review should roughly parallel Supreme Court review, but there are some salient differences. Full circuit review is perhaps more resource costly than Supreme Court review. Although the Supreme Court does not review many cases per year, accepting certiorari in some number of cases is its basic job. The very time-consuming basic job of circuit court judges, by contrast, is to work on numerous standard three-judge panels, so en banc review is analogous to overtime work without pay. Consequently, the probability of such review is also quite low; over 99% of decisions receive no en banc review.[20]

The en banc process also involves reviewing and reversing one's fellow circuit court judges, and frequent reversals might undermine collegiality in the circuit. Moreover, the en banc decision is not necessarily the final judicial word, as the decision may also be appealed to the Supreme Court. Indeed, the Supreme Court is relatively more likely to accept certiorari to take on an en banc decision than a regular panel decision, which means that the full circuit has its own strategic concern for reversal when it considers whether to reverse a three-judge panel. Circuit judges whose preferences differ from those of the full circuit but align with the preferences of the Supreme Court may therefore feel somewhat insulated from en banc reversal. Empirical evidence suggests that circuit judges are more likely to vote strategically in line with Supreme Court preferences when serving on an en banc panel than when serving on a typical three-judge panel.[21]

Although existing empirical analysis of en banc decision making is limited, Tracey George found that the process has an ideological component and a strategic component.[22] One analysis of the D.C. circuit en banc process found that it was highly ideological,[23] which might prompt three-judge panels to use a strategy that seeks to avoid en banc reversal. Given what is known about circuit court decision making, one would expect a strategic judge to at least contemplate the possibility of en banc review when rendering a decision. It seems likely, however, that the threat of en banc review would be less than that of Supreme Court review because circuit court decisions are less predictably ideological, en banc review has significant resource costs for the circuit, and en banc decisions may themselves be reversed on appeal to the Supreme Court.

Investigation of Strategic Compliance with the Full Circuit Court

The study of strategic compliance with the full circuit court follows the same approach used in the Supreme Court compliance analysis. The dependent variable was the ideological direction of the judge vote, and the independent variables included those for circuit court judge ideology, affirmance deference, the preferences of the current Supreme Court, the average preference of the Supreme Court for the previous five years, and the preferences of the full circuit. The ideological preferences for the full circuit of which the voting judge was a member was computed as CircuitCourt, and the average median preference for that full circuit for the previous five years was computed as OldCircuitCourt. The following list reports the results of the multiple regression for these variables on the ideological direction of the judge vote in all cases:

Variable	All Votes
SupremeCourt	−.21 (.000)
OldSupremeCourt	.18 (.006)
CircuitCourt	.002 (.001)
OldCircuitCourt	.006 (.003)
Ideology	.31 (.000)
LowerCourt	1.33 (.000)
N	
R^2	.122

All variables were statistically significant but the judges on the three-judge panels did not deal with full circuit preferences in the same way they did Supreme Court preferences. Current median circuit court preferences were a statistically significant determinant, though this is not necessarily explained by fear of reversal (because it might be due to collegiality within the circuit or other judicial interaction factors). Old preferences, which may represent precedents, were equally significant.

The negative association with contemporary Supreme Court preferences remains. The hypothesis that circuit courts are strategically pressing the Supreme Court to reveal its preferences and set national precedents remains viable. The three-judge panels do not have such a strategy with the full circuit, however. This difference might be expected, because the smaller panel is capable of setting full circuit precedent by itself and requires no en banc stamp of approval to have this effect. The three-judge panel also may be more familiar with the preferences of their colleagues on the full circuit and see less need for testing its intentions.

The judicial hierarchy apparently does create some interinstitutional strategizing by circuit courts. The strategy does not involve the generally hypothesized straightforward fear of reversal, though. Instead of merely responding defensively to the Supreme Court, circuit courts may be using the Court offensively as a tool to nationalize their own preferences when they believe the Court may be willing to do so. This behavior is significantly colored by the legal model, however, and the evidence on institutional strategy further demonstrates the importance of legal factors in circuit court decision making. The next question is the responsiveness of circuit courts to the preferences of other institutions, such as the legislative and executive branches of our government.

Strategy and Congress

Considerable attention and research have addressed the effect of Congress on judicial decision making. The seminal work is that of William Eskridge, who investigated the circumstances in which Congress has functionally reversed a Supreme Court statutory interpretation decision.[24] He found that Congress overrode 121 decisions between 1967 and 1991. In light of this threat of reversal, Eskridge also analyzed how strategic justices would adapt their decisions in response to congressional preferences. His theory is that justices, realizing that Congress might reverse their interpretation, modify their opinion sufficiently so that enough members of Congress find it acceptable and thus would block legislative action. Numerous other researchers, including Lee Epstein and Jack Knight, have considered this strategic adaptation by courts.

The theory of strategic adaptation to congressional preferences traces the basic theory of strategic adaptation to Supreme Court preferences. The differences in institutional procedures, though, create some distinctions between the theories. Unlike the Supreme Court, Congress may realistically ignore all circuit court decisions and need review none. But Congress may be more able to respond to circuit court rulings because it can theoretically reverse many more decisions than the Supreme Court can. Congress is also not dependent on a party appealing a particular case because Congress can set its own agenda and address whichever decisions it wishes.

Given these institutional differences, the theory behind the congressional reversal strategy hypothesis is in some respects weaker than the theoretical basis for concern over Supreme Court reversal. As with Supreme Court reversal, the realistic risk of congressional reversal is quite low. Passing legislation of any sort is difficult because our legislative process has created many roadblocks to enactment, such as committee screening and supermajority voting requirements, which are sometimes called pivot points. A 60% majority is required to overcome a minority filibuster in the Senate and a 67% majority is required to overcome a presidential veto of legislation. All these opportunities for the obstruction of legislative action give the courts more freedom to act on their own preferences, without regard to Congress. The circuit courts might worry about the median justice of the Supreme Court but need not worry so much about the median legislator, given the supermajority pivot points for legislative action. A measure of gridlock is considered an essential reality of the U.S. federal legislature.[25] Enacting legislation also has significant opportunity costs for federal representatives because any given bill draws time and resources away from other topics that Congress might address. Congress does pass bills, of course, including occasional bills responding to judicial decisions, but the likelihood of reversal of any given case remains quite low and this frequency is probably unpredictable. Thus, it is unclear why a strategic circuit court would choose to acquiesce in congressional preferences without a fight.

Much of the research on congressional reversal has involved the legislature's 1991 amendments, in response to conservative judicial decisions, to the Civil Rights Act. The history of this action negates the validity of the strategic judicial decision-making hypothesis. In this history, the Supreme Court first rendered a series of very conservative civil rights decisions, which the legislature reversed, indicating that the Court was not strategizing effectively before the law was passed. Then, after passage, the Court issued a string of conservative decisions that limited the scope of the 1991 law. For example, the Court made it more difficult for civil rights plaintiffs by ruling that an employer's failure to give a legitimate nondiscriminatory basis for its decision could not itself support a ruling for a plaintiff.[26] Thus, the Court did not strategically alter its decisions to fit the preferences of Congress even after the legislature had demonstrably disapproved of conservative civil rights decisions. This outcome also demonstrates another weakness of the legislative reversal theory: the courts get to interpret any statute attempting to reverse their decisions and consequently retain for themselves the last word on the law's implementation. The leading example for judicial strategizing in response to legislative preferences thus suggests that such strategizing does not occur.

The legislative reversal theory does have one strength compared with judicial reversal theories. Higher courts are generally unable to materially punish noncompliant lower court judges, save for reversing their decisions. The legislature has many additional tools with which to punish those courts that do not conform to congressional preferences. Congressional authority begins with impeachment power. Although Congress has seldom removed judges from office, threats of impeachment are not infrequent and, unlike reversal, impeachment carries a substantial sanction. The mere threat of impeachment may itself carry some stigma. Federal district court judge Harold Baer reversed his own decision on evidence admissibility in a criminal action after threats of impeachment and other public criticism. Congress may also seek to control the judiciary by stripping it of jurisdiction to hear certain types of cases. Although this type of legislation is fairly rare, studies have shown that it can not only reduce judicial power but also intimidate the federal courts more broadly and cause them to attend to legislative preferences.[27]

The most direct congressional influence over judges lies in the legislative funding power. Congress cannot cut judicial pay (and certainly cannot cut the pay of judges with whom it disagrees just for that reason), but Congress can withhold judicial pay raises and has great discretion in the appropriation of funds for the judiciary's necessary logistical support, such as support staff and courthouse facilities. The judiciary has frequently gone to Congress to plead for higher pay, more resources, and such other concerns as control over the judicial caseload. They have also lobbied for more judgeships. In response, Congress has exercised closer oversight over judicial expenditures and demanded more information from the courts. The judiciary has answered by showing greater concern about its relationship with the legislature. One empirical analysis found evidence that Congress has punished undesirable Supreme Court decisions with budget cuts and that the justices have responded with decisions more amenable to the policy goals of the legislature.[28] Congress does have tools to punish a judiciary that fails to conform to congressional desires, and those tools appear to have some effect on judicial decisions. The courts thus might have greater concern for legislative preferences, out of fear that the judiciary will be punished for a pattern of decisions that ignores those preferences.

The existing research on judicial strategic conformity to congressional preferences has focused on the Supreme Court, but the circuit courts should feel much the same influence of Congress, if indeed such influence exists. Circuit courts might be expected to feel less congressional influence simply because their decisions do not have nationwide effect and may be less likely to reach the attention of Congress. The circuit courts, however, issue many more decisions than does the Supreme Court and therefore have more potential for disrupting a congressional statutory plan. Moreover, if the Supreme Court does conform to congressional preferences, Congress could better focus its attention on objectionable circuit court rulings. Also, the Supreme Court can avoid ideological confrontations with Congress through their docket control (denying certiorari in problematic cases), whereas the circuit courts are generally compelled to take all appeals and therefore confront issues of salience to the legislature. Perhaps the limited geographic reach of circuit court decisions could actually encourage a legislative response, to ensure national unity in statutory construction. The possible effect of congressional preferences on circuit court judges thus requires analysis and is explored in the following discussion.

Once again, evaluation of the accuracy of these theories commands empirical investigations, and studies have been done on Supreme Court strategy with respect to Congress. An early study of Supreme Court rulings on labor law found some evidence that the Court considered congressional preferences.[29] But a much larger and more comprehensive study by Jeffrey Segal reached the opposite conclusion. Segal examined the Supreme Court's decisions in light of congressional preferences and concluded that the Supreme Court's preferences were seldom outside the congressional pivot points' protection and that individual justices voted their personal preferences regardless of the composition of Congress.[30]

Segal's findings have been criticized by researchers who contend that congressional preferences have constrained the Supreme Court's ability to be ideological for at least some periods in the twentieth century.[31] These researchers found that congressional preferences appeared to affect Supreme Court decisions for these limited periods when the Court's preferences were outside the congressional ideological mainstream. Another study looked at the degree to which Supreme Court decisions showed deference to other institutions, such as Congress and the president, even when such deference was not legally directed.[32] The effect varied by justice and was not as significant as ideology, but the effect was a statistically significant factor for nearly all the justices. There is some evidence, albeit limited, of judicial concern for congressional preferences, but this evidence has been confined to the Supreme Court level. One other study of D.C. circuit decisions on health and safety law found ideological judicial decision making but no effect from the party controlling Congress or the presidency.[33] The results of the existing research on the Supreme Court are mixed. The next section of the chapter examines circuit court rulings to see whether judges appear to be adapting their outcomes to congressional preferences.

Investigation of Strategic Compliance with Congress

The preferences of the legislature must be captured quantitatively to empirically assess the effect of the legislature on judicial decision making. Extensive political science research on Congress has provided measures of ideological preferences for the legislators. The most common is probably the Americans for Democratic Action (ADA) score, which reflects the voting record of legislators on key votes tracked by the ADA and which was incorporated into the ratings for judicial ideology. Thus, there is a score available to measure the ideology of the median member of both the House and the Senate and how that ideology has changed over time. The median member of a legislative body may not be the relevant member, however. Under the pivot points analysis, numerous veto points in the legislative process give control to someone other than the median legislator. The next need is to identify the preferences of the pivotal legislator.

Political scientists have come up with various theories to identify this key legislator, whose preferences must be satisfied to avert affirmative legislative action. One approach is called the committee-gatekeeping (CGK) model, which incorporates the preferences of the Senate and House judiciary committees to determine the pivotal voting congressperson. Another slightly more elaborate approach is called the multiple-veto (MV) model, which also includes the preferences of the House Rules Committee, the Speaker of the House, and the Senate majority leader. A third approach is the filibuster-veto (F-V) model, which presumes that the key roadblocks to legislative action are the filibuster in the Senate and the vote required to override a presidential veto. In this model, the key votes depend on whether the president approves a bill, in which case one need only get sixty votes in the Senate, or disapproves the bill, which requires a two-thirds majority in both the House and Senate. A final model, with a different approach, is the party-caucus (PC) model, which reflects the importance of political party organization. This model is based on evidence that policymaking is determined by party caucuses rather than the preferences of committees,

TABLE 4.2
Congressional preferences and ideological votes

Variable	(1)	(2)	(3)	(4)
SupremeCourt	−.82 (.000)	−.95 (.000)	−.69 (.000)	−.82 (.000)
OldSupremeCourt	.72 (.000)	.80 (.000)	.58 (.000)	.56 (.000)
CircuitCourt	.001 (.045)	.001 (.141)	.001 (.018)	.001 (.038)
OldCircuitCourt	.007 (.002)	.002 (.000)	.004 (.144)	.009 (.003)
Ideology	.29 (.000)	.28 (.000)	.27 (.000)	.28 (.000)
LowerCourt	1.35 (.000)	1.35 (.000)	1.36 (.000)	1.35 (.000)
F-V UB	.000 (.741)			
F-V LB	.002 (.002)			
CGK UB		−.001 (.210)		
CGK LB		.009 (.000)		
MV UB			.001 (.087)	
MV LB			−.001 (.455)	
PC UB				.001 (.167)
PC LB				.004 (.001)
N	19,982	19,982	19,982	19,982
R^2	.129	.129	.128	.129

so that parties drive legislative outcomes. Available data identify the ideological points for legislative capacity for each of the distinct models of the legislature and investigate whether changes in relevant legislative ideology have any influence on judicial votes.[34]

Although some have argued that the F-V model should be the most accurate, there is no consensus about the model that best describes congressional action, so this chapter considers each model. For each of these models (F-V, CGK, MV, and PC), the annual lower bound (conservative) and upper bound (liberal) veto points were included. For example, the F-V liberal upper bound is expressed as F-V UB and the conservative lower bound is expressed as F-V LB. The other models have similar designations. Separate regressions were run for each theory, and results are reported in Table 4.2. The dependent variable is the ideological direction of the judge vote, and the analyses contain the control variables for judge's ideology, affirmance deference, and preferences of the other judicial institutions that might affect decisions.

The results of Table 4.2 shed some light on the interface of the circuit courts and congressional preferences. First, there is little difference between the four models in their predictive capacity. Second, in three of the four models (F-V, CGK, and PC), the conservative veto point had a statistically significant association but the liberal veto point did not. This finding might suggest that liberal legislation is more likely to occur in response to court decisions, so it is the conservative veto point that effectively shelters those decisions. Alternatively, the conservative members of Congress may be the ones who are more closely monitoring circuit court decisions. The finding was reversed, however, in the test using the MV model, which calls into question either the result or the validity of that model.

The broader picture, though, suggests the insignificance of the congressional constraint, regardless of the model adopted. Although a few of the congressional variables were statistically significant, they did not contribute to the R^2 term and were not substantively important in determining circuit court judge votes. At this point it is also worth noting that the basic associations identified earlier (such as circuit court judge ideology, affirmance deference, Supreme Court preferences, and past Supreme Court preferences) remain consistently significant even as new variables are added to the equation and the N changes. This is a sign of the robustness of those relationships and the relative immateriality of legislative preferences as a constraint on the courts.

The test reported in Table 4.5 might be too broad to capture the desired effect. Under the Eskridge theory, the courts have to conform to a fear of congressional statutory amendment, which would not apply in constitutional rulings of the courts. A direct test of this hypothesis would consider only the statutory decisions of the circuit courts. The study just discussed was modified to be limited to statutory decisions of these courts. The results of this multiple regression are reported in Table 4.3.

The liberal upper bound of Congress has no effect on circuit court statutory decisions. The conservative lower bound appears to have an effect in three of the models (but not in the MV model). The strong association with judicial ideology and affirmance deference remain, and the associations with current and past circuit court preferences also remain. The associations with past and current Supreme Court preferences remain but are somewhat weakened.

These regressions show some evidence of strategic circuit court deference to at least the conservative veto points in Congress. The effect of congressional preferences is a relatively small one, but perhaps this is to be expected. Congress could not monitor and correct all of the thousands of circuit court statutory rulings. The marginal effect would be consistent with a theory claiming that the courts attend to congressional preferences in a small number of especially salient cases, in which a congressional override (or other punishment) might be a realistic concern, but not in other cases.

TABLE 4.3
Congressional preferences and ideological votes in statutory decisions

Variable	(1)	(2)	(3)	(4)
SupremeCourt	−.71 (.000)	−.78 (.000)	.59 (.000)	−.69 (.000)
OldSupremeCourt	.77 (.000)	.77 (.000)	.54 (.000)	.60 (.000)
CircuitCourt	.001 (.176)	.001 (.341)	.001 (.085)	.001 (.172)
OldCircuitCourt	.008 (.002)	.009 (.002)	.004 (.205)	.009 (.013)
Ideology	.32 (.000)	.30 (.000)	.30 (.000)	.31 (.000)
LowerCourt	1.35 (.000)	1.35 (.000)	1.35 (.000)	1.35 (.000)
F-V UB	−.002 (.188)			
F-V LB	.008 (.008)			
CGK UB		−.001 (.467)		
CGK LB		.007 (.005)		
MV UB			.000 (.485)	
MV LB			−.002 (.084)	
PC UB				.001 (.501)
PC LB				.003 (.052)
N	13,160	13,160	13,160	13,160
R^2	.127	.127	.126	.127

One further refinement in the analysis might focus on particular case types. This could help capture the sort of cases in which the circuit courts attend to congressional preferences. The next analysis considers the effect of congressional preferences on circuit court decision making in three key legislative areas—criminal law, civil rights law, and economic regulation. This analysis is limited to cases decided on statutory grounds and by the particular type of case. It uses the variables of the earlier regressions, but includes only the F-V model of congressional preferences. Table 4.4 reports the results.

The isolation of different case types doesn't reveal much effect for strategic acquiescence with congressional preferences. The one apparent association is a response to the conservative veto in civil rights cases. This happens to be the one area in which Eskridge's analysis claimed to find a similar effect for reversal of Supreme Court decisions. Perhaps very limited judicial strategizing occurs in one or a few areas of legislation. The overall effect of statutory reversal, though, generally seems to be insignificant in circuit court decisions.

Strategy and Opinion Length

Even if strategic considerations are not significant determinants of case outcomes, they might still influence other aspects of circuit court deci-

TABLE 4.4
Congressional preferences and ideological votes by case type

Variable	Criminal	Civil rights	Economic
SupremeCourt	.040 (.164)	−.189 (.000)	−.056 (.037)
OldSupremeCourt	−.011 (.707)	.148 (.000)	.026 (.333)
CircuitCourt	.024 (.132)	.003 (.894)	.052 (.000)
OldCircuitCourt	.052 (.004)	.096 (.002)	−.026 (.107)
Ideology	.039 (.007)	.056 (.014)	.010 (.451)
LowerCourt	.083 (.000)	.042 (.062)	.258 (.000)
F-V UB	−.015 (.570)	−.113 (.020)	.042 (.068)
F-V LB	.027 (.260)	.150 (.001)	.011 (.621)
N	4,658	1,949	5,471
R^2	.013	.024	.073

sion making, such as opinion writing. This section examines the effect of the preferences of other institutions on circuit court opinion length. The measure of opinion length has not been studied much, and no established theory suggests that the ideology of other institutions should alone have any necessary impact on opinion length, but the exploration begins with this general analysis. Table 4.5 reports the effects of the current Supreme Court and old Supreme Court ideologies on opinion length, with and without controls.

The results are clearly significant but difficult to explain. Circuit courts write longer opinions as the Supreme Court is more conservative and also write longer opinions when OldSupremeCourt, the proxy for Supreme Court precedent, is more conservative. As a general matter, there is no obvious reason for this finding, which may be attributable to random chance.

There are some theories of how strategic institutional issues could influence circuit court decision writing. Emerson Tiller suggests that circuit courts may write their opinions in a way that better insulates them from reversal by other institutions. Under this theory, one might expect a circuit court to write longer opinions when the reviewing entity was adverse, to make reversal by that entity more difficult. Thus, a circuit court might have a more extensive factual analysis that could complicate reversal or might simply devote more time to legal analysis, perhaps including independent alternative grounds for its finding. With the second possibility, the ideologically adverse Supreme Court would have to do relatively more work to reverse the circuit court holding. Empirical analysis has found that fact-based opinions are consistently longer than those focused on the rules of law.[35]

TABLE 4.5
Supreme Court preferences and opinion length

Variable	(1)	(2)
SupremeCourt	−.147 (.000)	−.134 (.000)
OldSupremeCourt	−.123 (.000)	−.129 (.000)
Reversal		.108 (.000)
Ideology		.056 (.000)
N	9,818	9,818
R^2	.066	.084

TABLE 4.6
Supreme Court preferences and opinion length by ideology

Variable	Liberal	Conservative
SupremeCourt	−.162 (.000)	−.107 (.000)
OldSupremeCourt	−.083 (.000)	−.177 (.000)
Reversal	.040 (.011)	.160 (.000)
N	3,992	5,769
R^2	.058	.106

To find this possible strategic effect displayed in opinion length, I broke down the circuit court opinions into liberal and conservative opinions. Table 4.6 reports the effect of Supreme Court preferences on opinion length for opinions of different ideologies, with a control variable for reversal and for the preferences of OldSupremeCourt. Under this theory, one would expect liberal opinions to be longer as the Supreme Court was more conservative, with the opposite effect for conservative opinions.

The results generally do not prove the theory that longer opinions are written to insulate decisions from reversal. The association is as predicted for liberal decisions but not for conservative rulings. The results offer some support for the hypothesis—the size of the negative coefficient for SupremeCourt is distinctly larger for liberal circuit court opinions than for conservative ones. This finding suggests that liberal authors may be going to some extra effort to write longer opinions as the Court is more conservative. The association for conservative opinions, however, is not at all what the theory would predict. As the Supreme Court grows more liberal, conservative circuit court opinions get shorter. This suggests that any finding is an artifact of judicial norms variance over time, rather than a strategic action. Table 4.7 introduces full circuit court preferences into the regres-

TABLE 4.7
Other Court preferences and opinion length by ideology

Variable	Liberal	Conservative
SupremeCourt	−.151 (.000)	−.100 (.000)
OldSupremeCourt	−.075 (.004)	−.148 (.000)
CircuitCourt	−.004 (.829)	−.072 (.000)
OldCircuitCourt	−.033 (.050)	−.029 (.000)
Reversal	.041 (.011)	.161 (.000)
N	3,698	5,290
R^2	.054	.105

TABLE 4.8
Congressional preferences and opinion length

Variable	Liberal	Conservative
SupremeCourt	−.149 (.000)	−.101 (.000)
OldSupremeCourt	−.076 (.007)	−.145 (.000)
CircuitCourt	−.003 (.859)	−.072 (.000)
OldCircuitCourt	−.033 (.054)	−.028 (.052)
F-V UB	.000 (.986)	−.009 (.713)
F-V LB	−.033 (.894)	.008 (.706)
Reversal	.041 (.011)	.161 (.000)
N	3,698	5,290
R^2	.054	.105

sions. The same strategic reasoning that could apply to the influence of Supreme Court preferences might also apply to the effect of full circuit preferences, given the possibility of en banc review.

The inclusion of circuit court preferences does not add much information. Although the associations are statistically significant for conservative opinions, the R^2 terms are smaller after including these variables.

The final analysis of the potential effect of judicial strategy on opinion length considers congressional preferences. It seems less plausible that courts would alter their opinion length in response to congressional preferences than that they would alter it in response to the preferences of other courts. Congress is presumably more interested in the substance of the decision than in the details of its legal analysis and would be less responsive to the court's effort to write a longer opinion. A longer opinion might, however, provide more information to persuade the legislature, thus avoiding a congressional reversal. Table 4.8 includes the independent congressional variables of the F-V model in the multiple regression on opinion length.

As expected, congressional preferences have no apparent effect on opinion length. The association with the Supreme Court's conservatism remains, however. That association is a curiosity, requiring theoretical analysis and further empirical examination.

Conclusion

The studies of strategic compliance with other institutions do not confirm the conventional theories of the significance of judicial strategy at the circuit court level. The data are contrary to any hypothesis that circuit courts passively moderate their rulings to conform to the preferences of the Supreme Court. Indeed, the findings regarding the Supreme Court suggest, if anything, a much more elaborate strategy, in which some circuit court judges may use a strategy of affirmatively attempting to manipulate the Supreme Court's dockets and decisions. There is also a clear association between a more conservative Supreme Court and longer opinions by circuit court judges, though there is no apparent strategic explanation for this phenomenon. Full circuit preferences show some influence on circuit court panels but not a substantial one. The legislature does not appear to have much effect on circuit court decision making, though there is a hint of such an effect for some discrete types of cases.

Besides examining the findings on the strategic effects of adaptation to other government institutions, the analyses in this chapter shed light on the significance of legal model decision making. The preferences of past Supreme Courts are a proxy for the state of substantive legal precedents, and the significance of the old Supreme Court preferences is further evidence of the importance of the legal model. Moreover, given the extreme imprecision of the measure of past precedents, the presence of a statistically significant association with a respectably sized correlation coefficient might be considered evidence of remarkable power for the legal model. Only an exceptionally strong variable would be expected to produce such consistent significant results in the presence of unavoidably substantial specification errors.

FIVE

Litigants and Circuit Court Decision Making

Judges are potentially subject to external influences besides other govern-ment institutions. The most obvious external influence would come from the parties and lawyers who appear before the judges. Circuit court judges lack agenda control. Unlike legislators, judges cannot take up a legal issue and render an opinion on its proper resolution. Circuit courts cannot issue advisory opinions in the absence of a true case. Instead, judges are limited to deciding the cases and controversies brought to them by disputants. Conse-quently, judges are generally constrained by the issues these parties present to them. This litigant control has many implications for the judicial system.

Because parties control the cases presented to judges, one cannot assume that the cases represent any sort of random sample of important legal issues. Moreover, the ability of parties to control the judicial agenda suggests the possibility that litigants might try to manipulate the judiciary into rendering particular decisions. It is well accepted in political science that the ability to structure an institution's agenda has significant effects on institutional outcomes. The adversary system and the constitutional jurisdictional requirement that parties to litigation have a genuine dispute should help prevent such manipulation, but they do not entirely exclude the possibility, as I discuss later. The structure of appeals also means that parties have the power to frame the issues for the judiciary; parties can raise certain issues and preclude consideration of others. The structure of litigation provides considerable space for party strategizing in a way that may affect judicial decisions. A broad study of the expansion of individual rights around the globe argued that the expansion was attributable to the mobilization of interest group litigants, rather than to the ideological interests of the judiciary.[1]

Economists have done considerable research on the effect of litigants on judicial decision making. Unfortunately, this research has frequently failed to account for the substantial political science research on judicial decision making, and the political scientists have often failed to acknowledge the economic research. Generally, economists have focused on the role of the parties to litigation (typically in private law cases at the trial level), whereas political scientists have focused on the role of the judges (typically in public law cases at the appellate level). This chapter will attempt to integrate the two approaches and determine the relative influence of litigants on circuit court decision making.

The Selection of Cases for Litigation

Cases do not spontaneously arise before the circuit courts. For a court to hear a case, a plaintiff must have filed suit, pursued the case to trial, and received a final judgment. Then, either the plaintiff or defendant must decide to appeal that judgment and pursue that appeal to a circuit court ruling. At many steps in this process, one party might abandon his or her efforts or reach a consensual settlement with the other party. When this occurs, there will be no circuit court ruling. Most cases settle, and only a small subset of filings advance to a circuit court decision. The process by which cases are weeded out before a decision is commonly known as the selection of cases for litigation.

Law and economics researchers have explored the selection of cases for litigation in some detail. Since the early 1980s, a theory known as the 50% hypothesis has prevailed in the literature. This theory, propounded by George Priest and Benjamin Klein, claimed that only the close cases will result in litigation.[2] The close cases are those in which it is difficult to project a winner, making the outcome more uncertain and correspondingly complicating settlement. According to the theory, the easy cases, in which one side has a much stronger basis, will generally settle because the parties will not want to bear the expense of litigation when the outcome is already known. If the parties are in rough agreement about the likely outcome, both win by settling and avoiding the costs of litigation. The weaker party in an easy case may well extract a monetary settlement in exchange for eliminating the litigation costs of the stronger party and to account for the small probabilistic risk of an unexpected outcome, but the case will settle and not go to a decision. The parties are self-interested, are operating in a sort of financial market, and will act to optimize their financial outcome. More than 90% of filed cases settle before a decision, which demonstrates that the parties are evaluating their prospects and negotiating a decision. Because only the small fraction of cases that are close will proceed to final resolution, Priest and Klein hypothesized that plaintiffs and defendants should each win about 50% of the time.

The selection of cases theory presumes that each party can create a reasonable estimate of the quality of its case and of the probability that it will succeed in court. The theory typically focuses on the factual and legal strength of the case and ignores the political science evidence on the ideological effect of judges in decision making. The theory can easily accommodate the political science research, though, because informed parties would be aware of the ideological effect and factor that into their assessments of probabilistic trial success.

Since the original 50% hypothesis article, the theory has been elaborated. One elaboration accounts for asymmetric information between the parties.[3] Under this theory a party might misperceive its prospects in litigation. If information about the probability of success is asymmetric, some litigants will mistakenly pursue weak cases, believing them to be strong, to a decision. The party with the superior information about the case will not settle because it will realize that its trial prospects are promising; likewise, the other party will not settle for a realistic amount because it overestimates its chances of success. Under the asymmetric information hypothesis, plaintiffs and defendants would not necessarily win about 50% of the time. If plaintiffs were systematically less well informed than defendants about case prospects, plaintiffs would push relatively weak cases to a judicial outcome and would win less than 50% of the time. Research suggests that, in some cases, plaintiffs are less well-informed than defendants.[4]

Most of the theorizing and most of the research on these hypotheses has focused on trial-level district court rulings rather than appellate circuit court determinations. The asymmetric information hypothesis makes more sense at the trial level. At this level, parties have the benefit of discovery to ascertain case facts, but the discovery process itself is expensive and may not elicit all the necessary information to equalize the parties' assessment of posttrial value.[5] Consequently, some informational asymmetry may remain, forcing unequal cases to judicial decision.

Some parties also may be particularly subject to decision-making errors. The field of behavioral economics suggests that human decisions are not always rational but may be subject to biases.[6] These biases, or decision heuristics, can render individuals poor calculators of probability. One relevant bias is known as the self-serving bias, which proposes that individuals overestimate their abilities (or the strength of their case). Emotional litigants may commit decision-making errors and may not make financially rational choices in deciding whether to litigate but may base their decisions on considerations of justice.

The asymmetric information theories make less sense in the context of appellate decision making. By the time litigants reach the appellate stage, the parties have sometimes had the facts ventilated at trial; they have a trial court decision and should thus be relatively well informed of their prospects. Moreover, appellate courts usually take the facts as found by the trial court and correct only legal mistakes made by that court. Although parties may have asymmetric information about the facts, it seems less likely that they have asymmetric information about the law. The preexisting law is readily and inexpensively available to both parties. It is also relatively easy to ascertain the judges' ideological predilections, if only from the party of the appointing president. Consequently, decisions whether to appeal and whether to settle an appeal should be based on relatively symmetric information and therefore the assumptions of the original 50% hypothesis would stand. The behavioral theories of error would still be relevant to appellate decisions, however.

Still other elaborations explain why, even under the theory, one would not expect exact 50% win rates between the parties. For example, the case might be an easy one on liability but a close one on the amount of damages to be awarded to the parties. In this circumstance, the parties would drive the case to a judicial decision to determine the recoverable damages. Such events are not reflected in data on simple win rates on the liability determination. Because of this, one would expect plaintiffs to have a higher win rate.

One possible but commonly overlooked shortcoming of the general hypothesis is its presumption that parties to litigation care only about the financial outcome of the proceedings. Litigants may have noneconomic aims and be emotionally driven, such that they are not seeking to maximize their financial returns, which upsets the market for settlements and the associated 50% hypothesis. A party may reject possible settlement out of a desire for formal judicial vindication or even a desire to punish the other party.[7] Studies of appellate litigation have found that these noneconomic motivations were significant.[8] Parties so inclined may refuse to settle even a clear case to obtain a final ruling. Unless such motivations were equally distributed between plaintiffs and defendants, one could no longer project a 50% win rate.

If the classic economic selection model were operating, either with 50% win rates or with adjustments for such factors as asymmetric information, it would inform studies of judicial decision making. For example, some have claimed that appellate decisions are overwhelmingly ideological, so the law does not matter significantly. The 50% hypothesis raises the possibility that the law is important, even if decisions are overwhelmingly ideological. Decided cases are not a random sample of disputes or legal resolutions. Ideology is most likely to matter if a case is very close on the legal issues. If only the close legal cases reach decisions, ideology would appear significant, but this could be misleading. A study of decisions would involve only the tip of the iceberg and fail to explain the outcome of most litigation. The importance of the law might be found in the settlements, which are not studied.

The Strategic Selection Hypothesis

Another important elaboration of the selection of cases hypothesis involves legal strategizing and manipulation of judicial decisions. The basic theory assumes that parties have an interest only in the outcome of the particular case, that is, whether they will have to pay or whether they will receive damages and in what amount. The strategic selection hypothesis suggests that some parties have an interest that goes beyond the outcome of the particular case because they are interested in similar future cases. Consequently, they have additional interest in the state of the law and the legal precedent that the decision may produce. Because the parties have different stakes in the outcome of the case (one party cares about more than simple damages), the party with the greater stakes will go to greater lengths to ensure victory.

Strategic selection readily occurs through a process similar to that described in the 50% hypothesis. Suppose a company is a tort defendant in three cases and the estimated probability of plaintiff success in those cases is 30%, 50%, and 70%. Under the 50% hypothesis, the defendant and plaintiff would settle the cases with the 30% and 70% success probabilities and more likely litigate the 50% case. If the company cares about the precedent set by the decision, however, its logic shifts. The company would settle the 50% and 70% cases and litigate the 30% case, which offers the greatest promise of yielding a favorable precedent. A favorable precedent means that the company is at less risk of liability in future cases and, consequently, should be able to settle those cases for less when they do arise. Moreover, the "repeat players" with an interest in the state of the law will also typically have the resources to devote to quality legal representation to ensure their victory in most cases.

This strategic case selection process is well recognized in the legal research under a different name. Some strategic litigants have carefully designed "test cases" in hopes of advancing their legal agenda. Perhaps the best-known example of this is when the National Association for the Advancement of Colored People (NAACP) legal defense team cautiously pursued appellate litigation in the 1950s and 1960s as part of a long-range civil rights plan. To establish a pattern of precedents that would lead to further advances in civil rights, the NAACP carefully screened cases according to their underlying facts and the makeup of the reviewing court. The success of the NAACP stands out as the classic example of strategic selection of cases for litigation. The American Civil Liberties Union (ACLU) and now–Supreme Court justice Ruth Bader Ginsburg embarked on a similarly successful strategy in gender rights litigation. These civil rights examples are the best known but not the only instances of such strategic litigation. Paul Rubin's historic study of nineteenth-century nuisance law suggests that "factories and firms" manipulated cases to drive the law to more defendant-favorable rulings.[9] A longitudinal study of more than a century of litigation found that large companies used litigation aggressively and that the "powerful entities" of our society "use the system to engineer legal doctrine that suits their interests."[10]

Economists have also considered the significance of strategic selection. One theoretical analysis explains how precedents will evolve to favor the concerns of parties with the greater interest in precedent but recognizes that this tendency may be frustrated if the judiciary is ideologically predisposed against those parties.[11] Although this theory centers around long-run legal changes, its operation should be noticeable in a pattern of judicial decisions. The theory logically would show up in circuit court decisions because they can have considerable precedential effect.

The strategic selection model implicitly assumes that the legal model has significance in judicial decision making. It presumes that precedent-setting has some significance. If judges were purely ideological, there would be no value to setting favorable precedents because the precedents would not influence future decisions. Sufficient evidence shows that legal rules matter to courts, though, so the strategic hypothesis has plausibility.

If the strategic litigation hypothesis is operating, the implications for judicial decision making are substantial. Under this model, the judges are essentially tools being used by the parties to produce favorable law. The ideology and background of judges would still have some importance because they would facilitate or complicate the efforts of litigants to produce favorable law. But judges themselves would not be controlling decision making, and the ability of parties to settle and prevent the judge from reaching a decision could confound a judge's ability to produce ideologically pleasing policy.

Alternative Theories of Litigant Influence

Although sociologists and political scientists have paid little attention to the economic research on the selection of cases for trial, they have considered the possible influence of litigants on judicial outcomes. Marc Galanter produced a classic exposition of litigant influence in which he discussed why the "haves" typically prevail in court over the "have nots."[12] The haves were litigants who were richer and more powerful and who were more often repeat players in the litigation process. Although Galanter proposes a number of reasons, including resource advantages, why haves are more likely to prevail, one of his theories for the disproportionate success of haves, the ability to "play for rules," is essentially the economic strategic litigation hypothesis. The haves are more interested in the state of precedent.

Political scientists have also studied how interest groups can use the judicial system to advance their political agendas. They have focused more on the political than the economic issues and have explored topics such as test cases. Much of the political science research examines amicus curiae briefs, in which nonparties argue that the court should rule in a particular way. Such outside participation in litigation suggests that private parties might attempt to manipulate decisions and the resulting course of the law.

A separate theory of litigant influence is specific to the government. The belief is that the government, especially the federal government, has particular influence as a litigant. This may be a variation of the strategic theories described in Chapter 4. The federal government has many powers over federal courts; one of the most significant of these is the appropriations power on which the judiciary depends for much of its resources. Judges may therefore be loathe to antagonize the federal government. Moreover, as officers of the federal government themselves, judges may feel some solidarity with and sometimes socialize with other federal officers.[13] Some have described this as a sort of "regime deference" by judges, in which they act as agents of the government, at least on a broad functional level.[14] The federal government also has the repeat player and party capability advantages discussed earlier. Bolstering this theory is a widespread belief and supporting empirical evidence that the U.S. solicitor general is a particularly successful litigant at the Supreme Court level.

The Amicus Opportunity

Much of the research on litigant influence dwells on the original parties to the dispute, but outsiders may also have some influence. In some limited circumstances, the federal procedural rules allow entities to intervene in litigation that may affect them. Outsiders have a much greater opportunity to participate as amici (friends of the court). Amici are those who are not parties to the litigation but who nevertheless file briefs arguing that the court should rule for one side or the other. Courts are generally liberal about allowing entities to file such amicus briefs.

The very existence of amici is significant and potentially validates the strategic selection hypothesis. Why would an outsider care enough about the outcome of a case in which it was not involved to bear the expense of filing an amicus brief? The obvious reason is that the outsider cares about the state of the law and the precedential consequences of the decision. Thus, the outsider tries to influence the decision to shape the path of the law it creates. This is the generally accepted theory of amicus participation. The theory is further validated by the cases in which amici appear. There are more amici at the Supreme Court level than at the circuit court level and more amici at the circuit court level than at the trial court level. This corresponds to the relative importance of the precedents created at those court levels.

The amicus effect could well be more profound than that of strategic case selection by the parties. When an individual party, such as a company, strategically litigates to set a favorable precedent, much of the benefit of that precedent will inure to others, including the party's competitors. If Ford Motor Company strategically achieves a favorable precedent, the precedent will probably benefit Chrysler, General Motors, Toyota, and other auto companies. The presence of external free-rider benefits somewhat reduces the party's incentive to strategize precedent creation. An amicus permits all the auto companies to join together, in a trade association or otherwise, and share the costs of mutually beneficial precedent creation. The economic incentives for strategy by amici are therefore greater.

Of course, amici may appear on both sides of a case and consequently cancel each other out. If this is common, amicus participation may be more a defensive measure than an opportunity to manipulate the judicial outcome. One study found little overall impact of amici at the Supreme Court level, in part because of this effect.[15] On closer scrutiny, that same study showed that amicus participation by some entities, such as the solicitor general and the ACLU, did have a significant influence on Court outcomes. This suggests that amicus briefs from experienced litigants do have an effect.

The strategic opportunities for amici are limited because they cannot directly settle cases. They may, however, participate in settlements. This ability is well illustrated by the case of *Piscataway Township Board of Education v. Taxman*.[16] In this case, a school district was sued by a white teacher who challenged its affirmative action policy. After losing before the third circuit court of appeals, the board of education appealed to the Supreme Court. Civil rights groups feared that the appeal would enable the conservative Supreme Court to issue a powerful anti–affirmative action ruling with nationwide effect. These groups raised the necessary money to settle with the teacher before such a decision, so the case was dismissed.

Even when amici cannot participate in a settlement, their resources and litigation skills can improve their favored litigant's chances for success. Research has found that amici can cancel out the repeat player advantage enjoyed by the haves in appellate litigation.[17] One study of federal appellate decisions on environmental common law claims found that, even controlling for judicial ideology, amici played a significant role in the ability of business to obtain decisions restricting such claims.[18] The very existence of amici is a testament to the potential success of strategic litigation.

Empirical Research on Litigant Influence

The theories of litigant influence on judicial decisions has been the subject of considerable empirical investigation. At its most basic, the 50% hypothesis is easy to empirically test because it predicts that plaintiffs will win about 50% of the time. This simple theory has been disproven.[19] In most areas of tort litigation, plaintiffs win far less than 50% of the time, with their win rates generally below 40%. In other areas of the law, including some contract and intellectual property litigation, plaintiffs win at a rate much higher than 50%. A 50% win rate is an atypical outcome in litigation.

The results in the earlier chapters of this book also disprove the simple hypothesis. According to this hypothesis, there should be no systematic differences among judges (by their ideology, their personal characteristics, or even the state of the law, such as affirmance deference) because the parties would have already accounted for those inclinations in their probabilistic estimate of outcome success. Indeed, such political science research is the best refutation of the hypothesis because the results cannot be explained by most of the theoretical elaborations of the hypothesis (although the strategic litigation hypothesis is potentially consistent with the decision-making results, a possibility explored later in this chapter). The data clearly show that the simple 50% hypothesis is not empirically valid.

Because the basic 50% win rate obviously does not prevail, researchers have sought to test the elaborations of the basic model. One study examined the asymmetric information and strategic litigation hypotheses in circuit court decisions.[20] The study considered the possible effect of factors such as different stakes in the litigation outcome, differences in party sophistication, the possibility that litigation focused on the amount of damages, agency problems with the parties' lawyers, risk aversion, and others. The authors concluded that, once these possible distorting factors were eliminated, the basic presumptions of the 50% hypothesis appeared to be operating. These findings were only tentative, though, and some of the authors' coding decisions are debatable.

The strategic litigation hypothesis has seen some indirect empirical testing. Researchers have noted that big-business interests, who are among the most likely to strategically litigate, win the overwhelming proportion of cases in which they participate.[21] This is confirmed by Galanter's research on the success of haves in litigation. A study of circuit court litigation likewise found that large enterprises are much more successful on appeal than are individuals and that the effect was greater in federal circuit courts than in state or federal supreme courts.[22] The research has not consistently shown the effect to be extremely powerful. A broad study of state decisions found that stronger parties won more often but not much more often.[23] A study at the Supreme Court level, though, found dramatic variations in the success of different categories of litigants.[24]

The strategic selection of cases analysis should intersect with the findings on judicial ideology. If the theory is correct, one would expect that strategic haves would settle cases when faced with ideologically unfavorable judges but refuse to settle cases when they have a judge that is predisposed to favor their position. This theory has not been extensively studied but one test of the strategic litigation hypothesis found that New York judges who generally favored defendants in tort litigation also rendered many more tort decisions.[25] This was a statistically significant association that did not appear in other types of cases, such as contract and property disputes. The results are what would be predicted if one assumes that the defendants in tort cases are more likely to be large corporations who have a greater interest in precedent than do the individual plaintiffs in these actions.

Identifying the Litigant Effect

As noted earlier, the classic 50% hypothesis should not necessarily produce any particular pattern of judicial decisions beyond the 50% outcomes. The strategic litigation theory, by contrast, does yield testable hypotheses about outcomes. This theory suggests that the haves will win more cases, to produce favorable precedents, than the have nots. Testing for this effect is possible with the courts of appeals database, but the test also requires the isolation of other potential decision determinants.

Testing the hypothesis necessitates the identification of the haves who are likely to participate in such strategic litigation decision making. The classic example of such a have is a big-business interest, and studies have shown that such businesses are indeed more likely to prevail in court.[26] Large interest groups, particularly those who participate as amici, might also be regarded as haves.

Although previous studies have often focused on organized business interests as the haves who will prevail and drive the direction of the law, the federal government is certainly also such a have. The federal government is a party to many disputes and occasionally appears as an amicus in purely private litigation. One study of tax court settlements and trials, a legal area in which the government interest is surely considerable, found only limited evidence that the Internal Revenue Service (IRS) successfully engaged in strategic settlement behavior.[27]

One might expect the government to engage in strategic behavior in criminal cases. Although the government cannot appeal an acquittal, it can appeal decisions such as judicial exclusion of evidence. If the government appeals only those cases in which its claim is unusually strong, it would set favorable precedents for future prosecutions, though the difficulties of settling subsequent appeals brought by convicted defendants could interfere with the strategic litigation process. In other areas of law, such as antitrust,

TABLE 5.1
Party frequency in circuit court

Party type	Appellant	Respondent
Federal government	10.3%	45.0%
State government	2.4%	8.3%
Substate government	2.1%	4.7%
Business	28.4%	27.4%
Association	4.4%	3.5%
Person	53.2%	15.1%

NOTE: Numbers total more than 100% because some cases had multiple categories as appellant or respondent.

the federal government has a disproportionately high success rate.[28] At the Supreme Court level, the U.S. solicitor general does quite well when called on to represent the interests of the federal government.

The courts of appeals database codes for the identity of litigants. The major categories for litigants are natural persons, businesses, associations, the federal government, the state government, a substate government, and fiduciaries. The database also codes for whether the parties were appellants or respondents in the litigation. One can assess from this data the role of particular classes of litigants in driving judicial decision making. Table 5.1 reports descriptive statistics on the frequency with which these parties appeared before circuit courts. For each party category, the table gives the percentage of cases in which the party appeared as either an appellant or respondent.

Obvious disparities show in the results, which qualify any assessment of party effects on outcomes. The federal government appears far more often as a respondent than as an appellant. This may be due to its overwhelming success at the lower court level or to its strategic selectivity in choosing cases to appeal. A similar effect is seen for state governments, and the reverse effect appears for natural persons. The results suggest the possibility of strategic litigation to manipulate the path of the law; this prospect is explored in the rest of the chapter.

The functional power of the law and of precedent is the necessary precondition of the strategic litigation behavior discussed earlier, but the law can also make such strategic behavior more difficult to implement. Affirmance deference complicates the strategic litigation theories.

A party wishing to manipulate the path of the law would be expected to appeal adverse decisions to favorable circuit court panels, in hopes of

TABLE 5.2
Party effects on affirmance

Party type	Appellant	Respondent
Person	.013 (.091)	−.006 (.476)
Business	.000 (.993)	.004 (.683)
Association	−.007 (.409)	.002 (.805)
Federal government	.042 (.000)	.002 (.832)
State government	.038 (.000)	.009 (.259)
Substate government	.010 (.204)	−.026 (.001)
Fiduciary	−.014 (.112)	.011 (.215)

obtaining a reversal and precedential opinion. Affirmance deference interferes with this strategy, however. As shown in Chapter 2, circuit court judges affirm even ideologically unaligned lower court rulings more than 64% of the time. Thus, an appellant takes a substantial risk of creating an adverse precedent, even when appealing to an ideologically favorable panel.

Table 5.2 reports the effects of various parties on circuit court affirmance rates. Each cell reports the increased (or decreased) probability of affirmance by party and, in parentheses, whether that difference was statistically significant.

Only the federal and state governments appeared to have much success as a strategic litigant. This success appears only when these party types are appellants, which suggests that the appellant's strategic prospects are greater. The respondent's single opportunity for strategy is in settlement, and settling nonfinancial (e.g., criminal) actions may be difficult. Even in financial actions, noneconomic motives of appellants may also obstruct strategic settlement. Moreover, though statistically significant, the size of the advantage for the parties was small. Of course, this simple analysis does not take into account the party on the other side of the litigation or the frequency with which a party appears as appellant or respondent. It also does not take into account different case types.

The net effects from Table 5.2 fail to take into account the nature of the opposing party. The overall effect could obscure significant effects in cases between, say, the federal government and business. Moreover, the findings in Table 5.2 may be influenced by the relative number of times a party appears as an appellant or a respondent, which differs greatly by litigant category, as demonstrated in Table 5.1. The associations reported in Table 5.2

TABLE 5.3
Net party success rates

	Federal government	State government	Business	Association	Person
Federal government	—	+20.9%	+36.0%	+17.4%	+35.5%
State government	−20.9%	—	+16.0%	+33.9%	+33.0%
Business	−36.0%	−16.0%	—	−13.0%	+5.4%
Association	−17.4%	−33.9%	+13.0%	—	+12.6%
Person	−35.5%	−33.0%	−5.4%	−12.6%	—

could be biased (in either direction) because of the different frequencies with which the categories appealed.

Table 5.3 displays the net success rate of the primary litigant categories when appearing on appeal against other litigants. The net success rate is calculated as a category: % success as appellant versus other category + % success rate as respondent versus other category − 100. This formula neutralizes any effect of affirmance deference on the relative success rates. The numbers in Table 5.3 display the relative success rate of the party in the vertical column versus the party in the horizontal column. Thus, when the federal government appears in circuit court against a state government, it has a positive net success rate of 20.9%.

The results show significant litigant effects on success. Clearly, the federal government is by far the most effective party in appellate litigation because it has an overwhelming advantage over every other category of litigant. State governments are also quite effective, with a considerable net advantage over every class of party except the federal government. Natural persons are clearly the least successful on appeal, though businesses do not do well either. The theory that business interests commonly prevail, through strategic litigation or otherwise, is refuted by the results, with business litigants having net success against only natural persons and even then at a relatively low level. Government appears to be the category of party that has the greatest success on appeal, possibly because of its strategic choice of appellate litigation.

When considering Table 5.3, remember that it treats the percentage of success rate for appellants and respondents equally when calculating the net effect and does not account for the number of cases in each group. The federal government appears far more often as a respondent than as an appellant. On the infrequent occasions that the federal government is an appellant, however, it tends to be very successful, winning more often than it loses, despite the general affirmance deference of circuit courts. This suggests that the federal government may be engaging in strategic appeals. But the federal government's relatively infrequent appearance as an appellant may also illustrate the limitations of such a strategy. The high success rate of the federal government may be due to its extreme selectivity in appealing.

The effect of litigants may be influenced by the presence of amici. Unfortunately, the courts of appeals database contains only very limited coding for amicus participation. It provides data on the number of amici in a case but not on their identity or even on the side for which they appeared. The available information does show that 97.1% of the cases in the database had no amici participation, so the presence or absence of data on amici should not greatly alter the results. The exclusion of cases with amici results in only a miniscule change in the net party success rates presented in Table 5.3.

Federal Litigant Effect in Criminal Decisions

Incorporating litigant effects into the basic decision-making tests used in previous chapters is difficult, because the dependent variable is an ideological one and the parties on appeal may be on either the conservative or liberal side of the appeal. The courts of appeals database does not directly report which parties favored the conservative or liberal positions. One way that ideological and party variables can be integrated into the same study is to find types of cases in which a specific category of litigant is systematically associated with a particular ideological position. This occurs in criminal appeals, in which the government is juxtaposed against criminal defendants and decisions favoring defendants' rights are coded as liberal. In these cases, the government is by definition pursuing a conservative legal outcome. The next analysis reports the outcome of the standard multiple regression model, with Ideology, LowerCourt, SupremeCourt, OldSupremeCourt, CircuitCourt, and OldCircuit Court as base variables and with the additional variable of whether the respondent was the federal government. If the federal litigant effect was important, one would expect Federal-

Respondent to have a negative coefficient with statistical significance. The results are as follows:

Ideology	.36 (.000)
LowerCourt	.67 (.000)
SupremeCourt	−.38 (.062)
OldSupremeCourt	.44 (.023)
CircuitCourt	.002 (.171)
OldCircuitCourt	.002 (.650)
FederalRespondent	.004 (.451)
N	7,074
R^2	.018

The federal government as respondent shows no real effect in criminal cases. The power of the available variables is generally lower in criminal actions than in other case types (perhaps because of the significance of particular case facts in criminal cases). Ideology shows only marginal significance, and the significant factors are affirmance deference and contemporary circuit median. The federal government has relatively little control over appeals when it is a respondent. The strategic litigation effect may be more likely to appear when the federal government is the appellant, choosing to appeal a loss. A regression with this variable is reported in the following list:

Ideology	.38 (.000)
LowerCourt	.82 (.000)
SupremeCourt	−.39 (.061)
OldSupremeCourt	.41 (.032)
CircuitCourt	.002 (.246)
OldCircuitCourt	.002 (.559)
FederalAppellant	−.40 (.011)
N	7,074
R^2	.020

These results may show some effect for the federal government as appellant, though the effect does not quite reach statistical significance. In criminal actions, the federal government is apparently having little unique success as a strategic litigant. Considering the criminal context, though, this analysis is really measuring the relative effect of the federal government against state governments (because the other categories of litigants do not usually participate in criminal prosecutions). Hence, the limited effect of federal participation can show only that it is scarcely more successful than state governments, but states themselves are generally interested and effective parties in the circuit courts, so the study does not negate the possibility of federal government influence.

The structure of this study could well understate the strategic litigation effect by including Ideology as a control variable. Strategic litigation might occur by manipulation of ideology on deciding circuit court panels. The federal government could choose to pursue an appeal only after calculating that the circuit court panel ideology appeared promising for that appeal. To test this possibility I analyzed the cases to determine the composition of the panels hearing criminal cases and to determine those hearing criminal cases in which the federal government was a party.

The next analysis presents the panel composition for criminal cases, with varying levels of federal government participation. The descriptive statistics include the mean Ideology, which is taken from the cumulated Ideology numbers for the full panel. The data are converted from the original ratings, so that higher numbers mean more liberal judicial ideologies. The following list presents the mean TotalIdeology for all criminal actions in the courts of appeals database, those in which the federal government was an appellant, those in which the federal government was a respondent, and those in which the federal government did not participate:

All criminal	.0213
Federal appellant	.1206
Federal respondent	.0119
No federal party	.0343

These results are precisely the opposite of what strategic litigation theory would predict. The federal government is pressing criminal appeals before panels that are somewhat more liberal, and therefore presumably unfavorable, than the panels ruling in other criminal cases. The federal government remains a relatively successful appellant in criminal actions, though, and may be pursuing a more complex strategy in these appeals. Perhaps a conservative decision from a comparatively liberal panel carries enhanced credibility and therefore produces greater precedential weight in future cases or suffers a lower risk of rejection by other institutions. If so, the government would be pursuing favorable cases on the facts, before apparently unfavorable panels, to obtain a decision with particularly great credibility.

Federal Litigant Effect in Labor Decisions

One other area of the courts of appeals database in which there is an association between ideology and litigant category is in labor law decisions. In these cases, the federal government is most commonly associated with the liberal position (rather than the conservative position of criminal law). Many of these cases involve the federal enforcement of union rights against businesses. In some cases, the federal government may have been enforcing against a union, but the government is considered liberal in these cases also, perhaps because the cases involved the enforcement of individual rights of union members.

The next analyses track those used earlier for criminal law. To test the effect of the federal party, I ran a multiple regression on the ideology of the individual vote, with judicial ideology, affirmance deference, and strategic control variables. The following list reports the results for the federal government as respondent:

Ideology	.045 (.012)
LowerCourt	2.07 (.000)
SupremeCourt	−1.74 (.001)
OldSupremeCourt	1.42 (.001)
CircuitCourt	−.001 (.779)
OldCircuitCourt	.042 (.000)
FederalRespondent	−.012 (.031)
N	2,739
R^2	.299

In labor cases, the federal government is particularly ineffective as a respondent; its participation is associated with a statistically significant reduced likelihood of success. Bear in mind that this effect is relative to the other parties who may defend the liberal position in labor cases (e.g., unions). The federal government's lack of success is not necessarily inconsistent with strategic litigation, because unions may have a greater interest in the state of labor law precedent than does the federal government. This hypothesis is impossible to test directly, though, because the courts of appeals database does not contain separate coding to distinguish unions from other associations.

This analysis of labor votes highlights some other aspects of judicial decision making. The R^2 term, while not high, is distinctly higher than in earlier regressions and dramatically higher than for criminal cases. This suggests that the database has better captured the key variables in labor law cases and that individualized case facts may not be as significant in these disputes. The measures for the law are quite powerful (both affirmance deference and old court variables) and judicial ideology has material power. The strategic variables do not explain the decisions, because the SupremeCourt strategic variable is significant and negative, as in the results for other case types. The following list reports the results of the same analysis for cases in which the federal government appeared as an appellant:

Ideology	.45 (.011)
LowerCourt	2.07 (.000)
SupremeCourt	1.77 (.000)
OldSupremeCourt	1.51 (.000)
CircuitCourt	−.001 (.755)
OldCircuitCourt	.042 (.000)
FederalAppellant	−.016 (.034)
N	2,739
R^2	.298

With the federal government's enhanced case selection opportunities, it remains ineffective, even when appearing as an appellant. Clearly, the general success of the federal government in circuit courts does not extend to labor law disputes. The other variables retain the same general significant associations as before and the R^2 term remains relatively high.

Effects of Collectivity

Up until now, the analysis has not distinguished between the absolute number of parties appearing as respondent or appellant. In a significant number of cases, however, multiple entities appeared as litigants. A single state might appeal a lower court judgment but, alternatively, a number of states might appeal a decision of broader interest or one of more intense concern to state governments. The number of representatives of a category of litigant could have some effect on their relative success.

Table 5.4 presents descriptive statistics for the litigant makeup of cases in the courts of appeals database. Each column gives the percentage of total cases in which a primary litigant category appeared (as either appellant or respondent) with one, two, or more than two representatives.[29]

Although most cases do not involve multiple representatives of a given litigant category, a material number of cases do have such multiple representatives. These cases may be especially significant ones that merit further investigation.

The breakdown of litigant types in the regressions presented earlier used the basic categories without any differentiation in each category. But such differentiation may be vital to identifying a litigant effect. For example, the business category does not distinguish between a party that is a small auto parts store and a party that is General Motors. The courts of appeals database enables some differentiation within categories because it includes the absolute number of category representatives in a case. Thus, the database distinguishes between cases in which a single business is a party and those

TABLE 5.4
Number of party representatives

Party	One	Two	More than two
State appellant	1.4%	0.3%	0.7%
State respondent	5.1%	1.0%	2.1%
Business appellant	21.2%	2.8%	4.5%
Business respondent	18.3%	3.4%	5.7%
Association appellant	2.3%	0.4%	1.7%
Association respondent	1.9%	0.4%	1.3%
Person appellant	42.4%	5.0%	5.8%
Person respondent	9.7%	1.8%	3.6%

in which a dozen businesses are parties. The latter cases are more likely to produce strategic litigation.

The effect of multiple parties within a case category can be tested in an analysis that checks for this effect on success. The number of representatives of a litigant category could serve as a proxy for the category's interest in the litigation and its possible associated strategic litigation. The next regression uses as independent variables the number of representatives for the categories of natural person, business, association or group, and state. The dependent variable is affirmance rate. The analysis distinguishes whether the relevant parties were appellant or respondent, and the Align variable controls for the effect of judicial ideology. For each of the independent variables, a positive sign means that higher numbers produce greater success in court. The following list reports the results:

Person appellant	−.012 (.022)
Business appellant	.002 (.667)
Association appellant	−.003 (.566)
State appellant	.039 (.000)
Person respondent	−.014 (.010)
Business respondent	.006 (.269)
Association respondent	.007 (.179)
State respondent	.009 (.087)
Align	.068 (.000)
N	38,741
R^2	.007

The results suggest two meaningful associations. The number of state government parties to an action is positively associated with greater success. This is consistent with the general findings about the disproportionate success of state governments and possible strategic litigation. Interestingly, there was also a negative significant association between success in the circuit court and the number of individual natural persons as parties. Although there is no obvious reason for this, the number of persons possibly serves as a proxy for the financial consequences of the case for the opposing party (which may be business or government) and thus drives that party to put more effort into winning. As in all the earlier studies on litigant effects, the practical significance of even the statistically significant associations is very small, explaining well below 1% of the outcomes.

Litigants and Opinion Length

As with the other decision-making factors discussed in previous chapters, litigant influence might show up in the content of opinions, for which our only proxy variable is length. The nature of the litigants might influence opinion length for two reasons. Perhaps appeals brought (or defended) by certain categories of litigants, such as the federal government, are taken more seriously by courts and therefore yield longer opinions. Also, certain types of litigants might pursue more complex cases that require longer opinions. Table 5.5 reports the mean page length of the case opinion when various categories of litigants appear as parties to the appeal. The data are broken down by whether the case outcome was liberal or conservative.

There are some apparent differences in page length, with the most striking being the relatively long opinions issued in cases in which an association was a party, especially an appellant. This finding is probably a proxy for case significance. These descriptive statistics are too simple to offer plain conclusions, however. They do not account for an effect from other parties in the case or consider the number of such parties. To explain these potentially confounding factors, I performed a multiple regression in which the number of parties representing each litigant type is introduced as a quantitative independent variable for the dependent variable of opinion length. The

TABLE 5.5
Identity of parties and mean opinion length

Party	Liberal	Conservative
Person appellant	4.626	4.143
Business appellant	4.848	4.846
Association appellant	6.997	6.122
Federal appellant	4.727	4.533
Person respondent	5.136	4.553
Business respondent	4.823	4.248
Association respondent	5.136	4.923
Federal respondent	4.923	4.533

TABLE 5.6
Number of parties and opinion length

Party	(1)	(2)
Person appellant	−.008 (.379)	−.006 (.475)
Business appellant	−.007 (.414)	−.009 (.314)
Association appellant	.034 (.000)	.033 (.000)
State appellant	.015 (.088)	.010 (.243)
Federal appellant	.013 (.026)	.006 (.492)
Person respondent	.000 (.980)	−.001 (.897)
Business respondent	−.003 (.756)	−.003 (.785)
Association respondent	−.010 (.275)	−.010 (.296)
State respondent	.010 (.272)	.010 (.228)
Federal respondent	.045 (.000)	.045 (.000)
Reversal		.124 (.000)
Ideology		.025 (.004)
N	13,368	13,368
R^2	.004	.021

regression was done with and without controls for reversal and ideological case outcome. Table 5.6 reports the results.

Litigants do not appear to have much effect on opinion length. Clear evidence shows that courts write longer opinions in cases that have associations as appellants or the federal government as a respondent. Even in these cases, however, the absolute effect is not great. There is some evidence that courts treat cases involving these parties more significantly, but presumably not because of the litigant itself, given the lack of significance for cases with association respondents or federal appellants. Perhaps the significant party associations are linked to cases of greater complexity or social consequence.

Amicus participation might also influence opinion length. Cases with amici are likely the more important ones. Given the cost and effort associated with filing an amicus brief, amici probably participate in only the most socially significant actions, which courts might recognize by writing longer opinions in such cases. The following list incorporates amici as an independent variable for opinion length:

Amici	.146 (.000)
Reversal	.120 (.000)
Ideology	.022 (.013)
N	13,400
R^2	.039

These results indicate that opinion length is clearly associated with the presence of amici. Cases with more amicus participation produce longer opinions; this correlation is statistically significant and appears to be substantively significant also.

Although the implications of many of this book's findings on opinion length are uncertain, the findings for amici are potentially quite valuable for future research. The longer opinions in cases with more amici suggest that courts do prioritize their opinion-writing efforts and focus on the more socially salient cases. The findings also indicate that amicus participation might serve as a useful proxy for case significance in future research. One limitation of much empirical research is that all cases are treated as equivalent, even though some decisions are considerably more significant than others. Earlier studies have probably not differentiated by case significance because there was no clear basis for doing so. The presence of amici as a proxy for case significance could be used in future studies to find out whether other determinants of outcomes vary depending on the relative social importance of a case.

Conclusion

Contrary to many economic theories, litigants do not appear to play a major role in driving judicial decisions. Some categories of litigants are distinctly more successful in the circuit courts. The federal and state governments are the most successful categories of litigants, and individuals are consistently less successful. The number of government entities and the presence of amici also have some effect on judicial opinions. Attempting to integrate litigants into the explanatory model created in previous chapters, using legal and ideological variables, does not yield much, however. Consequently, litigant influence seems not to be a central determinant of circuit court decisions. Litigants are necessary to enable judicial action but they do not appear to drive the outcome of that judicial action.

Panel Effects and Circuit Court Decision Making

The overwhelming majority of circuit court decisions are rendered by panels of three judges. Until now, this book has proceeded as if each judge was an atomistic individual, unaffected by the opinions of others, except so far as the judge somehow might be punished by outsiders. This chapter considers the possibility that a judge's vote might by influenced by the other judges on the panel, a phenomenon called panel effects. These panel effects involve the intrapanel dynamics of the circuit court judges, who seek to persuade or otherwise influence their colleagues.

In the conventional ideological attitudinal model of judicial decision making, judges are not amenable to persuasion. The judges of this model know their own preferences and can be straightforward in voting to implement those preferences. The judge with the median preference will always prevail. There is no a priori reason to reject the possibility of panel effects, though. If the law matters in decisions, a strong legal argument from a judge's colleagues might alter his or her decision. Considerable psychological and sociological evidence demonstrates the possibility that decisions may be influenced by others.

Given the absence of quantitative evidence on the internal workings of circuit court panels, the exact nature of panel effects cannot be precisely tested. We can, however, indirectly examine the possibility of panel effects. The presence or absence of dissent on a circuit court panel is one clue to the presence of panel effects. Such effects might also be observed by testing whether differences in the nature of a judge's panel colleagues appear to influence the way that judge votes. This chapter examines the presence and significance of panel effects in circuit court decision making.

Median Voter Theorem

The median voter theorem is a simple but classic theory of political science. Attributed to the early work of Duncan Black, the theorem essentially states that in democratic group decision making, the preferences of the median decision maker will rule.[1] The theorem requires certain basic assumptions for its validity, though. It presumes majority rule, in which each decision maker has independence and a vote of equal weight. More critically, it depends on the decision makers' single-peaked preferences, which in turn presumes that those preferences lie along a two-dimensional spectrum. Figure 6.1 illustrates the circumstances of the median voter theorem.

In this figure, there are three judges, A, B, and C, with a range of ideological preferences on the horizontal axis. Their utility declines as they get further in either direction from their ideal preference point. The median voter theorem states that when these three judges are jointly reaching a majority decision, the outcome will be at point X, the ideal preference point of B. Decision maker B has no need to compromise his or her preferences because he or she has no risk of being outvoted. A and C cannot combine on any outcome that both would prefer to the outcome at the median member's preference (point B). The exact positions of A and C do not matter—as long as one is to the left of B and the other to the right, B's preferences will prevail.

Although the logic of the theorem seems obvious, at least given its assumptions, there are some reasons to question its applicability. The basic median voter theorem is applicable only when the voters have preferences

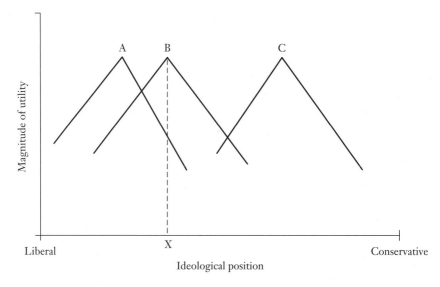

Figure 6.1 Operation of Median Voter Theorem

in a single dimension, such as a liberal to conservative ideological spectrum, and single-peaked preferences that consistently decline in both directions. If the voters have preferences in multiple dimensions, there may be no true median voter. B might have the median preferences in the ideological dimension but A might be the median voter in some other dimension, such as legal preferences.

The theorem also essentially eliminates the possibility of persuasion or other collegial influence. It does not admit the possibility that decision maker A could make a convincing argument, by providing additional information or for some nonideological reason, that point A should be preferred by decision maker B. In the basic theorem, decision maker B knows exactly what his or her preferences are and exactly how a given outcome would conform to those preferences. This assumption of the theorem might also be questioned. People occasionally do change their minds. But the median voter theorem has been subjected to empirical social scientific testing, usually in the legislative context, and the tests have generally demonstrated its validity.[2] Thus, the median voter theorem is widely accepted as a valid method for describing the outcomes of democratic group decision making with simple majority rule. The theorem at its basic level admits to no effects from colleagues because the median decision maker unilaterally controls the outcome.

The median voter theorem is generally applied to majority decision making in such bodies as legislatures but it could also be applied to court decision making. Indeed, Supreme Court decision making appears to be consistent with the theorem. In the Rehnquist Court, Justice Sandra Day O'Connor was often considered the crucial justice because she stood at the ideological center of the Court and was therefore the median voter.[3] In this context the use of median voters for the Supreme Court or other judicial panels has intuitive appeal but only if one assumes that judicial decisions are purely ideological. To the extent that they are multidimensional, with some effect for law, the straightforward median voter model may not apply. It has sometimes been assumed that the median voter theorem is also applicable to circuit court decision making, but this assumption has not been proved.

Evidence of Panel Effects in Circuit Court Decision Making

According to the classic median voter theorem, the median preferences are the only ones that matter. Thus, on a three-judge panel, the most moderate of the three would dictate the decision. The preferences of the other two judges would be utterly irrelevant because the median voter would choose the outcome regardless of their preferences. But some empirical research on circuit court decision making questions the accuracy of this model in judicial decisions.

Richard Revesz performed a multidecade study of environmental decisions in the D.C. circuit court of appeals and found that the outcomes were significantly affected by a judge's own ideology.[4] He also found, however, that the composition of the full panel strongly affected judge votes. Contrary to what the basic median voter hypothesis would project, under some circumstances the ideological preferences of a panel member's colleagues had as strong an effect on his or her votes as the panel member's own ideological preferences. This research provided strong support for panel effects and called into question the presumptions of the median voter theory.

At around the same time, Emerson Tiller and I studied a group of D.C. circuit administrative law decisions interpreting a crucial Supreme Court precedent.[5] The study tested for the ideological direction of the court decision and for whether that decision showed deference, as the Supreme Court precedent directed, to the administrative decision that the court was reviewing. The central finding of this research was that composition of the full circuit court panel had a significant effect on outcomes. Unified panels (those composed of judges appointed by presidents of the same party) were distinctly more ideological and less likely to show deference to an administrative decision that was ideologically disparate from their preferences. By contrast, split panels (those composed of two judges from one party and one from the other) were less ideological and more likely to defer to ideologically contrary administrative decisions. Although, as the median voter theorem would predict, the two aligned judges could easily outvote the one judge from the other party and have their preferred ideological outcome, even on a split panel, they were much less likely to do so. The presence of one judge appointed by a president of the other political party made a significant difference in outcomes.

Although both these studies were independently conducted at about the same time, they used different approaches and different sets of cases. Neither study directly tested the median voter theorem but both produced results that called the theorem into question as an explanation for circuit court decision making. The preferences of the nonmedian members of the circuit court panel appeared to have an important effect on outcomes, which were thus not entirely based on the preferences of the median panel member. The authors theorized about the possible reasons for this effect, but the results did not provide a clear explanation for why nonmedian voter preferences were so salient. Moreover, both studies used the defensible but somewhat crude measure of party of appointing president as a proxy for judicial ideology, which made it impossible to identify a true median voter on the panel.

Some more-recent research further confirms the presence of a panel effect.[6] This research examined circuit court decisions in thirteen discrete areas, ranging from abortion rights rulings to capital punishment. In most of these areas, the authors found clear evidence of panel effects on judicial decisions. They concluded that the ideological preferences of the other panel judges were every bit as important in predicting a judicial vote as were the preferences of the voting judge. The effects were not universal, though; in abortion and capital punishment cases, judges voted their own ideology. This finding suggests that some topics are so ideologically charged that judges' votes cannot be altered by their panel colleagues. In a few other areas, the votes were entirely nonideological. But this study suffered the same shortcoming as the two described earlier, in that it could not identify a true median member of each panel but relied instead on the split versus unified panel distinctions.

The panel effects identified in the existing research are contrary to the standard median voter theorem's predictions but should not be too surprising in the context of circuit court decision making. As discussed earlier, the median voter theorem depends on the decision makers having single-peaked preferences along a single dimensional spectrum. If the decision makers are purely ideological, and the issues lie along a typical liberal to conservative spectrum, the theorem has great plausibility. As soon as a second dimension, such as concern for the law, is introduced, however, the assumptions underlying the median voter theorem break down. If the law and ideology both matter, one would not expect the theorem to be predictive. Moreover, as I discuss later, there are other psychological reasons to question the real-world validity of the median voter theorem. When individuals participate in group decision making, they may be influenced by the attitudes of other group members and not driven entirely by their own attitudes.

Minority Influence

Psychologists and sociologists have conducted considerable research on the ability of a minority to influence majority opinion (and vice versa). Under the standard basic political theories, such as the median voter theorem, each decision maker knows his or her preferences and has no reason to be influenced by minorities. The median voter theorem allows no room for one decision maker to convince another to become more conservative or more liberal in a particular decision. Yet there is ample anecdotal evidence that some decision makers, such as those who serve on juries, are influenced by minority persuasion. Psychologists have conducted studies into how and when this may be the case.

The classic study of minority influence was done in the 1960s.[7] In this research, small groups were called on to declare the color of slides, which were plainly blue. The authors had two group members insist, however, that the slides were green. They convinced a small but statistically significant number of the other group members to change their minds and call the color of the blue slides green. The study demonstrated that a minority could persuade a majority to adopt a clearly "wrong" opinion and that the power of the minority might be expected to be greater when the decision is more ambiguous. Our real-world experience certainly suggests that individuals may be persuaded to change their minds. Were it not so, politicians, advertisers, and others would not devote such great resources to attempts at persuasion.

Persuasion and related panel effects might be expected in judicial decision making. Consider the possible role of a minority member of a circuit court panel. The social etiquette of the court requires that the majority listen to the minority judge. He or she can argue that the law compels a decision contrary to that preferred by the majority and can support that opinion with reasoned argumentation. This argument creates for the majority a potential cognitive conflict to which they must respond. This response process forces them to grapple with the validity of the minority's claim. Moreover, in attempting to comprehend and respond to the minority opinion, the majority may effectively validate that opinion. The minority may expose the majority's underlying, unconscious biases and force the majority to confront the conflict and potentially resolve it in the minority's favor.

Minorities might be expected to use the materials of the law to persuade the ideological majority that once their preferred decision is subjected to rigorous analysis, it is legally unsustainable. Chapter 2 has shown that the law is an important determinant of circuit court decisions. Research on juries confirms the plausibility of this legal effect. Juries are instructed that under the law they must give the defendant the benefit of any reasonable doubt. Jury studies have found that an initial minority advocating acquittal is more likely to persuade a majority than is an initial minority favoring conviction.[8] Thus, jurors seem to take seriously the directions of reasonable doubt and modify their decisions accordingly. This finding is evidence of the power of legal rules for enabling minorities' persuasive efforts. The earlier-described Cross and Tiller research on administrative deference decisions is likewise consistent with the view that ideological minorities can use legal doctrines to persuade ideological majorities.

Some research on the Supreme Court also shows minority influence. This empirical research has found that the Court's majority opinions use more complex reasoning in cases in which they are confronted with a dissent.[9] This finding is not evidence that the minorities persuaded an initial majority to change their decision (though anecdotal examples of such change can be readily found) but it does show that the presence of a minority influences the majority's decisional process. Even if that influence does not produce a change in the case's outcome, a change in the case's opinion can be significant in its own right.

There are many reasons for the minority's ability to use the law to persuade an ideologically contrary majority. The most obvious is simple rational persuasion within the group, which might be called internal whistleblowing. The minority is blowing the whistle on the majority's motivated reasoning, that is, the majority's allowing their ideology to override good law. Once the internal whistle has been blown, the majority must confront the cognitive conflict between its ideology and the best understanding of the law, and the majority may sometimes bow to the latter. Another reason for minority persuasion, external whistle-blowing, involves the threat of dissent to publicly expose the majority's infidelity to the law. This theory is discussed later.

Minorities may also have more indirect influence on the group's conclusions, short of a total reversal of position by the majority. The minority opinion could trigger the consideration in the group's analytical process of other alternatives that might provide a middle-ground answer. A series of studies has shown that "when confronted with minority solutions to problems, the solutions generated by research participants are more creative and novel," because "minority positions are evaluated objectively, appraised, and one's own positions (and biases) are thus re-evaluated."[10] This conclusion is confirmed in the judicial context by the research discussed earlier on Supreme Court opinions. The minority effect may be greater for circuit court panels than for other groups because the minority position is occupied by a close colleague, an in-group member, whose opinions presumably are based on jointly shared values and considered worthy of serious consideration.[11] Because panel composition changes, each member of the majority knows that he or she may be in some future minority, so judges may have an implicit deal to treat minority opinions seriously.

Judge Harry Edwards has examined, in his discussions of "collegiality," some of these panel factors in the context of circuit court decision making.[12] He rejects straightforward ideological explanations of judicial behavior in the circuit courts, in part because they fail to account for collegiality. Although collegiality may make judges more willing to compromise for the greater good, Judge Edwards notes that a comfortable level of collegiality may also make it easier for a judge to disagree with the position of his or her colleagues. These disagreements can then be debated respectfully within the three-judge panel. Judge Edwards believes that, both within the panel and throughout the entire circuit, the collegial process of appellate decisions can mitigate the role of judicial ideology.

A more traditional strategic analysis of decision making would involve external whistle-blowing. Rational choice social scientists might be dubious of the vague psychological effects associated with collegiality and seek a more pragmatic, self-interested explanation for the minority effect and apparent violation of the predictions of the median voter theorem. The threat of a dissent could provide such an explanation. A minority who threatens to issue a dissenting opinion can publicly expose the weaknesses of the majority's ruling. This in turn might call the case to the attention of another institution, such as the Supreme Court, and cause that body to overturn the decision. The results from Chapter 4, however, call into question the degree to which circuit courts need fear overruling from other institutions. That finding casts doubt on this theory, which direct research has also failed to confirm. A dissent might have other adverse consequences for the majority, though, beyond mere fear of reversal. The majority might be embarrassed if the scholarly legal consensus lined up behind the dissenting opinion. A dissenting opinion might also reduce the precedential impact of a ruling, a subject I investigate in Chapter 8.

Another potential path for minority influence on circuit court panels would be through logrolling, or vote trading. This practice is considered to be common in legislatures. Logrolling occurs when decision makers trade votes among themselves according to each decision maker's relative preference intensity for particular issues. Thus, if a liberal legislator especially cares about issue A, that legislator will be willing to cast a conservative vote on issue B (about which he or she cares less) in exchange for a vote from a conservative legislator on issue A (because the conservative cares more about issue B). The legislator sacrifices a vote on a matter of less importance to him or her to prevail on a matter of greater importance. In the context of circuit courts, a liberal might give a vote on a takings clause case, for example, to win a conservative vote on a privacy rights case. Judicial logrolling is considered inappropriate, though, and its existence in judicial panels has never been demonstrated.[13] Although no one can prove a negative, the absence of any hint of logrolling is reasonable testimony that it is, at most, a rare occurrence.

Circuit court judges who find themselves in the minority have some opportunities to influence the majority and perhaps even prevail on the case outcome. The conventional strategic rational choice theories, such as logrolling or threat of dissent, would not appear to be very influential. The opportunities for persuasive influence show more potential. Psychological research has demonstrated that minorities can sometimes persuade majorities to change their minds. The effect of judicial collegiality on circuit court panels might further this effect.

Group Polarization

The flip side of minority influence is consensual group polarization. The previously discussed research on motivated reasoning shows that an individual views information in a light consistent with his or her prior values. But this effect is constrained by the reasoning process, especially if a devil's advocate argues the other side. A panel consisting of three individuals with roughly the same values is unlikely to face this constraint because there is no devil's advocate. Moreover, if like-minded individuals engage in motivated reasoning, the effect might be stronger than that for a single individual. John Turner and his colleagues gave an apt description of the phenomenon: "like polarized molecules, group members become even more aligned in the direction they were already tending."[14] Each individual's particular doubts might be overcome by the others' confidence in the conclusion.

Psychological research into the concept of group polarization has found evidence of this effect. When one's opinion is met with agreement, one's confidence in one's beliefs may be strengthened, which has been shown to encourage more extreme beliefs.[15] Research on group decision making has found that when the deliberators hold similar biases, the deliberation process can exacerbate those biases rather than moderating them.

Group polarization has also been identified in a concept commonly known as risky shift. This phenomenon was identified in the early 1960s by James Stoner and has frequently been replicated. The research finds that people acting in a group will make decisions that involve greater risks than they would when acting as isolated individuals. The presence of a like-thinking group can bolster the self-assurance of individual group members and perhaps help mitigate their self-doubt. Moreover, the company of a like-minded group helps shift some of the responsibility for a risky error, should that error come to pass. In the context of judicial decision making, such a risk might take the form of an ideological departure from the apparently contrary dictates of the law. Thus, an ideologically aligned group, such as a politically unified panel, might be expected to be especially ideological and less legal in its decision making because the judges only reinforce one another's preferences. Judge Edwards has confirmed from personal experience that when ideologically like-minded judges sit together on a panel, "they might use the occasion to tilt their opinions pursuant to their partisan preferences."[16]

The findings about group polarization and risky shift might seem to call into question the value of using three-judge appellate panels rather than having a single judge conduct the review. Such polarization could drive appellate opinions to more extreme results than would individualized review. The research on group decision making is not that simple, however. Such research extensively shows that group decisions are often superior to the decisions made by individuals. On relatively technical matters, groups can use the skills of the most technically proficient group member and possibly enhance those skills. Under some circumstances, group decisions do not produce extreme outcomes but can lead to the opposite—a depolarization effect.[17] The value of group decision making, though, seems to be contingent on group diversity. When a group contains potential dissenters, or at least internal devil's advocates, the minority position can highlight the counterarguments to the majority position and its associated risks, thus moderating the majority. Research has found that when decision-making groups had a minority advocating a position that diverged from the majority preference, the result was that the group made less extreme and less polarized strategy decisions.[18] When members of a group all share the same proclivities, though, they lack this moderating counterweight. Other research has confirmed this effect and found that appointing a devil's advocate to join a group improved the quality of that group's decision-making processes, the quality of their decisions, and their ultimate commitment to those decisions.[19] These findings suggest that a minority can influence a majority to make a better decision by some relatively objective standard, such as the law.

Dissent in Circuit Courts

The decision-making process of circuit court panels is opaque. Judicial discussions are not disclosed. But one small window into the process occurs when a judge dissents from the majority opinion. A recent study sought to predict the likelihood of dissent from a circuit court panel member.[20] When the authors considered various factors as determinants of dissent, the judicial ideological factor predominated. Certain case features also played a role; dissents were more likely in disputes that were especially salient or legally complex. Racial minority judges (but not female judges) were also more likely to dissent. There was no evidence, however, of hierarchical reversal strategizing in the judge's decision to dissent or not.

Although this study examined the relative probability of dissent, it did not address issues around the absolute frequency of dissent. If a circuit court panel includes judges of materially divergent ideologies, as most do, the political theory of decision making suggests that they will tend to reach different conclusions regarding the proper outcome of a case and that the outvoted ideological minority would render a dissenting opinion. Such dissenting opinions, however, are relatively rare in circuit court decisions, even when the panel's judges have plainly differing ideologies. Some have suggested that this is strong evidence that ideology does not drive circuit court decisions, because judges of very different ideologies commonly join in a single opinion.

The low rate of dissent is often attributed to a sort of panel effect, called the norm of consensus. One of the various possible reasons for this effect, some have suggested, is that circuit court panels have a strong desire to avoid issuing rulings with a dissenting opinion. Consequently, they endeavor to reach unanimous holdings. This effort to reach panel unanimity could involve either minority capitulation to a majority, to avoid boat-rocking dissents, or some degree of majority conciliation, giving the minority something of precedential value in the opinion, if not the actual desired outcome, to stave off a dissenting opinion. The first explanation could be considered simply a variant of the median voter theorem, whereas the second would involve true panel effects. The hypothesized norm of consensus alone does not suggest which of the two behaviors is most likely.

Some have argued for a slightly different explanation, based on judicial norms, for the relative paucity of circuit court panel dissents.[21] Judges may face social pressure not to file a dissenting opinion. This norm may be motivated by a general concern for protecting the court's credibility and preserving the image of the nonideological nature of decision making. Alternatively, dissent may be suppressed, given the absence of practical ideological benefits, by its very loneliness and the possibility of subsequent individual embarrassment. There is a slight difference in the general but not absolute norm of consensus effect, though, in that it to some degree empowers the potential dissenter. The majority might be willing to make some compromises, at least in opinion language, to avoid provoking the minority into one of the rare dissents. But if the majority is indifferent to dissent, there would be no incentive to make such compromises.

The relative absence of dissent neither truly counters the ideological theory of decision making nor demonstrates panel effects, once the circuit court judge's circumstances are considered. The pattern of unanimity is potentially consistent even with individual judicial voting being driven primarily by personal ideology. Suppose that you are the lone liberal on a circuit court panel and are outvoted by two conservative judges, with all the judges being ideological and unamenable to persuasion on the law. You have the opportunity to write a dissenting opinion, opposing the majority's decision and expressing your liberal legal position. Writing such a dissenting opinion, though, takes time and can demand considerable effort but, unlike a majority opinion, has no automatic practical effect, either directly over the parties or indirectly through its precedential effect. Thus, the outvoted judge must consider whether to make the effort to dissent, given that no obvious real-world benefit will result from the dissent. This cost/benefit evaluation is colored by the fact that circuit court judges have an extremely heavy workload, regardless of whether they dissent. Under the circumstances, it is unsurprising that circuit court judges seldom expend the resources to issue a dissenting opinion, even when they ideologically disagree with the majority's opinion. Thus, the constraints of workload and effort on circuit courts would naturally suppress dissent, even absent any panel effects. The fact that "circuits that publish a lower percentage of terminated appeals also have a higher percentage of published dissents" is consistent with this theory.[22]

The mere absence of dissent, then, is not necessarily contrary to the general theory of ideological judicial decision making. This absence also need not be considered persuasive evidence of some psychological decision driven by panel effects. Instead, it could be a simple economic decision about the judge's strategic deployment of his or her scarce resources. Consequently, one must be cautious when interpreting empirical results that appear to show panel effects. The theorized purely economic decision means that the empirical research on individual judge votes will tend to understate the ideological effect of decisions (because minority ideologies will go along with the majority out of practical necessity). The possibly economic decision on dissents also means that the empirical results may overstate the true significance of panel effects. When an ideological minority goes along with a majority opinion, the minority's vote may appear to be influenced by panel effects, though it is truly influenced only by the practical decision that dissenting is not worth the effort. Any study of panel effects must account for this confounding economic effect.

Some of the existing studies have sought to avoid the confounding effect of dissent by focusing not on individual votes but on full panel decisions and the consequences of diverse panel composition. These studies have not confirmed the median voter theorem and have found some panel effect. Because of this effect I have previously argued that all circuit court panels should be split panels, with at least one panel member appointed by a Republican president and at least one appointed by a Democratic president.[23] Although this proposal has not been adopted by any circuit, many panels are in fact politically split and the effect of such a split can be empirically assessed.

The Circumstances of Dissent

The first investigation of this chapter further examines the circumstances under which panel members dissent from a majority opinion. Although dissents are not typical in the cases contained in the courts of appeals database, they are frequent enough to be studied. Judicial ideological preferences are not the sole determinant or even the most significant determinant of circuit court outcomes but they do have a statistically significant association with outcomes. It would be interesting to see if the dissenters were predictably ideological, that is, if a Republican dissented from a liberal decision by a majority Democrat panel. Unfortunately, the database does not allow for identification of which judge was the dissenter, so no analysis of dissenter characteristics is possible.

We can understand some circumstances of dissent, though, by examining the rates of dissent in different categories of cases. Table 6.1 reports for the courts of appeals database cases the rate of dissent by case type and the absolute number of cases for each type.

Dissent on circuit courts is not as rare as sometimes assumed. The frequency of dissent differs by case type and seems to depend most significantly on the number of cases heard. Legal areas with relatively fewer total cases appear to have a higher proportion of dissents. Dissent seems far more likely on certain constitutional issues that seldom come before the courts, such as First Amendment and privacy issues.

This finding on dissent frequency is potentially consistent with the economic model discussed earlier. If, as one might expect, constitutional First Amendment and privacy issues are more ideologically or legally salient, a judge would be more willing to expend resources on such cases. This incentive would be enhanced if these are the cases that are most likely to reach the Supreme Court and in which a dissent might trigger closer review by the Court. The relative infrequency of these cases might also motivate the judge to writing a dissenting opinion. Such an opinion might be largely overlooked in the vast body of criminal circuit court opinions but get more notice and have more indirect impact in an area of constitutional law with fewer cases and thus fewer binding precedents.

Just as the subject area of the case influences the probability of dissent, so might the nature of the decision. One might expect a reversal to be more

TABLE 6.1
Frequency of dissent by case type

Case type	Dissent rate	Absolute number of cases
Criminal	8.3%	3,825
Civil rights	11.1%	1,077
First Amendment	22.4%	165
Due process	12.0%	150
Privacy	19.0%	21
Labor relations	10.5%	974
Economic	6.8%	7,112

likely to engender a dissent because of the standard of affirmance deference. The following list reports the rates of dissent by decisions, according to whether they were liberal or conservative and whether they were a reversal or an affirmance of the lower court:

Outcome	Dissent Rate
Liberal reversal	12.3%
Conservative reversal	10.0%
Liberal affirmance	7.2%
Conservative affirmance	6.1%

Reversals are obviously more likely to provoke dissents than are affirmances. This is consistent with the expectations of the legal model and the psychological internal whistle-blowing hypothesis. Because of the procedural rules directing deference to affirmances, reversals are on average the legally more suspect category of cases and are more subject to claims of error. Also, liberal outcomes are apparently more likely to provoke dissent than are conservative ones. The reason for this is not obvious; possibly the liberal decisions are the most legally aggressive and questionable and therefore more likely to produce dissents or possibly the conservative circuit court judges are more ideologically aggressive and prone to dissent from an ideologically contrary decision.

The next descriptive statistics consider dissent rate by type of panel. If group polarization effects were operating, one would expect to see fewer dissents on unified panels and more dissents on ideologically split panels.

The following list reports the dissent rates according to the panel's ratio of party of presidential appointments:

Panel Ratio	Dissent Rate
3–0 D	7.5%
2–1 D	8.3%
2–1 R	9.6%
3–0 R	6.7%

As anticipated, dissents are somewhat more frequent on split panels than on unified panels, though the difference is small. The observed behavior of circuit court dissents can display only the tip of the iceberg of interpanel decision making on circuit courts. It is possible that a minority could have an impact on case outcomes and therefore would not need to dissent. The dissent rates would be more evidence of failed minority influence, rather than proof of panel effects. Most cases have no dissents but individual judges may still internally influence the panel's outcome in those cases without dissent. Such cases are examples of successful minority influence. The following section considers the presence of such panel effects on circuit court decisions.

Ideological Diversity Panel Effects

As noted earlier, several studies have found that split panels apparently produce less ideological decision making than do unified panels. The median voter theorem may not govern individual judicial decisions, though the previous research did not directly test that theorem. This section will directly test the median voter theorem and examine the nature of panel effects on circuit court outcomes. The research here cannot fully capture possible panel effects because it considers only case outcomes. It is distinctly possible that panel minorities could influence the language of the judicial opinion, even when it does not alter the outcome, and that the opinion could be significant, but the data cannot capture this effect. Nonetheless, the outcome-based results should provide partial evidence of existing panel effects.

TABLE 6.2
Effects of other judge ideology

Variable	(1)	(2)	(3)
Ideology	.020 (.106)	.381 (.000)	.08 (.148)
OtherIdeology	.086 (.000)	.071 (.000)	.30 (.000)
LowerCourt		1.33 (.000)	1.34 (.000)
SupremeCourt			−.65 (.000)
OldSupremeCourt			.59 (.000)
CircuitCourt			.002 (.008)
OldCircuitCourt			.006 (.002)
N	22,236	22,237	19,651
R^2	.005	.122	.128

The first study examines the effect of the ideology of other panel judges on the vote of each panel judge. This involved the construction of a new variable (OtherIdeology) that measures the total ideological score of the other judges on the panel. OtherIdeology is added to the basic regression of determinants of the ideological direction of the judge vote. The effect of this variable is shown in Table 6.2. Column (1) of the table gives results for the Ideology and OtherIdeology variables alone, Column (2) introduces the effect of affirmance deference as a control variable, and Column (3) adds the effects for other judicial institutions. The dependent variable is the ideological direction of the individual judge's vote.

These dramatic results appear to show distinct panel effects. The ideological preferences of the other panel members are consistently statistically significant and the introduction of these preferences in the model reduces the ideology of the judge to only marginal statistical significance. The other judges' ideologies do not entirely overwhelm the preferences of the individual judge but they do appear to be a greater factor in the individual judge's vote than his or her own ideology. The introduction of other legal and strategic control variables does not alter this finding.

Because of the economic costs of dissent for the judge, however, these results still do not conclusively demonstrate panel effects. The judge in question might simply have been outvoted by his or her colleagues and have chosen to go along with their ruling rather than taking the effort to write separately. This reasoning seems unlikely as an explanation for the full effect but it cannot be ruled out. The degree to which the economic costs of dissent explain away the panel effects associated with OtherIdeology can

TABLE 6.3
Effects of median ideology and full panel ideology on decisions

Variable	(1)	(2)	(3)
MedianIdeology	.04 (.816)	.09 (.623)	.15 (.464)
TotalIdeology	.087 (.003)	.27 (.003)	.20 (.051)
LowerCourt		1.33 (.000)	1.35 (.000)
SupremeCourt			−.55 (.001)
OldSupremeCourt			.40 (.002)
CircuitCourt			.002 (.062)
OldCircuitCourt			.006 (.040)
N	9,851	9,851	8,683
R²	.008	.124	.130

be assessed by looking at the determinants of full panel opinions instead of just judge votes.

The best test for whether the individualized median voter theorem, without panel effects, drives judicial decision making is to analyze the preferences of the full panel and its decision in the case. Doing so involves a study that uses the ideological preferences of the panel median voter as one independent variable and a measure of the full panel ideology (TotalIdeology), which cumulates the Ideology rankings for all three judges, as a second, separate independent variable. There will be some collinearity between these variables but the regression should resolve whether it is the median or the full panel ideology that matters most in determining judicial decisions. Table 6.3 reports the results of this analysis, using the same three columns as in Table 6.4, on the ideological direction of the case outcome.

The results are striking in their demonstration of panel effects. Once there is a control for the ideology of the full panel, the ideology of the panel's median voter is insignificant in all the separate equations. The median voter theorem appears entirely inapplicable to circuit court panels. The total cumulated ideological score of the full panel provides the statistically significant results in each of the equations.

The significance for the total ideology component and lack of significance for median ideology is substantial. This finding demonstrates the importance of each judge, not just the ideologically median voter. In some cases an ideological minority judge is presumably tugging the median voter to his or her side via devil's advocacy, whistle-blowing, or some other persuasive psychological tool. The results also lend support to the group polarization hypothesis of decision making. As the full panel is increasingly ideologically aligned (with the corresponding exaggerated TotalIdeology), the effect on the ideology of decisions increases. The median voter is more likely to render an ideologically aligned ruling when he or she is accompanied by two relatively like-minded colleagues.

To expand on this analysis, next I consider whether the party composition of the panel matters. Many previous studies have relied only on party identification of the judges. This measure has been considered too crude, which led to the creation of measures such as Ideology that seek to more precisely capture judicial ideology. But party identification matters in legislatures, even beyond legislator ideology, and the earlier panel effects research found an effect associated with split panels. The definition of a split panel was based on party of appointing president. The use of party ratio enables us to better identify the truly split panels. One might expect the panel effects to be more pronounced when there was an opposite party representative on the circuit court panel to serve as the devil's advocate. To test for a residual party effect beyond total panel ideology, I repeated the analyses of Table 6.3 using the ratio of Democrat to Republican judges in place of MedianIdeology. The results are reported in Table 6.4.

These results illuminate both the nature of judicial ideology and the nature of the panel effects. Because TotalIdeology is based in substantial part on the ideology of the appointing president, the combined use of this variable with PartyRatio may distinguish only party identification effects that go beyond the effects of the individual judge ideology measurements. The

TABLE 6.4
Effects of party ratio and full panel ideology

Variable	(1)	(2)	(3)
PartyRatio	.16 (.033)	.18 (.021)	.12 (.177)
TotalIdeology	.24 (.000)	.27 (.000)	.24 (.000)
LowerCourt		1.33 (.000)	1.35 (.000)
SupremeCourt			−.59 (.000)
OldSupremeCourt			.53 (.001)
CircuitCourt			.001 (.111)
OldCircuitCourt			.006 (.046)
N	9,997	9,997	8,820
R^2	.009	.126	.132

TotalIdeology measurements appear to better capture ideology than does the simple party affiliation association. There is some suggestion of an effect for party affiliation over and above TotalIdeology, but the effect lacks statistical significance with the strategic variables in the full model of equation (3). Party ratio is a better determinant than is individual Ideology in these equations. The introduction of party variables also slightly increases the size of the R^2 term. These results provide additional support for the existence of panel effects. Regardless of the panel's party breakdown, the total ideological preference of the panel was a significant determinant of outcomes.

The findings that all the judges on the panel clearly affect outcomes is consistent with Judge Harry Edwards's theory that "collegiality plays an important part in mitigating the role of partisan politics and personal ideology by allowing judges of differing perspectives and philosophies to communicate with, listen to, and ultimately influence one another in constructive and law-abiding ways."[24] That the relative ideologies of the panel members were the determinative variables might imply that the law was not driving the collegiality effects. But given human psychological tendencies, such as motivated reasoning and group polarization, the findings might well demonstrate the ability of ideological judges to invoke the nonideological law as a persuasive argument that overcomes ideological preferences. If *only* ideology mattered, the median voter theory should predict the results, and it plainly does not. Indeed, the need to use ideological variables to capture nonideological effects could indicate that the panel effects are greater than those found in the regressions because of some obvious specification error.

Background Diversity Panel Effects

Ideology is only one possible source of panel effects. Some have argued that the circuit courts should have a minimum number of women and racial minority judges, precisely for the panel effects they may bring to decision making. This argument is consistent with general theories of the values of diversity in making decisions; panel members with different personal or occupational backgrounds may bring to bear their experiences in a way that informs and influences the other judges on the panel. If the psychological theories of panel effects are operating, one might expect some effects of having minorities or women on the panel.

The argument for background diversity panel effects presumes that the background differences are material ones, which influence judicial decision making. The empirical evidence of the relatively minor effect of personal background variables on individual judge votes, as reported in Chapter 3, could cause one to question the importance of background diversity. The finding on individual judge votes does not resolve the question, though, because the individual judge votes are themselves influenced by the other panel members. The very thesis of the panel effects hypothesis is that individual judge votes, divorced from the rest of the panel, are not reliable guides to decision-making determinants.

One recent study examined the effect of the presence of women and racial minorities on circuit court panels in the context of employment discrimination cases.[25] The study found no panel effects for nonwhite circuit court judges but found a distinct effect on outcomes from having one woman on the panel. There was no additional effect of having two women on the panel, which is a clear sign of a background panel effect rather than a median voter effect. This empirical finding is suggestive but it is limited to a relatively small sample (only four hundred cases over two years) and to cases in the discrete area of employment discrimination law, in which such a background characteristic panel effect would be most likely.

To more broadly measure background diversity panel effects, I used the basic ideological control variable of TotalIdeology, which has the clearest association with outcomes. Consequently, these analyses use the panel means for race and gender to attempt to capture panel effects. Table 6.5 includes an independent variable for the mean number of minority representatives on a panel (MinorityMean) and again measures the dependent variable of the ideological direction of the decision outcome.

The mean number of minorities on a panel obviously has no impact on outcomes. Chapter 3 found that race was not a strong background determinant of individual judge voting but it showed some small effect, which disappears in the examination of panel effects from minority presence. The lack of panel effects for minority representation may be due to

TABLE 6.5
Minority representation and panel decisions

Variable	(1)	(2)	(3)
MinorityMean	−.003 (.979)	.02 (.898)	.10 (.481)
TotalIdeology	.29 (.000)	.32 (.000)	.027 (.000)
LowerCourt		1.33 (.000)	1.35 (.000)
SupremeCourt			−.59 (.000)
OldSupremeCourt			.56 (.001)
CircuitCourt			.02 (.04)
OldCircuitCourt			.06 (.049)
N	14,194	14,194	14,194
R²	.009	.126	.132

this relatively weak association between minorities and ideology or to a lack of panel effects for the minority representatives. Panel effects can depend in part on shared backgrounds or values among the full panel, which may undermine the persuasive effects of minority judges with different backgrounds. In addition, the relative lack of affirmance deference for minority judges might also compromise their ability to make a powerful argument in favor of their preferred outcome. The dearth of evidence of minority judge panel effects must be qualified, though, by noting that the dependent variable is just the ideology of the panel decision. Minority panel effects might appear stronger with some other dependent variable.

The next consideration is the panel effects for gender, which showed a significant effect on individual judge votes in some of the analyses of Chapter 3. This analysis is the same as that for race but with a variable for the mean female representation (FemaleMean) on the circuit court panel and the effects of that mean on the decision outcome. Results of the regressions are shown in Table 6.6.

After I controlled for panel total ideology and other legal and strategic variables, these results show some suggestive panel effects for gender representation. FemaleMean had statistical significance in the full model of equation (3), pushing decisions in a more liberal direction. One might expect to see a greater effect if the data were broken down into particular case types. Gender diversity seems to influence decisions, probably through panel effects, beyond the simple effects of ideology and survives the ideological screening conducted by appointing presidents and confirming Senates. Gender appears to have a small effect on decision outcomes.

TABLE 6.6
Gender representation and panel decisions

Variable	(1)	(2)	(3)
FemaleMean	.32 (.050)	.28 (.104)	.04 (.037)
TotalIdeology	.29 (.000)	.31 (.000)	.26 (.000)
LowerCourt		1.33 (.000)	1.35 (.000)
SupremeCourt			−.060 (.000)
OldSupremeCourt			.061 (.000)
CircuitCourt			.002 (.030)
OldCircuitCourt			.006 (.050)
N	14,194	14,194	14,194
R^2	.009	.126	.132

Effect of Extremes

The next analyses reconsider judges with the most extreme ideological positions and their effects on panel decision making. The analysis in Chapter 1 showed that the median panel voter's relative extremity has a roughly linear effect on individual judge votes and that ideology is not significantly increased or muted as a determinant as it becomes more extreme. The panel effects of ideological extremes of nonmedian panel members merits investigation. Those of more ideological extremity might be less persuasive within the panel, precisely because their minority opinions would be considered more ideological and less objective and grounded in the law. But those at ideological extremes might be more dedicated to influencing the other panel members to reach a desired outcome. Some psychological research suggests that the conviction of minority advocates gives their position greater influence.[26] The more ideologically extreme panel members might be expected to exhibit such conviction in their persuasion. Other psychological research indicates that political extremists have opinions of greater cognitive complexity that are better integrated into a coherent theory, which could make them more persuasive advocates for a minority position.[27] The significance of TotalIdeology suggests that the nonmedian extremes may be influential in determining panel decisions but a direct test of the effect of extremes is possible.

To study the relative effect of extreme panel members, I created two new variables—LiberalExtreme (the Ideology rating for the most liberal panel member) and ConservativeExtreme (the Ideology rating for the most

TABLE 6.7
Ideological extremes and panel decisions

Variable	(1)	(2)	(3)
MedianIdeology	.26 (.051)	.27 (.047)	.20 (.192)
LiberalExtreme	.10 (.298)	.15 (.136)	.14 (.214)
ConservativeExtreme	.26 (.011)	.27 (.011)	.30 (.012)
LowerCourt			1.35 (.000)
SupremeCourt			−.56 (.001)
OldSupremeCourt			.49 (.003)
CircuitCourt			.002 (.077)
OldCircuitCourt			.007 (.025)
N	14,194	14,194	14,194
R^2	.008	.124	.130

conservative panel member). These variables were introduced into the basic regression equations, with MedianIdeology used as a control variable. MedianIdeology is a more appropriate control variable for this regression than is TotalIdeology because TotalIdeology needlessly double-counts the effects of the most liberal and conservative panel members and becomes nothing more than an indirect placeholder for MedianIdeology on three-judge panels. The analyses reveal the relative weight of each panel member on the ultimate decision. The results of these regressions are reported in Table 6.7.

These results are again striking. The outcomes of circuit court panels are better predicted by the preferences of the extreme conservative than even by the preferences of the median panel member. The median member loses statistical significance in the full model of equation (3) but the conservative extreme member retains clear significance in all models. Moreover, these data show that not only does the most conservative panel member wield the greatest power in panel decision making but that that power appears to grow proportionately as the most conservative panel member becomes even more ideologically conservative (according to the Ideology scale). The effect of the liberal extreme judge, by contrast, is not statistically significant.

These results show obvious panel effects in circuit courts, as the median member clearly does not dictate outcomes. Although the liberal extreme had no statistical significance, its association was consistently positive and the liberal extreme presumably exercises some effect. The effect of the more conservative panel member was much more profound. Conservatives are apparently much more effective in promoting their minority view within

TABLE 6.8
Panel effects on differing panel compositions

Variable	3–0 D	2–1 D	2–1 R	3–0 R
MedianIdeology	.95 (.230)	.18 (.538)	.52 (.128)	.64 (.225)
LiberalExtreme	.27 (.657)	.00 (.987)	.35 (.077)	.22 (.484)
ConservativeExtreme	.02 (.967)	.32 (.134)	.17 (.646)	.38 (.364)
LowerCourt	1.32 (.000)	1.33 (.000)	1.44 (.000)	1.30 (.000)
SupremeCourt	−.57 (.186)	−.10 (.738)	−.87 (.013)	−1.03 (.018)
OldSupremeCourt	−.04 (.929)	.004 (.990)	1.03 (.003)	.84 (.036)
CircuitCourt	.005 (.029)	.000 (.775)	.004 (.038)	.000 (.863)
OldCircuitCourt	−.007 (.445)	.009 (.184)	.003 (.595)	.007 (.251)
N	1,265	2,522	2,057	1,652
R^2	.130	.121	.152	.126

the panel. The most influential judge on these panels seems to be the most conservative one.

The above analysis does not discriminate between different categories of panels, however. According to the group polarization and minority effect theories, one would expect different panel effect results for ideological extremes, depending on the nature of the panel majority. The earlier-described full model analysis described earlier is therefore broken down into different types of panel ratios according took the Republican and Democratic composition of the circuit court panel. Table 6.8 reports the results of the full equation (3) regression for each different panel types.

The statistical strength of the associations is weaker when the panels are broken down in this fashion but the nature of panel effects appears to be roughly as predicted by the polarization theories and the previous legal research on panel effects. The effect of the most ideologically extreme judge becomes distinctly more powerful on 3–0 panels than on 2–1 panels (though the association does not reach statistical significance by itself). On split panels, however, the most significant determinant of decisions is the position of the minority judge. On panels that are 2–1 Republican, the most liberal judge (typically if not universally the Democrat) is the most influential for outcome. On 2–1 Democrat panels, the most conservative judge (the Republican) is the most influential. The particular effects for conservative extreme in the previous regression may be due to the relative frequency of different panel compositions in the sample and because the conservative extreme shows greater effects (though not statistically significant ones) on other types of panels than does the liberal extreme.

The results also shed some light on the manner in which the minority may be persuasive. Although affirmance deference is a highly significant predictor for all types of panels, it is slightly stronger for split panels than for unified panels, which suggests that minorities may occasionally use the legal standard of affirmance deference to mute the ideological impulses of panel majorities. This finding provides at least a hint that, as hypothesized earlier, panel minorities can use procedural legal arguments to counter the ideological motivated reasoning of the panel majority. Minorities can presumably also use other legal arguments, though other substantive legal arguments are difficult to capture in the courts of appeals database.

The results of this analysis show that ideological minorities are influential on circuit court panels. The results also suggest that, because the ideological scale for minorities is linear, as the minority panel representative becomes relatively more ideological (either conservative or liberal) he or she appears to wield more influence on the ideologically opposed panel majority. Truly disaggregating the effects of ideological extremes, though, requires creation of a new variable that can separate moderate from relatively extreme ideological positions. The extreme conservative on a given panel might possibly be a moderate conservative judge. By squaring the ideological ratings for the ideological extremes using the variables LiberalExtreme^2 and ConservativeExtreme^2, I could discern the relative effect of greater ideological extremity on panels. In Chapter 2 the data showed that the more extreme ideological panel members were only proportionately more ideological. The regression for Table 6.7 was run with the addition of the two new variables. A positive association would show that the most extreme members were disproportionately more influential on panels. Results are reported in Table 6.9.

The identifiable ideological effects are attributable to the median judge on the panel, especially for the particularly extreme conservatives. When the most conservative member of the panel was a moderate, the directionality of the effect was liberal. In the sample, the Reagan and Bush appointees were generally the most conservative, and Table 6.9 testifies to their effect on judicial outcomes. By contrast, the most liberal panel member showed no statistically significant effect in any of the analyses. For whatever reason, there seems to be a difference between the parties' appointees; the most conservative Republicans seem to be the most effective advocates for a

TABLE 6.9
Panel effects with squared extreme values

Variable	(1)	(2)	(3)
MedianIdeology	.003 (.053)	.003 (.049)	.002 (.192)
LiberalExtreme	.001 (.564)	.003 (.344)	.002 (.493)
LiberalExtreme^2	.000 (.901)	.000 (.743)	.000 (.839)
ConservativeExtreme	−.002 (.334)	−.003 (.230)	−.002 (.601)
ConservativeExtreme^2	.001 (.031)	.001 (.016)	.001 (.096)
LowerCourt		1.33 (.000)	1.35 (.000)
SupremeCourt			−.57 (.001)
OldSupremeCourt			.46 (.006)
CircuitCourt			.002 (.090)
OldCircuitCourt			.007 (.027)
N	9,851	9,851	8,683
R^2	.009	.125	.131

preferred ideological outcome. This finding requires the further breakdown of decisions by case type, panel composition, and other factors.

Panel Effects and Opinion Length

One might expect to see panel effects appearing in the content of opinions as well as in decisional outcomes. The presence of a dissenter could cause the majority to write a longer opinion. The accompanying dissent will doubtless raise factual matters or legal claims that the panel majority will feel compelled to address in greater detail than would be required if there were no published dissent. The following list presents the mean lengths of majority opinions in cases with and without dissent:

Dissent	5.6062
No Dissent	4.3821

As expected, majority opinions are longer in the presence of a dissenting opinion. This finding might not be attributable to the existence of the dissent; perhaps more significant cases are more likely to produce dissents. But one could reasonably believe that dissents force majorities to write longer opinions. This effect could sway panel dynamics and help explain minority influence. I noted earlier that dissents could be suppressed by the simple resource costs associated with writing them. If a dissent requires a longer majority opinion, with associated increases in time and effort, that could give the dissenter some leverage during intrapanel negotiations. The threat of a dissent might induce the majority to give up something of value to the minority to avoid the dissenting opinion.

Panel effects could have opinion length consequences in other circumstances. If unified panels engage in group polarization while split panels more carefully evaluate the law, one might expect split panels to produce longer, more thoughtful opinions. The following list presents the mean opinion length by panel composition by party affiliation of the judges:

Panel Composition	Opinion Length
3–0 D	4.1510
2–1 D	5.1441
2–1 R	3.5307
3–0 R	5.1009

Although the differences in opinion length by panel composition seem substantial, they don't suggest any explanatory theory. There is no consistent association of opinion length with party affiliation or with split versus unified panels. Panel effects surely influence opinion content but they do not appear to have any clear association with opinion length. But opinion length may reflect a variety of factors, ranging from carefully limited decisions to decisions intended to create expansive precedent. Perhaps some effect of panel composition can be discerned if these varied explanations for opinion length can be disaggregated.

Conclusion

The findings of panel effects are among the most profound in the book. Much of the existing research on judicial decision making treats judges as atomistic maximizers of personal preferences, whether those preferences be ideological or something else. The research does not consider the environmental panel effects as a determinant of the judge's vote. The results in this chapter make clear that those panel effects are enormously important in determining the judge's vote and the case outcome. The differing ideological and background characteristics of a single panel member can affect the group's decision. Future research needs to account for the panel effects, rather than relying on the vote of the individual judge or the panel's median voter.

Judicial decision making clearly involves a mix that includes some ideological influence, considerable legal influence, and undoubtedly other factors. The dissent behavior apparently shows some pragmatic, self-interested economic influence. The true understanding of judicial decisions requires an appreciation of how these potentially conflicting determinants interact. The research on panel effects has revealed some aspects of the interaction of ideological and legal variables. Persuasive evidence, often using legal variables, can apparently sometimes temper the ideological impulses in decision making. The ideology of the persuaders matters, however, and there is evidence that ideologically conservative extreme judges may be particularly influential on circuit court panels.

SEVEN

Procedural Threshold Effects and Circuit Court Decision Making

The previous chapters have demonstrated that some legal standards, such as those commanding affirmance deference, have a significant impact on circuit court decision making. The power of this variable clearly exceeds all the other variables that have been tested. Although it is difficult to objectively capture the substantive content of the law as a determinant in judicial decision making, other legal procedures may be analyzed for their effects. This chapter considers a series of legal requirements that may be considered threshold rules.

A threshold rule is a procedural barrier that plaintiffs must surmount before their case is judged on the merits. There is no intrinsic ideological component to the threshold rules themselves, but their application may be ideological for the judiciary. Judges may use these procedural threshold rules to decide for the party they prefer. But this conclusion does not explain *why* judges would issue a politically desirable ruling on procedural requirements, rather than using substantive issues to reach the same ideological end.

Previous quantitative empirical research has generally overlooked such questions as the effect of procedural threshold requirements. Social scientists have focused on the "sexier" questions, such as the constitutionality of government action. Legal academics are well aware of the practical importance of procedural threshold issues but their empirical research has likewise eschewed the procedural for the substantive. Although the procedural requirements do not appear to be ideological on the surface, they clearly influence ideological outcomes of court decisions and, consequently, merit study. Indeed, the surface neutrality of these rules makes them in many ways a more interesting subject for study.

The Nature of Threshold Issues

Courts have established several distinct threshold devices for screening the cases that come before them. The threshold issues considered in this chapter are jurisdiction, standing, mootness, exhaustion of administrative remedies, and the political question doctrine. Some of these threshold issues are designed to ensure that the case before the court is a true adjudicatory dispute and not a request for the court to issue an abstract ruling, divorced from the facts of a particular controversy, on the law. Others have more pragmatic purposes.

Investigating threshold issues is crucial to an examination of judicial politics. Even those who argue that judging is ideological recognize that, because of judicial procedures, it is ideological in a slightly different way than legislative or executive branch decisions. The federal courts are limited to the resolution of cases and controversies—actual litigation between two parties. Unlike the courts of some other nations, our federal courts cannot issue advisory opinions that address the scope or constitutionality of a law in the abstract. Instead, they can rule only after a plaintiff brings a case on particular facts in search of particular relief; in that context the courts can address the scope or constitutionality of a law.

Jurisdiction is the most basic procedural threshold issue. Judges have limited authority to render legal decisions and cannot render decisions against all parties or in all types of cases. One important aspect of this limit is known as in personam jurisdiction. A court can render a binding decision only if it has jurisdiction over the parties to a case; there are some restrictions on exercising jurisdiction over foreign defendants, those from outside the state or the nation. If such defendants lack minimum contacts with the forum jurisdiction, the court lacks the jurisdiction to rule in their case, absent their consent. Most courts also have limited subject matter jurisdiction. Federal courts, for example, cannot hear cases that involve only state law unless there is diversity jurisdiction, that is, the plaintiff and defendant are from different states and the case is sufficiently significant. Like any other legal issue, jurisdiction is commonly contested and subject to judicial discretion, especially when it comes to the extent of contacts with the judicial forum that suffice to provide in personam jurisdiction for that court. Federal jurisdiction is also governed by subject matter jurisdiction, which involves the legal basis of the action.

Of the threshold issues, standing is probably the most controversial and most researched, from an ideological perspective. The standing rules require that a plaintiff have a sufficient personal interest in a dispute to establish a true case or controversy that the court may hear. Under traditional English law, citizens could maintain actions to enforce the law, even if they had suffered no direct injury from that violation. This traditional rule gave way to the standing limitation during the New Deal era in the United States. The doctrine may have been created "to insulate progressive New Deal legislation from frequent judicial attack."[1] Subsequently, however, standing has typically been used by conservative justices to prevent citizen plaintiffs from aggressively enforcing federal statutes (such as the Endangered Species Act) against business interests. Of all the procedural threshold issues, standing is the one that looks most suspiciously ideological. And, standing doctrine is sufficiently vague, sometimes called incoherent, that it allows considerable judicial discretion in its application to particular cases.

Another procedural threshold doctrine is mootness, which derives from the same case-or-controversy requirement that spawned standing doctrine. Some disputes, once active cases, may be mooted by time and circumstances. Suppose two individuals were litigating over the ownership of a piece of property, during which time that property was destroyed. The individuals might still pursue their litigation for some reason but a court could refuse to rule in the case because any decision had become moot—without meaningful remedy. Mootness doctrine also admits to some room for judicial discretion. Even if the case itself is mooted by events, a court might still render a decision if the case is "capable of repetition, yet evading review."[2] For example, a case on the right to an abortion may take so long to reach a judicial conclusion that the fate of the pregnancy is inevitably resolved before this occurs. Such cases are not considered moot because, if they were, the legal rights in question could never be enforced.

In some cases, exhaustion of administrative remedies may be a procedural threshold that plaintiffs must surmount. This doctrine frequently involves disputes with the federal government and applies when an executive branch entity is assessing the plaintiff's claims. Judicial review is not available until the entity has ruled and all available executive appeal opportunities have been completed. The purpose of the doctrine is to limit judicial review to cases where it is necessary and relief cannot be achieved in any other forum. Exhaustion of administrative remedies is not universally required and, even when required, it admits to exceptions, as does mootness. Exhaustion may be excused if the completion of remedies could prejudice the subsequent court action, if the executive agency could not grant a complete remedy, or if the agency is biased.[3]

The Supreme Court also created the political question doctrine, which may serve as a procedural threshold barrier to a ruling on the merits of litigation. This doctrine is intended to neuter the politics of the courts. Even in cases in which a plaintiff may have a valid legal argument, the court may eschew ruling because the matter in question is deemed too political for the courts to decide. Courts may decline to rule on legal issues when the Constitution commits the resolution of those issues to another branch of government, when the resolution requires nonjudicial discretion, or when it is vital for the government to speak with only one voice. The doctrine has been invoked in such cases as those challenging the lawfulness of a decision to go to war, of other sensitive foreign policy matters, or of rules regarding the procedures of impeachment.

These five issues are the most common and most controversial procedural threshold issues, though other procedural requirements may sometimes have a threshold effect. What the rules have in common is that they address whether the court should even hear and decide the underlying legal merits of the case. They permit courts to dispose of actions, without considering the merits, because the plaintiff has failed to surmount the threshold requirement. If the plaintiff does satisfy the procedural threshold barrier, though, the court must address the substantive legal merits of the plaintiff's claim. The rules operate only to bar plaintiffs. Although procedural rules may preclude defendants from raising certain types of arguments, they generally do not bar any defense to an action.

The Theories of Threshold Issues

The classic legal theory of threshold issues is that set forth in the preceding discussion. Each of these rules, save possibly for the political question doctrine, has a reasoned legal basis entirely unrelated to ideology, strategy, or other extralegal considerations. Indeed, courts and commentators could cite these procedural threshold rules as evidence of the significance of the traditional legal model of decision making. The legal process school of jurisprudence, which emphasizes such procedural rules, arose in response to the legal realists, who assert that the law is political. The legal process adherents claim that the significance of neutral legal rules demonstrates that law is more than mere politics.

The claim that such procedural rules as threshold requirements demonstrate the independent importance of law appears to have some surface validity. Such rules have no obvious ideological content; they may bar either a conservative or liberal litigant from pursuing his or her claims. Judge J. Harvie Wilkinson III argued that "it is critical for law to aspire to agreement on process—a task both more achievable than agreement on substance and more suited to our profession than waving the banners of ideological truth."[4] These seemingly neutral procedural rules ignore the substantive political content of the case in favor of the procedural legal principles underlying the adjudicative process.

The very existence of these threshold rules may be considered testimony to the importance of the law, as opposed to politics, to judicial decision making. Why would ideologically oriented judges choose to devote their time and effort to neutral, nonideological principles? Truly political judges probably would prefer to grapple with the ideological substance of a case, rather than with some neutral, qualifying rule. And, any decision on that predicate rule presumably sets a neutral, nonideological precedent for future decisions, rather than establishing an ideological path for future courts. Consequently, judicial reliance on procedural threshold requirements would seem to evidence an independent concern for law.

Some political theorists have challenged the neutral legal theory of procedural rules, though, and explained how the rules might be used for extralegal reasons. For such realists, procedural rules are simply another device enabling judges to reach their preferred outcomes. A conservative judge may reach a conservative outcome in a case with a procedural rule. But it is unclear why an ideological judge would use such rules to reach his or her decision if, as realists typically claim, the substantive rules could be likewise manipulated to produce the preferred outcome. If the law exercised some constraining power, however, procedural rules could increase ideological decision making. There may be cases in which the law is so clear on the substantive merits that a judge cannot reach an ideological result on them. Here, the opportunity to use less legally clear procedural threshold requirements could enable an ideological decision that was otherwise impossible under the substantive law of the case. The procedural requirements, therefore, become a tool for judges to avoid rendering a politically undesirable decision and its associated undesirable precedential effect when there was no realistic alternative on the merits. Thus, there may be cases in which the government violated the law but the court likes the government policy and invokes a procedural threshold doctrine to save this substantively unlawful outcome.[5]

Another explanation, which also accepts the importance of the legal model, focuses on the structural effects of procedural rules. Although such rules do not innately favor one ideological side over another, their use in practice may produce some systematic ideological effect. If, for example, most plaintiffs pursued liberal ends in litigation, the sincere nonideological legal application of a threshold issue that barred a certain proportion of plaintiffs would have a systematic conservative impact on the law. Some have argued that "proceduralism has historically played a conservative legal, political, and cultural role."[6] Unlike the traditional political theories of decision making, this hypothesis suggests that the legal model does affect at least some judicial decisions, in which ideological judges manipulate procedural legal rules to force certain ideological outcomes in future cases. Setting precedents on procedural threshold requirements could be *more* ideologically salient than ruling on the merits of the law. For example, a decision on standing that makes it more difficult for private plaintiffs to bring a citizen suit enforcing the Clean Water Act could set a precedent for all citizen environmental suits and have a greater policy effect than a substantive statutory interpretation of one particular subsection of the act. A truly ideological Supreme Court might first prefer to choose an apparently neutral procedural requirement that would have systematic ideological effects when applied by other courts. Reliance on procedural rules might also help further an illusion that courts are acting according to law when in fact they are ideological.

Yet another theory of the procedural threshold rules is a strategic one. If circuit court judges wanted to reach a particular decision but feared that such a decision would expose them to reversal or retribution from other institutions, they might choose to use a procedural rule. This seems especially logical for judges concerned about a legislative response. If a panel produced a particular interpretation of tax law, Congress might react by changing the law. If the panel instead achieved the same result simply by barring a challenge to a contradictory interpretation, Congress might be less likely to respond. Procedural rules might also be used to manipulate Supreme Court oversight. The use of procedural rules to decide an action could make the case less interesting to the Court or add decision costs to the Court's review.[7] If a circuit court rules on a substantive issue and the case is appealed to the ideologically disapproving Supreme Court, the Court may reverse and issue a ruling that directs the substantive content of the law. If the circuit court rules on a threshold issue, though, the Supreme Court may reverse the procedural ruling but generally can at best remand for consideration of the substantive issues, rather than declaring the law. The threshold ruling forces the Supreme Court to burn its effort and resources on a nonsubstantive procedural matter that lacks ideological power, which may in turn mean that the Court does not bother to accept certiorari in the case.

Each of these theories has some preempirical plausibility. Although each theory can find support in anecdotal case examples, a reliable test would require greater analytical rigor. Most of the social science research to date has not addressed legal procedures but has focused on major substantive legal concerns. But some tentative empirical research published on procedural issues is discussed in the following section.

Empirical Research on Threshold Issues

As so often happens, the classic legal theories have not been subjected to much empirical testing, and political scientists have not closely examined the role of procedural threshold issues. Legal research has produced some limited examination, though without statistical testing, of the effect of such procedural threshold rules, especially standing doctrine.

Richard Pierce hypothesized that standing doctrine was ideological, such that "a liberal judge would give standing to environmentalists, employees, and prisoners, but not to banks, while a conservative judge would give standing to banks, but not to environmentalists, employees or prisoners."[8] He then examined five major Supreme Court standing rulings of the 1990s and found that his hypothesis predicted the outcome of each case and of thirty-one of the thirty-three individual justice votes. He also examined thirty-three circuit court decisions during the same period and found that Republican judges voted to deny standing to environmental plaintiffs 43.5% of the time, while Democratic judges voted to deny standing to environmental plaintiffs only 11.1% of the time.[9] This research suggests that standing, like other legal issues, may be manipulated for ideological ends.

Pierce's analysis supports the pure legal realist theory that standing doctrine is manipulated to achieve preferred ideological outcomes. Moreover, his results contradict the hierarchical structural theory of procedural threshold rules. Given the ideological disparity in the circuit court rulings in the cases he studied, the Supreme Court's standing doctrines apparently have not substantially constrained the circuit courts' outcomes. The research did not consider the possibility of strategic effects.

An unpublished paper by Christopher Banks empirically examined the effects of standing doctrine in the D.C. circuit court of appeals.[10] Much like Pierce, Banks found that standing was used ideologically by the judges. Liberal judges were far more likely to grant standing, though other factors, such as the identity of the litigants, were also significant determinants of granting standing. Banks's paper did not differentiate between liberal and conservative plaintiffs, but we will see that plaintiffs dismissed on procedural threshold grounds are disproportionately liberal.

Another unpublished paper of mine considered the ideological circuit court effects of a particular Supreme Court expansion of standing doctrine.[11] The paper examined circuit court decisions rendered before and after the Supreme Court decision in *Lujan v. Defenders of Wildlife*,[12] which was widely considered a seminal decision that strengthened standing doctrine to bar some citizen environmental suit plaintiffs from the courts. The decision did not affect the number of citizen suits brought to court alter the ideology of voting by circuit panels (as measured by ratio of Republican to Democrat judges), or materially increase the probability of a case being rejected for want of standing. *Lujan* did increase the likelihood that standing would be an issue; there was a corresponding increase in the absolute number of cases dismissed for lack of standing, producing an overall pattern of more conservative results. In the eight years after *Lujan*, standing was an issue in more than twice as many environmental enforcement cases, and the number of cases dismissed on standing rose by 130%. This research suggests that the significance of standing doctrine could be found in the hierarchical structural theory but the investigation involved a relatively small number of circuit court decisions. The study did not look for any external strategic rationale for the decisions.

The existing research on the empirical consequences of procedural threshold issues is quite thin. The quantitative research on decision making has been extensive on some substantive legal issues, especially constitutional ones, but has largely ignored the role of procedural issues, though these issues are clearly common and important. Procedural issues are quite worthy of study and may contribute to an understanding of the intersection of legal and political concerns of the circuit court judiciary. The rest of this chapter explores this intersection.

Operationalizing the Study of Threshold Procedures

The courts of appeals database provides coding for various legal procedural questions, including the procedural threshold issues that can determine outcomes. The database provides the coding for jurisdiction, standing, mootness, exhaustion of remedies, the political question doctrine, and "other threshold issues." The database codebook provides no information on the

TABLE 7.1
Frequency of threshold issues

Threshold issue	Issue met	Issue not met
Jurisdiction	468	370
Standing	87	92
Mootness	68	49
Exhaustion	145	77
Political question	11	7
Other threshold	173	137

nature of these other threshold issues. For each threshold issue category, the database contains coding for the cases in which the issue was raised on appeal and for how the case was resolved. This coding enables integration of the threshold issues into the broader analysis of legal and political influences in circuit court decision making.

Table 7.1 presents data on the number of cases in which the threshold issues were presented and the resolution of those cases. The columns are broken down into rulings that found the threshold issue was met (so the plaintiff could proceed to the merits) and those in which it was not met (so the defendant prevailed on the threshold issue).

Threshold issues were raised in just over 10% of the cases in the courts of appeals database. Plaintiffs survived the threshold issue slightly more than half the time but a significant percentage of cases were dismissed on the issue. By far the most common threshold issue is jurisdiction, which was a factor in about half the cases. The political question doctrine, by contrast, is virtually never invoked by the circuit courts. The frequency of threshold issues in general has not varied much over time. From 1925 to 1960 the yearly number of threshold cases in the database ranges only from 97 to 144. In 1961 the database began coding more cases per year, so the total number of cases jumps but the annual range for threshold cases is only from 239 to 289. The frequency did change for some types of threshold issues, though. From 1925 to 1960 only 28 total cases discussed standing. In the 1970s alone there were 53 standing decisions. Different types of threshold issues may have different types of significance but the number of cases for each issue is relatively small, so this chapter's analysis generally lumps them together as threshold issues.

Procedural Threshold Issues and Ideological Outcomes

The analysis begins with descriptive statistics on the outcomes in which procedural threshold issues were present and the ideological results of each of these cases. This simple test can inform on the ideological importance of the use of procedural threshold issues. These data do not account for the number of threshold issues in a case, just for whether at least one threshold issue was raised. The next analysis provides data for the full courts of appeals database on the mean ideological outcome of cases in which there was no threshold issue, in which a threshold issue was present, in which that threshold issue was met by the plaintiff, and in which the case was barred for failure to satisfy the threshold issue. The numeric score is on a scale of 1 to 3, on which 2.0 is perfectly ideologically neutral. The following list gives the results:

No threshold issue	1.8237
Threshold issue	1.9121
Threshold issue met	2.1857
Threshold issue not met	1.6579

Some preliminary conclusions can be drawn from this basic finding. The first conclusion, which is consistent with the structural hypothesis, is that the use of procedural threshold issues to bar plaintiffs from reaching a decision has a substantially conservative effect. The most conservative outcomes occur when the threshold issue was raised and not met. The second conclusion, which is not particularly consistent with any hypothesis, is the unusually liberal outcomes that result when the threshold requirements were satisfied by the plaintiff and, to a lesser degree, when a threshold issue was present. There is no apparent reason why the mere raising of a threshold issue should produce more-liberal results, so this curious finding requires further investigation.

The anomalous result might simply be due to the case categories in which threshold issues generally arise. These might be cases in which judges tend to be more liberal on the merits. Investigation shows that the threshold cases are not randomly spread throughout the case categories. They are far more common in civil rights cases than in any other category. Yet the civil rights cases generally yield more conservative results than do the cases in the full courts of appeals database. So the liberal results are not merely an artifact of case types in which threshold issues are generally present.

The effect of procedural threshold issues may be found most remarkably at the lower court level, picked up in circuit court results because of affirmance deference. The database does not code directly for the lower court's resolution of the threshold issue, but it is possible to create ideological coding for that lower court decision. Hence, the following results do not reflect the district court's ruling on a procedural threshold issue but simply report the district court's ruling in cases grouped by whether the circuit court considered a procedural threshold issue. The next list presents the results at the district court level, converted to the same scale as in the preceding list:

No threshold issue	1.7220
Threshold issue	1.7656
Threshold issue met	1.8294
Threshold issue not met	1.7006

The effect of procedural threshold issues at the lower court level is similar in direction to the effect at the circuit court level but much weaker. The circuit courts have more conservative results in cases in which the threshold issue barred the action but much more liberal results in cases in which the procedural threshold issue was satisfied. Such issues clearly have some direct effect on circuit court decision making and not merely a derivative effect carried over from the district court level.

The basic results of procedural threshold issues remain unusual. The data plainly demonstrate that the direct net effect of such issues is conservative: when cases are resolved because the threshold requirements were not satisfied, the results are relatively conservative. Yet cases with procedural threshold issues on balance yield more liberal results because of the especially liberal results on the merits in the cases in which the threshold issue was satisfied. The rest of the chapter explores possible explanations for this odd consequence.

Litigants and Procedural Threshold Issues

The results of Chapter 5 suggest that the general characteristics of litigants did not generally have a major effect on circuit court outcomes. Litigant decisions could possibly explain the results for procedural threshold issues, however. Suppose that relatively conservative defendants are interested in winning their cases and in the precedent that those decisions set. If so, a conservative defendant might selectively choose to raise procedural threshold issues, depending on the strength or weakness of his or her case on the merits. If the conservative defendant believed that he or she had an especially weak case on the merits, the defendant would try to prevail on the threshold issues. When he or she failed on the threshold issue, the results on the merits would therefore appear to be unusually liberal. Of course, the ability to raise a legitimate threshold issue is somewhat fact dependent and not purely a matter of party choice. But the threshold doctrines admit to some ambiguity and, in some cases, a party may have the option to raise or not raise such an issue.

If litigant decision making does explain the results in procedural threshold matters, the association should generally be found in connection with repeat player defendants. The earlier findings show that the failure to meet a threshold issue is associated with conservative results and the satisfaction of the issue is associated with liberal results. Table 7.2 reports the effects of introducing variables in which certain repeat player parties—business and the federal government—are also involved in the litigation. The table provides the results for two separate regressions, one for cases in which the threshold issue is met and one for cases in which it is not. The ideological outcome is the dependent variable.

TABLE 7.2
Litigant effects, ideology, and procedural threshold issues

Variable	(1)	(2)
Threshold issue met	.096 (.000)	
Threshold issue not met		−.054 (.000)
Business appellant	.041 (.000)	.044 (.000)
Business respondent	−.005 (.571)	−.004 (.618)
Federal appellant	.026 (.002)	.029 (.000)
Federal respondent	.003 (.717)	.009 (.289)
N	14,193	14,193
R^2	.012	.006

Although there are significant associations based on party identity (business and federal appellants are both associated with liberal outcomes), the substantial association with the outcome of the threshold issue remains. This includes the unusual finding that cases in which a plaintiff raises and meets a threshold issue yield very liberal outcomes.

The results of the earlier investigations are at least somewhat consistent with the 50% hypothesis, which otherwise is generally not confirmed by judicial outcomes. Some cases that are clear on the merits for plaintiffs and that would otherwise settle are nevertheless tried and appealed because the defendants believe they may prevail on a procedural threshold issue. The especially conservative results when the threshold was not met and the especially liberal results when the threshold was met are precisely what this settlement-based hypothesis would predict. Hypothetically, this theory could explain the liberal results in cases in which the threshold issue was met (though not the relatively liberal net results when a threshold issue was raised). Other explanations are also possible and are considered in the following sections of this chapter.

Judicial Ideology and Procedural Threshold Issues

One obvious factor that could explain the use of procedural threshold issues and related ideology of circuit court decisions is the ideology of the panel judges. With threshold issues producing conservative results, one might expect conservative judges to disproportionately use such issues to bar plaintiffs. To examine the association of ideology and employment of procedural issues, I used, in a simple regression, the individual judge's ideological preference (Ideology) as an independent variable and judge votes that the threshold issue was satisfied as the dependent variable. Although we don't know the lower court's ruling on the threshold issue, the ideological direction of the lower court ruling (LowerCourt) is a control variable. The results are for those cases in which threshold issues were decided. Results are found in Table 7.3.

These results indicate that judicial ideology is a factor in the decision of whether the threshold issue was satisfied but that it is not a particularly strong one. The correlations are less significant than for most regressions on ideology and the R^2 term is quite low. The reliance on threshold issues

TABLE 7.3
Ideology and votes on procedural threshold issues

Variable	(1)	(2)
Ideology	.023 (.026)	.023 (.024)
LowerCourt		.14 (.055)
N	3,532	3,532
R²	.002	.003

is not merely ideological. For some reason, affirmance deference is much weaker on these issues.

Judicial ideology may still play a role in the application and effect of threshold issues. The anomalous liberal results of the cases in which threshold issues were met might still simply be an artifact of the panel's ideology in that particular set of cases. Perhaps the cases in which the threshold issue was satisfied by happenstance had a more liberal panel than typically found in other cases. This coincidental association is not implausible. Plaintiffs may be pushing the envelope on such issues as jurisdiction to have the case heard by an unusually favorable panel. If the plaintiff's jurisdictional stretch succeeds, one might expect that panel to look especially favorably on the plaintiff's case on the substantive merits.

The next set of analyses adds two control variables, judicial ideology and direction of the lower court holding; the second variable was to control for affirmance deference. The measure for judicial ideology is the total Ideology score for the full panel (TotalIdeology, which explained outcomes better than would have the ideology of the median panel voter). Table 7.4 reports the results of the two regressions of the threshold issue effect on ideological outcome, with LowerCourt as a control variable.

Controlling for panel ideology and affirmance deference does not explain the ideological effects of threshold issues. Clearly, decisions dismissing cases on threshold issues have a conservative effect, independent of the ideology of the panel. The curiously liberal results when threshold issues are satisfied are further strengthened by the addition of these two control variables. With controls for judicial ideology and affirmance deference, cases in which a threshold issue is raised and met produce much more liberal decisions.

To investigate the possibility of ideological panel effects, I consider in the next analysis individual judge votes rather than panel outcomes. The

TABLE 7.4
Ideological effects of threshold issues and panel ideology

Variable	(1)	(2)
Threshold issue met	.87 (.000)	
Threshold issue not met		−.49 (.000)
TotalIdeology	.32 (.000)	.32 (.000)
LowerCourt	1.34 (.000)	1.33 (.000)
N	10,019	10,019
R^2	.130	.139

TABLE 7.5
*Ideological effects of threshold issues and panel
ideology on judge votes*

Variable	(1)	(2)
Threshold issue met	.95 (.000)	
Threshold issue not met		−.53 (.000)
Ideology	.32 (.000)	.31 (.000)
Other Ideology	.30 (.000)	.30 (.000)
LowerCourt	1.34 (.000)	1.35 (.000)
N	22,594	22,594
R^2	.129	.141

effect of threshold issues is assessed on the ideology of judge votes, with multiple regressions including the judge's ideology, the ideology of other members of the panel, and the ideological direction of the decision being reviewed. Table 7.5 reports the results.

The ideology of both the judge and the other panel members are significant but do not alter the basic findings about the effect of rulings on legal threshold questions. The association of liberal outcomes and threshold issues being met is robust, standing up to multiple forms of testing and many different control variables. Tables 7.4 and 7.5 suggest that the association is greater than that of judicial ideology itself. Something about these cases in which threshold issues are satisfied is causing judges to vote contrary to their ideological preferences.

The analyses do not clearly confirm any of the general hypotheses about procedural threshold issues. The classic legal process model of neutral principles is not supported because the application of these procedural matters is not neutral—their use depends on judicial ideology and has systematic ideological effects. The absolute realist position finds support in that judicial ideology matters in threshold issue cases, but the magnitude of this effect is not great and the presence of the issues has a substantial impact over and above judicial ideology. The structural ideological theory finds clear support in the association of conservative outcomes with decisions on procedural threshold issues. But this theory is confounded by the distinctly liberal results in cases that surpass the procedural threshold requirements; these outcomes are much more liberal than those in cases that presented no procedural threshold issues.

At this point the results don't provide a clear answer to questions about procedural threshold issues but they suggest a hypothesis. The threshold effect findings are consistent with a combination of the legal model and the 50% hypothesis. Suppose that conservative defendants are deciding whether to settle a case or appeal it. Suppose also that the law is a major determinant of appellate outcomes and that the threshold issues offer some hope of a defendant victory, even with a weak case on the merits. One would expect defendants to settle extremely weak legal cases on the merits, unless those defendants had some realistic hope of prevailing anyway because of a threshold issue. The results are consistent with this supposition because defendants win a significant percentage of appeals on the threshold issue but, when they lose on the threshold issue, they lose a disproportionate number of cases on the merits, even independent of judicial ideology. In these latter cases the legal argument is so weak that even a favorable ideological panel rules against the defendant. If this hypothesis is true, the case outcomes may be driven less by judicial preferences than they are by the law and litigant case selection.

If the case selection/legal model hypothesis is correct, it adds to our understanding of the role of these procedural threshold issues. They are not strictly ideologically manipulable because they significantly influence outcomes regardless of judicial ideology. The threshold issues themselves have a distinctly conservative effect but they appear to yield liberal outcomes in cases in which the threshold issues are litigated and satisfied. Threshold issues do seem to play a structural ideological role in outcomes, enabling the defendants to win some cases that they would otherwise lose (or settle). Before embracing this conclusion, though, strategic considerations should be examined.

Strategic Concerns and Procedural Threshold Issues

The results for cases with procedural threshold issues may be explained by strategic considerations. Two distinct types of strategy should be examined. The first strategy operates only at the circuit court level. This strategy could involve judges using procedural threshold issues to avoid rendering ideologically undesirable rulings on the merits. The second strategy is that of the risk of reversal from other institutions, which is higher in the judicial hierarchy explored in Chapter 4.

To begin the analysis I explore the effect of threshold issues by contrasting cases of affirmance with cases of reversal. Given the presumption and demonstrated power of affirmance deference in circuit courts, reversals involve relatively activist decision making. A reversal that relies on a procedural threshold issue may involve a conservative judge's use of the legal procedural "escape hatch" to avoid a liberal decision on the merits.

To examine this possible use of legal strategy, I first separated the cases into affirmances and reversals, then ran regressions for individual judge votes using the effects on ideological outcomes of judge ideology and decisions in which the threshold issue was not met. Table 7.6 reports the results.

The basic association of judicial ideological preference and use of a procedural threshold issue is the same for affirmances and reversals but the relative power of conservative rulings for the defendant on threshold issues is significantly greater in reversals. This is somewhat consistent with the conservative escape hatch theory. But the independent significance of the threshold issue not being met is evidence that even some liberal judges are employing the procedural threshold variables to reverse and produce conservative results. To further examine the possible use of legal strategy, I conducted the same analysis on the effect of cases in which the judge found that the threshold issue was satisfied. Results are reported in Table 7.7.

The association remains strong between liberal results and threshold issues being met. A conservative judge may use the threshold issues as an escape hatch but the hatch is obviously very small. Many cases survive the procedural threshold issues and yield liberal outcomes on the merits, even after I controlled for judicial ideology. These issues have an effect on outcomes that goes beyond ideological manipulation.

TABLE 7.6
Effect of threshold issues not met by affirmance/reversal

Variable	Affirmance	Reversal
Ideology	.21 (.000)	.43 (.000)
Threshold issue not met	−.28 (.001)	−.75 (.000)
N	15,308	7,306
R^2	.003	.020

TABLE 7.7
Effect of threshold issues met by affirmance/reversal

Variable	Affirmance	Reversal
Ideology	.22 (.000)	.42 (.000)
Threshold issue met	.82 (.000)	.56 (.000)
N	15,308	7,306
R^2	.013	.016

Threshold issues might be deployed strategically to avoid or invoke the review of such other institutions as the Supreme Court. Up until now the analyses have consistently shown a negative association between circuit court outcomes and Supreme Court preferences, results that contravene the classic fear of reversal hierarchical control hypotheses. Some have argued, however, that the circuit court concern for reversal manifests itself in the structure and theory of the opinion, rather than in the outcome. If so, the procedural threshold issues might be used to avoid reversals, or at least reversals on the substantive merits of the action.

To investigate strategic effects with the Supreme Court, I incorporated the variables for the current Supreme Court preferences and old Supreme Court preferences as independent variables in the regression on the effects of procedural threshold issues on individual judge votes. Other variables were for affirmance deference, the voting judge's ideology, and the ideology of the other panel judges. Again, the dependent variable was the ideological direction of the judge vote. Results are reported in Table 7.8.

The addition of Supreme Court strategic variables does not alter the statistically significant effects for threshold issues. The direction and significance of the associations for the Supreme Court variables are the same as in previous studies without threshold effects—there is a statistically significant negative association between circuit court votes and the current

TABLE 7.8
Effect of Supreme Court preferences and threshold issues

Variable	(1)	(2)
Threshold issue met	.98 (.000)	
Threshold Issue not met		−.53 (.000)
Ideology	.28 (.000)	.28 (.000)
OtherIdeology	.27 (.000)	.28 (.000)
LowerCourt	1.37 (.000)	1.37 (.000)
SupremeCourt	−.57 (.000)	−.62 (.000)
OldSupremeCourt	.71 (.000)	.66 (.000)
N	20,619	20,619
R^2	.148	.135

TABLE 7.9
Effect of other institutional preferences and threshold issues

Variable	(1)	(2)
Threshold issue met	.98 (.000)	
Threshold issue not met		−.56 (.000)
Ideology	.25 (.000)	.26 (.000)
OtherIdeology	.24 (.000)	.25 (.000)
LowerCourt	.136 (.000)	1.37 (.000)
SupremeCourt	−.71 (.000)	−.77 (.000)
OldSupremeCourt	.70 (.000)	.67 (.000)
CircuitCourt	.001 (.098)	.001 (.168)
OldCircuitCourt	.005 (.025)	.006 (.005)
F-V UB	−.001 (.707)	−.001 (.338)
F-V LB	.007 (.002)	.009 (.000)
N	19,964	19,964
R^2	.149	.137

Supreme Court preferences and a statistically significant positive association between circuit court votes and preferences of the recent past Court.

The Supreme Court is not the only institution of hierarchical concern
to circuit court panels. The use of threshold issues might be attendant
to the preferences of other potential reviewing entities. Table 7.9 reports
the results of the basic regressions, with the inclusion of measures for
the preferences of the F-V veto points of Congress and of the full circuit
court.

The introduction of the additional institutional variables does not considerably alter the results, though there is an intriguing consistent and statistically significant association with the lower bound (conservative) side of
the F-V model. This finding suggests that the conservatives in Congress
may be monitoring the circuit courts and that the courts are to some de-

gree responding. As the conservative lower bound grows more liberal, the courts are more willing to render a liberal decision. As the conservative lower bound grows more conservative, the courts are more likely to reach a conservative decision on the threshold issue (rather than reach on the merits). One might expect this logical strategic response from the courts. The liberal upper bound in Congress does not have the same effect, however.

The institutional strategic response is not a great one, though, and the fundamental legal and ideological variables still explain most of the outcome, regardless of whether the threshold issue is met. The unusually liberal outcomes in cases in which the threshold issue is satisfied continues with statistical significance and is not explained by consideration of strategic factors.

Procedural Threshold Issues and Opinion Length

One would expect, as a legal matter, some effect of procedural threshold issues on opinion length. Opinions in cases in which the threshold issue is met should be relatively long because they require the circuit court panel to address an extra legal issue before reaching the merits. One might expect opinions in cases in which the threshold issue is not met to be relatively short because the court need not reach the merits, though opinion length in these cases would depend on the detail required to analyze the threshold issue itself. Opinion length might also be affected by other characteristics of the cases in which threshold issues are more likely to arise.

The association of threshold issues with opinion length might illuminate an entirely separate theory of judicial decision making—one of the economic, leisure-seeking interests of the judiciary. Under this theory, judges would prefer less work, including opinion writing. If so, judges could use threshold issues to avoid the need to grapple with the substantive law on the merits. The threshold issues offer a basic template, applicable across numerous legal areas, by which judges can readily dismiss cases, rather than making the effort to resolve the substantive issues and render an opinion on them. Opinion length might be considered a reasonable proxy for judicial work effort versus judicial leisure.

Before these various theories can be analyzed, though, some basic statistics on opinion length have to be measured. The following list reports the mean opinion length for threshold issue cases:

All cases	4.4852
Threshold issue met	5.7631
Threshold issue not met	4.0599

The results are as expected. Opinions for cases in which the threshold issue is met, requiring the judge to consider the merits, are distinctly longer than for all cases or for those in which the threshold issue is not met. But control variables should be incorporated in the analysis for us be confident in this conclusion because the longer threshold-issue-met opinions could be attributed in part to the fact that they tend to be liberal outcomes, which are also associated with longer opinions in other types of cases. To control for these factors I included threshold variables with other control variables in the next analysis, a multiple regression. Opinion length is the dependent variable. Table 7.10 reports the results.

These results with control variables refute the theories of the effect of threshold issues on opinion length. The logical, legal model theory that opinions should be shorter when the threshold issue is not met is unsupported by the results. Opinions are somewhat longer when the court must address both the threshold issue and the merits. The results are likewise inconsistent with the economic, leisure-seeking model of threshold issue use. Instead, they suggest that judges deploy some default amount of opinion-writing effort regardless of the issues in the case. The only

TABLE 7.10
Effect of threshold issues on opinion length

Variable	(1)	(2)
Threshold issue met	.018 (.072)	
Threshold issue not met		−.002 (.854)
Reversal	.014 (.163)	.016 (.121)
Ideology	.004 (.687)	.006 (.589)
SupremeCourt	−.008 (.633)	−.009 (.608)
OldSupremeCourt	−.038 (.024)	−.039 (.023)
N	10,315	10,315
R^2	.003	.003

consistently significant finding was that opinions were shorter when they were contrary to recent Supreme Court preferences. These results raise interesting questions about the effect of opinion length and why circuit courts might choose to write longer opinions. Chapter 8 considers these questions.

Conclusion

The evidence on the effect of threshold issues illuminates the application of these issues and, more generally, the determinants of judicial decision making. The consideration of threshold issues demonstrates the complexity of judicial decision making and the insufficiency of simple explanatory models, such as the political model. Procedural threshold rules are legal in nature and are without obvious ideological importance. Yet the data show that the application of these variables is somewhat ideological. Judges apply the threshold rules consistently with their own ideology, and the rules themselves appear to have some systematic structural ideological direction. But ideology does not fully explain the application of procedural threshold issues, which appear to exercise some classic legal tug that can override the ideological preferences of the judiciary.

The most interesting finding of this chapter involves the especially liberal outcomes in cases in which threshold issues were raised by a defendant but satisfied by the plaintiff. The empirical results do not provide a conclusive explanation for this effect but they suggest a logical answer that cannot be explained ideologically or strategically. The results are consistent with the claim that the substantive law, combined with the case selection hypotheses, matters in decision making. The addition of a procedural threshold issue to a case means that some typically conservative defendants with legally weak cases on the merits will nevertheless press an appeal in hopes of prevailing on the threshold issue. If they fail on the threshold issue, they consequently are likely to lose on the merits, regardless of judicial ideology, because the law clearly favors the plaintiff. This finding, combined with the independent significance of the threshold issues themselves, further suggests the importance of the law in circuit court decision making.

EIGHT

Circuit Court Decision Making and Precedential Impact

The overwhelming bulk of quantitative empirical analyses of judicial decision making, at any court level, has considered only individual case outcomes and their determinants. Outcome is the variable most readily captured in a form that can be reduced to quantitative measurement. But the case outcomes by themselves influence only the parties to the particular litigation and do not directly describe the path of the law. In the judicial system of the United States, case outcomes have an effect on the path of the law because they serve as precedents. Case outcomes should roughly correspond to the direction of precedents set. One cannot automatically assume, however, that a pattern of outcomes is associated with a corresponding particular pattern of precedents and the consequent state of the law.

If decisions are purely ideological and the law therefore irrelevant, studying judicial precedents might seem unnecessary. Purely ideological judges are unbound by precedents, which would be meaningless as a practical matter when describing the state of the law. Legal realists assert that there is a virtually limitless supply of precedents available to justify any decision that an ideological judge might prefer to reach. The preceding chapters have demonstrated, though, that the law does help determine future decisions, at least on the circuit court level. Because the law matters, the study of precedential impact is correspondingly important.

The close study of precedents and their impact is impossible with currently available or readily foreseeable empirical tools. The available data do enable preliminary tentative analysis of precedential impact. This chapter commences this analysis to discern the categories of decisions and determinants of decisions that are likely to have the greatest legal power. The following discussion attempts to cover many issues and is therefore only a preliminary analysis of the factors that may influence precedential impact.

The Nature and Significance of Precedent

Although precedent has seen relatively little quantitative empirical research, it is a crucial aspect of judicial decision making at the circuit court level. Precedent may be defined as a "decided case that furnishes a basis for determining an identical or similar case that may arise later, or a similar question of law."[1] Some legal systems, such as the civil law systems of continental Europe, do not rely on precedents as a source of law. But the common law system of the United States arose with the use of precedent for judge-made law; this use of precedent has since extended to statutory decisions. The legal importance of precedent gives greater potential impact to individual judicial decisions.

Technically speaking, a judicial decision resolves only a dispute between the particular litigating parties. Practically speaking, the decision may have far greater societal importance because of its precedential impact. When the U.S. Supreme Court decides that the broad prohibitions on abortion of a state law are unconstitutional, that decision directly strikes down the particular state prohibition in the case before the Court but functionally invalidates a wide range of additional laws in other states. Courts at all levels of the judiciary, including circuit courts, are to take the Supreme Court's ruling and apply it as governing law in future cases that challenge those other laws. They are to examine the facts of those other laws, apply the Supreme Court's reasoning, and thus determine if the other laws pass constitutional muster.

One type of precedential impact is vertical and hierarchical. When a higher court rules on a legal issue, that ruling controls subsequent decisions of lower courts. If the U.S. Supreme Court declares a particular statutory provision unconstitutional, that precedent prevents lower courts from legally applying and enforcing the provision. Circuit court precedents may also have this hierarchical governing effect. When a circuit court makes a ruling, such as declaring a statutory provision unconstitutional, that holding governs future rulings of district courts *located within the circuit* because they are vertically subordinate to that circuit court (e.g., district courts in Florida are governed by the eleventh circuit). District courts that are located outside the geographic perimeters of the particular circuit court are not legally bound by its rulings, though they may still use them in reaching a decision. Chapter 4 presented evidence that circuit courts were indeed bound by vertical precedent as reflected in recent rulings of the Supreme Court.

The issue of horizontal precedent is commonly raised because the nation has a dozen circuit courts that have different geographic coverage. Such precedents are not binding. A particular ruling by the fourth circuit court of appeals does not control a subsequent ruling on an identical issue by the sixth circuit court of appeals. Because circuit courts are horizontal equals their decisions are not controlled by precedents from sister circuits. Horizontal precedents may have a persuasive effect, however. Circuit courts may give some deference to the reasoned judgment of other circuits. Circuit courts may be loathe to directly contradict a decision from another circuit because doing so creates geographic disparities in the law. When the circuits disagree, a uniform federal statute may have completely different meanings in different states of the union, a consequence generally to be avoided. But such disagreements, often called circuit splits, among the circuits are by no means uncommon. If a circuit court believes that another circuit court got a decision wrong, it will not defer but will issue a contrasting ruling. Such a split may be resolved conclusively by the U.S. Supreme Court, with its vertical precedential power over all the circuits, or may persist.

Technically speaking, a circuit court is not even legally bound by the precedential effect of its own previous rulings. The court may reverse those earlier rulings if a subsequent panel believes them to be wrongly decided.

Such intracircuit overrulings are uncommon; panels usually treat previous decisions as though they provided binding precedent. Frequent reversals of circuit court precedent by circuit court panels could seriously destabilize the law. Legally, however, circuit court panels are not compelled to adhere to these earlier rulings.

The greatest effect of precedent may not be in its direct power, whether binding or persuasive, but in its broader indirect power. Much legal reasoning involves arguing by analogy, claiming that a given case should be decided one way because earlier similar cases were decided that way. The similarity may be factual or grounded in a broader principle. In the common-law judicial system of the United States, courts consider previous cases and use them as decision-making guides, even when those decisions have no binding authority. Circuit court panels commonly rely on and cite decisions from other circuits for persuasive guidance in rendering decisions.

Stability is one of the primary purposes for giving effect to precedents. Rather than revisit the same legal issue in every case, judges rely on precedents. This provides greater consistency in the law. Such reliance also should mitigate the possible arbitrariness associated with ideological judicial decision making because precedent should operate as a constraint on preferences. Citizens can better understand how the law is likely to be applied to their particular circumstances, and the system is more efficient because it avoids the need for repeated re-litigation of commonly contested questions. Reliance on precedents eases the task of judges and in the process "reduces individual workload and increases leisure time."[2] Consequently, precedents and especially patterns of precedents could be an important determinant in future case outcomes.

The significance of precedent in the U.S. legal system lends importance to the content of judicial opinions justifying the outcome of a particular decision. Although the original concept of precedent was focused on facts and outcomes and so was closely associated with the outcome, precedent today is found mainly in the language of opinions. Judges use precedents less in reference to the facts of the previous decision than as statements of the law to be applied. While deciding individual cases, judges create general rules, or perhaps governing standards, to be applied when similar factual circumstances arise in future actions.

Precedent remains somewhat tied to outcomes because dicta are not considered binding precedent. *Dicta* is the legal term for aspects of the opinion that are unnecessary to resolve the issue. Lawyers may distinguish between the opinion's holding, or *ratio decendi*, which are those conclusions necessary to resolve the dispute, and its dicta. Judges do not have authority to announce law in the abstract. Consequently, their dicta declarations of law do not possess legitimate authority and are not binding precedents.[3] Only those legal discussions necessary to the outcome may have precedential power. Many different approaches are available, however, for reaching a given result.

Opinions can be written in very different ways while reaching the same outcome. A court may set down a firm and clear legal rule that, if not reversed, should have a substantial effect on future decisions. For example, a court might hold that certain types of defenses cannot even be raised in particular statutory cases. Such a decision should minimize the discretion of future judges and perhaps bind ideologically contrary panels. Alternatively, the court may set out a balancing test, directing future courts to weigh numerous factors without any clear directions. This type of decision may have the same number of citations but would likely have less precedential power. Another approach is to write an opinion tied closely to the case facts; in such an opinion the court directs that the decision not be generalized as a powerful precedent. The Supreme Court did this in *Bush v. Gore*, in which it defined some equal protection clause rights connected with voting but cautioned that the Court's ruling was "limited to the present circumstances" of the 2000 election.[4] Such doctrine is often described as a "restricted ticket, good for this day and train only."[5] The approach is generally disdained because it suggests that the court favors a particular litigant in a particular dispute and consequently fashions law that it would reject in other contexts. Several circuit courts have sought to control the precedential impact of certain decisions by creating a rule that their unpublished decisions are not to serve as precedent.

Judges who write opinions may strive to influence the precedential impact of their decisions but future judges ultimately control this impact. A precedent may take on an active life of its own in the hands of future judges. Jerome Frank declared that a "case means only what a judge in a later case says it means."[6] Judges are commonly presented with precedents by both parties to the litigation and must choose the most apposite precedents on which to base their decisions. As precedents mount, judges may actually have greater discretion for ideological decision making because more legal tools are available for them to reach their preferred outcome.

The Limits of Outcomes Analysis in Quantitative Studies

As noted earlier, outcomes analysis, whether considered from either a legal or an ideological perspective, provides only a very crude approximation of the state of the law in the United States. This limitation can clearly be seen from the decisions on abortion rights. The first and most notorious Supreme Court case on abortion rights was *Roe v. Wade*.[7] The case involved a challenge to a Texas law prohibiting abortions. Besides the question of whether the law would be upheld or struck down, the Court confronted various legal theories for addressing the issue (including due process privacy rights and the equal protection clause) and various applications of those theories. Justice Harry Blackmun chose to strike down the law on privacy grounds but did not create an absolute right to an abortion. Instead he created the trimester system, permitting some regulation. Simple outcome coding would draw no distinction about the legal theory used and applied by the Court. Yet, if precedent matters, the theory may matter greatly. Outcome coding also would not identify the strength of the rule (e.g., the trimester analysis).

More recently, the Supreme Court reconsidered abortion rights in *Planned Parenthood of Southeastern Pennsylvania v. Casey*,[8] in which the Court declined to overrule its holding in *Roe* but modified its trimester analysis in favor of an "undue burden" approach for analyzing the constitutionality of state restrictions on abortion. The Court's decision in *Casey* was grounded substantially in the importance of adhering to precedent. There was little doubt, however, that the opinion in *Casey* substantially modified the rule set forth in *Roe* and generally reduced constitutional rights to an abortion. *Casey* upheld certain limitations on abortions but struck others and could be coded as conservative or liberal. A liberal coding would be inaccurate, because the decision was a shift from *Roe* in a conservative direction. Even a conservative coding would fail to capture the fact that the Court modified but did not overrule *Roe*. The key to *Casey* was the language of the opinion, not the outcome of the case.

Outcome coding inevitably suffers this shortcoming, which is difficult to overcome. Coding for the precise opinion content is extremely difficult on a case-by-case basis and surely impossible for such a large group of cases as contained in the courts of appeals database. But we should not ignore the importance of different opinions because of this difficulty. A decision that appears to be conservative on outcomes analysis and that is coded correspondingly might have a relatively liberal effect on future decisions (and vice versa). Different types of conservative decisions will have different effects on the future path of the law. A judge may write a decision to have great or little future impact.

Outcomes analysis fails to capture the range of significance of rulings. Some court decisions are seminal and set the path for a major change in the state of the law. Other decisions may be trivial and have little impact. The nature of the case plainly affects the significance of a decision but so may the opinion. The decision to reaffirm *Roe* was extremely significant, regardless of outcome. A decision creating a new constitutional right, striking down a statute as unconstitutional on other grounds, or reversing an earlier ruling of the court will be far more legally salient than will ordinary opinions. The effect of a decision on future cases is much more significant than merely looking at its outcome can show, and this effect can be captured to some degree.

Not all precedents are of equal importance in theory or in practice. Many factors can affect the power of a case as a precedent that can influence future decisions. One analysis of the "degrees of bindingness" of precedent listed the following relevant factors:

- The hierarchical rank of the court
- Whether the decision is merely of a panel or by a full bench
- The reputation of the court or of the judge writing the opinion
- Changes in the political, economic, or social background since the previous decision
- Soundness of the supporting arguments in the opinion
- The age of the precedent
- The presence or absence of dissent

- The branch of law involved (e.g., precedent is more weighty in property law than in the law of tort)
- Whether the precedent represents a trend
- How well the precedent is accepted in academic writings
- The effects of legal change in related areas[9]

Not all these factors are readily amenable to quantitative empirical testing. Some can be evaluated using the courts of appeals database, which also enables such testing for other factors that may influence the power of a precedent.

The Difficulties of Operationalizing Opinions and Precedential Impact

Although coding for opinion content is extremely difficult, some quantitative coding for precedential impact is readily available. Frequency of citation has been used as an indicator of judicial impact.[10] Two separate private services, Shepard's and Westlaw Keycite, provide lists of cases that have cited an opinion and give some information on the nature of that citation. They designate whether the succeeding opinion followed the precedent or sought to overrule or distinguish its application. An opinion with many citations and few distinguishing cases clearly has a major impact on the state of the law. An opinion that is overruled may have virtually no impact. The services are largely overlapping but some research suggests that Westlaw has slightly broader coverage of unpublished opinions and slightly more detail on the treatment of opinions, so I used Westlaw Keycite in the research for this chapter.

Although previous research has considered total citations, it has not considered the frequency of negative citations that overrule or limit the impact of an earlier holding. Westlaw's system has various signals for negative history that to some degree call into question the precedential value of a case. Under the Westlaw system a red flag means the case is no longer good law for at least one of the points that it contains. The case may have been overruled by a higher court or overridden by the action of some other institution, such as Congress. A yellow flag designates negative history, such as a limitation of the breadth of the decision's application, that is short of an overruling of the decision. The Keycite system also lists negative indirect history, which includes the cases that could have some negative precedential impact. Counting precedential impact has its own specification limitations. Practical limitations of such large-N analysis preclude coding the ideological direction of all the citing decisions. One study with a much smaller sample found a statistically significant association between the ideology of the precedent's panel and that of the citing panel, though this effect did not overwhelm other influences.[11] Cases may also be cited for reasons unrelated to the substance of the holding. But one would expect many citations to involve the substance of the holding, so an association should be statistically discernible.

Westlaw also provides some information on positive precedential history for cases. For citations that are not negative, Westlaw has depth-of-treatment stars, which range from one to four. Four stars means the case was carefully examined for a page or more, three stars means the case was discussed substantially in the text, two stars means the case was discussed briefly, and one star means the case was cited without any discussion, possibly in a string citation of many supporting precedents. For each decision, the Keycite system lists all the cited cases and assigns them the appropriate number of stars. For both negative and positive precedential treatment, the Westlaw system considers cases at all levels of the judicial hierarchy. Thus, the data incorporate citations from the Supreme Court, circuit courts, and district courts.

To operationalize precedential impact I have taken the cases in the courts of appeals database that were decided in 1971 or later (over four thousand cases) and coded them in four ways. The coding was binary for whether the case had a red flag or a yellow flag. I also coded for the number of cases with negative indirect history and the total number of positive citations in cases given two to four stars. (One star cases were omitted on the theory that the underlying cited case was not a significant factor in the subsequent ruling.) Although cases accumulate more precedents over time, the year of the underlying case was not a significant determinant of citations, probably because my citation counting occurred more than a decade after the most recent of the cases of the database.

Nearly all (98%) the cases had at least some citations as precedent. For total positive citations the number varied from 0 to 1,570 (in one outlying case). The mean number of such positive citations among the cases

TABLE 8.1
Interaction of precedent variables

Variable	Red	Yellow	Negative
Negative	.122 (.000)	.337 (.000)	—
Total	.038 (.013)	.306 (.000)	.346 (.000)

was 20.52. For negative indirect history citations the number ranged from 0 to 121, the mean was 0.97, and the median was 0, because most cases had no negative indirect history.

Before analyzing the negative and positive determinants of precedential impact, I examine the interaction of these precedent variables with one another. Table 8.1 reports the results of individual regressions of negative precedents and total citations against red flags, yellow flags, and total negative citations. I excluded the one case with 1,570 positive citations because it had more than three times the number of the next-most-cited case and could disproportionately affect the outcome of the analysis.

Total positive citations positively and significantly correlate with negative citations and with red and yellow flags. This finding suggests that one factor in both positive and negative citations may simply be case significance. Some decisions probably produce more citations, both positive and negative, because they involve recurring events. An alternative explanation for this result, however, has to do with opinion content. Perhaps judges can write particularly controversial opinions that are therefore more likely to yield both positive and negative citations. Such an explanation would suggest that opinion writing has a risk/reward association in which the opinions with the greatest positive precedential effect also have the greatest risk of reversal or limitation in future decisions. This alternative finds some support in research showing that the opinions of certain judges are cited more often.[12] The strong association between total negative citations and both red and yellow flags suggests that such dramatic decisions as reversals are not isolated events but tend to occur in tandem with a greater number of courts questioning the viability of a particular precedent.

Case types could also affect the nature of precedents. Some types of actions have many more cases brought before the court, with the opportunity for many more citations and, presumably, greater risk of negative interpretation or reversal. Alternatively, in categories with fewer cases, the fewer precedents might assume disproportionate importance. Table 8.2 reports

TABLE 8.2
Precedents by case type

Case type	Total	Negative	Red	Yellow
Criminal	18.17	0.68	0.05	0.29
Civil rights	24.30	1.01	0.05	0.35
First Amendment	28.12	0.84	0.04	0.47
Due process	25.11	1.04	0.06	0.42
Privacy	21.17	1.11	0.06	0.39
Labor relations	15.71	0.72	0.05	0.31
Economic	21.58	0.83	0.03	0.33
Miscellaneous	20.30	0.90	0.05	0.35

the mean score for each of the four precedential variables by the major case types in the courts of appeals database.

The precedential variables show some case type effects but not particularly dramatic ones. For each grouping, about one out of twenty cases is red flagged, though the lower rate for economic cases suggests that precedent may be treated as more significant in those cases. The most common case types in the database (including economic matters and criminal prosecutions) do not yield a particularly high number of precedents and are not particularly vulnerable to being overturned. The most apparent association from these descriptive statistics is the tendency for especially salient cases involving constitutional law to produce a greater absolute number of total positive citations and total negative citations.

To examine the effect of other variables on precedential impact, I needed to identify the types of actions most likely to produce more precedents. The next analysis thus considers as potential proxies for case significance the following binary variables: whether the case presented a federal statutory issue, whether it presented a federal constitutional issue, whether it was a class action, and the absolute number of amici who participated in it. The following list reports the results of a regression of these variables on the total citations measurement:

Constitutional	.035 (.021)
Statutory	.045 (.003)
Class action	.007 (.658)
Amici	.000 (.997)
N	4,331
R^2	.003

Class action status and amici participation are apparently irrelevant as measures of case significance if one uses the measure of total precedential impact. That the case addressed statutory or constitutional issues is a significant determinant of total precedential effect, though, and these two factors can be used as control variables in subsequent analyses of this effect.

Ideology and Precedential Impact

One obvious issue of interest is the degree of impact of liberal or conservative opinions. If judging were entirely ideological, one would expect the precedential impact to be governed by the judiciary applying the precedent. Thus, a more conservative judiciary would cite more conservative cases as precedents. Although this surely influences precedential treatment to some degree, we have seen in Chapter 1 and throughout the book that judicial ideology explains only a small fraction of outcomes. Consequently, precedential impact may be driven by more than the ideological preferences of the future circuit court panel that considers the precedent.

Judicial activism is often associated with ideological decision making but precedential measures may better capture the concept. As we observed in the Supreme Court decisions on abortion rights, the full ideological implications of a ruling are found in the language of the opinion, not just in the decisional outcome. A judge who reached ideologically consistent outcomes but wrote very narrow opinions might appear activist from the outcomes analysis but prove to be nonactivist when the precedential implications of those decisions were assessed. Conversely, a judge might seem balanced in outcomes but not in precedential effect. A liberal judge might render narrow opinions when casting a conservative vote but expansive and powerful opinions when casting a liberal vote.

The first analysis involves more descriptive statistics about the precedential consequences of liberal versus conservative circuit court decisions. Table 8.3 reports the mean of the four precedential variables for liberal and conservative decisions.

One sees little difference in these general statistics on precedential impact, though there is some suggestion that liberal decisions, with a slightly higher rate of reversal and general negative treatment, are more likely to

TABLE 8.3
Precedential impact by ideological outcome direction

Outcome direction	Total	Negative	Red	Yellow
Liberal	20.59	0.90	0.05	0.34
Conservative	20.43	0.73	0.04	0.31

TABLE 8.4
Precedential impact by panel composition

Panel composition	Total	Negative	Red	Yellow
3–0 D	18.70	0.79	0.04	0.33
2–1 D	17.63	0.65	0.05	0.28
2–1 R	22.44	0.79	0.04	0.34
3–0 R	23.25	0.80	0.03	0.35

be treated critically in future decisions. There was no material difference in total positive citations but an obvious difference in negative citations. This may simply be because the judiciary was relatively conservative during much of the relevant time period, from 1972 on.

The ideological composition of the circuit court panel could matter in addition to the ideological direction of the outcome. Table 8.4 contains descriptive statistics for the precedential variables by the panel composition according to party of the appointing president. Although there is a tendency for judges to vote ideologically, succeeding judges might be more influenced by the makeup of the panel than the simple decision. Thus, when a liberal panel renders a conservative decision, the nonideological nature of the outcome might make the opinion especially credible and more-often cited.

When ideology is examined by panel composition rather than outcome, there is no significant difference in negative treatment (though conservative panels get slightly fewer red flags). An obvious difference appears, however, for positive precedential treatment, with conservative judges receiving distinctly more positive citations.

Judicial activism has often been associated with liberal judges. The most dramatic expressions of judicial effect seemingly have been found in liberal rulings establishing abortion rights, gay rights, and so on. This anecdotal impression is not confirmed by the data, however. Conservative decisions, judging from the descriptive statistics alone, apparently have been given greater precedential power. I provide more-rigorous regression analyses of this effect after other variables have been examined.

Legal Treatment and Precedential Impact

The central legal treatment variable used in this book's analyses has been the decision whether to affirm or reverse the lower court or agency ruling. Even under the traditional legal model, one might expect legal treatment to have a significant effect on precedential import. A reversal is, by its nature, a ruling on the law. Appellate courts rarely review the facts decided at the lower court level. Typically, the reversal plainly declares the state of the law and maintains that the lower court got the law wrong. An affirmance, by contrast, does not state the law as clearly and may be more fact dependent (though this is not inevitably so). An affirmance might therefore be easier to distinguish as being confined to the particular facts found by the lower court; these facts are granted deference on appellate review. Thus, one would hypothesize that a reversal would have more legal impact and more total positive citations. One might also expect reversals of district court opinions to have more negative citations and be overturned more often because in these cases the circuit courts issued expansive rulings and showed less deference to the decision below. Table 8.5 provides the descriptive statistics for the precedential variables for each category of affirmance deference treatment.

These results seem to confirm the hypotheses. Reversals have a more substantial precedential effect than do affirmances. Reversals are cited at about a 15% higher rate than are affirmances. An even more profound effect

TABLE 8.5
Precedential impact by affirmance deference

	Total	Negative	Red	Yellow
Affirmance	19.30	0.67	0.04	0.29
Reversal	22.58	1.03	0.04	0.37

TABLE 8.6
Ideology and affirmance deference and precedential impact

Variable	Total	Negative	Red	Yellow
Reversal	.058 (.000)	.089 (.000)	.041 (.007)	.082 (.000)
TotalIdeology	−.015 (.336)	−.006 (.682)	−.013 (.387)	−.005 (.738)
Constitutional	.053 (.001)	.008 (.590)	.044 (.004)	.040 (.010)
Statutory	.047 (.002)	.054 (.000)	.033 (.035)	.037 (.016)
N	4,214	4,188	4,213	4,214
R^2	.008	.007	.005	.00

is found for negative treatment. Reversals also receive over 30% more negative citations than do affirmances, though the red flag variable shows that affirmances have no material difference in the rate of complete reversals. They are more likely to be distinguished, if not overridden in subsequent decisions. These results show some effect of the conventional nonideological legal model in opinions and their treatment as precedent.

The tables and list so far report only descriptive statistics without any controls. The ideological measures do not control for legal treatment, and the legal variables do not consider the ideological nature of the outcome or the ideological composition of the panel. The next analysis integrates these two variables in a multiple regression. Table 8.6 reports the results of regressions on the precedential variables, using independent variables of affirmance deference and ideology. Ideology is captured using the Total-Ideology score for the circuit court panel. Constitutional and statutory decisions are included as control variables. As in previous chapters, results are reported with coefficients and, following them, significance levels in parentheses.

The legal variable of reversal has significance when integrated but there is no apparent impact to the variable on the ideology of the deciding panel. Reversals have greater legal impact and are more likely to be positively cited in future cases. But reversals are also viewed dubiously by succeeding courts and are much more likely to receive negative treatment in future opinions. The ideology of the judicial panel appears to have no positive or negative effect on precedential impact. The overall power of these equations is small but there is a discernible effect of legal treatment on precedential treatment. Once again, the legal variable of affirmance deference transcends any effect of ideology when measuring precedents.

Judicial Background and Precedential Impact

The previous analyses have been based in the nature of the opinion itself or in the ideological composition of the deciding circuit court panel. Citing judges may also be influenced by other characteristics of the panel. Some judges may receive particular respect from their colleagues, so their decisions would be cited more frequently. Less-respected judges may be more likely to see their decisions reversed or overruled. But identifying such judges may be difficult.

There are some proxies that might be used for judicial prestige. The ABA ratings, described in Chapter 3, do not consider the judge's past performance on the bench but are meant to predict the future quality of that performance. Although the ABA ratings do not show strong associations with ideological outcomes or the degree of affirmance deference, they may be associated with precedential impact if "higher-quality" judges are more often cited and relied on or if their opinions are more persuasively written. Table 8.7 introduces the mean ABA rating of the panel into the regressions using ideology and affirmance deference.

The only consistently significant variable was whether the decision was a reversal, and, as reflected in total citations, the mean ABA score had no apparent impact on the positive effect of an opinion. The ABA ratings had one statistically significant effect—as reflected in the red flag numbers, panels with higher ABA ratings were less likely to have their rulings reversed. This may be because such judges are less likely to write bad opinions subject to reversal or may reflect some prestige effect that makes future courts less likely to reverse opinions issued by such judges. There was no general association of ABA ratings and overall positive precedential impact, though.

TABLE 8.7
ABA ratings and precedential impact

Variable	Total	Negative	Red	Yellow
Reversal	.057 (.000)	.060 (.000)	.081 (.000)	.041 (.008)
TotalIdeology	.015 (.327)	−.006 (.681)	−.005 (.740)	.013 (.389)
Constitutional	.053 (.001)	.008 (.584)	.040 (.009)	.044 (.004)
Statutory	.046 (.003)	.054 (.000)	.037 (.016)	.033 (.035)
ABAmean	−.025 (.107)	−.010 (.505)	−.031 (.043)	−.005 (.763)
N	4,213	4,187	4,213	4,212
R^2	.009	.007	.010	.005

TABLE 8.8
Precedents by circuit

Case type	Total	Negative	Red	Yellow
First circuit	18.18	0.59	0.03	0.31
Second circuit	29.28	0.81	0.04	0.37
Third circuit	26.64	1.04	0.05	0.38
Fourth circuit	19.63	0.77	0.03	0.32
Fifth circuit	17.80	0.59	0.05	0.31
Sixth circuit	20.20	1.19	0.04	0.30
Seventh circuit	27.07	0.82	0.05	0.34
Eighth circuit	12.54	0.53	0.04	0.22
Ninth circuit	19.32	0.76	0.06	0.31
Tenth circuit	18.35	0.74	0.05	0.31
Eleventh circuit	17.37	0.88	0.08	0.37
D.C. circuit	18.38	0.98	0.04	0.36

Lower ABA ratings were associated with more total citations at a level approaching statistical significance. This might imply that lower-rated judges are taking more risks in setting bold precedents, which could also explain a higher reversal rate.

Another proxy for judicial prestige might be based on the circuit rendering the decision. Precedents from different circuits can be expected to have different precedential impacts. Some circuits hear a higher number of absolute cases and therefore have many more opportunities for intracircuit citation. Also, particular circuit courts are generally regarded as being more prestigious, so their precedents might be cited more often even outside that circuit court. Some have suggested that the second circuit is especially influential. The D.C. circuit is often regarded as particularly important and prestigious but this is because of its unique jurisdiction over the lawfulness of various federal regulations, a factor that is less likely to influence the absolute number of positive or negative citations. Analyses of circuit court precedent are generally subjective, though one previous study found that the first circuit was the most prestigious in terms of absolute citation counts.[13] Table 8.8 reports the descriptive statistics for citations by circuit court.

The results show some plain circuit effects. Some circuits, especially the second, are cited more frequently, whereas others, such as the eighth, are very seldom cited. Other circuits have an unusually high rate of negative treatment. Eleventh circuit opinions were reversed at a rate more than twice as high as those of the first and fourth circuits. The third circuit

TABLE 8.9
Precedential impact controlling for circuit effects

Variable	Total	Negative	Red	Yellow
Reversal	.051 (.001)	.058 (.000)	.041 (.008)	.078 (.000)
TotalIdeology	−.006 (.682)	−.011 (.474)	−.013 (.413)	−.016 (.296)
Constitutional	.053 (.000)	.008 (.583)	.044 (.004)	.040 (.009)
Statutory	.040 (.009)	.053 (.001)	.032 (.036)	.034 (.028)
ABAmean	−.005 (.759)	−.006 (.713)	−.004 (.785)	−.021 (.186)
Circuit	.115 (.000)	.026 (.103)	.002 (.889)	.060 (.000)
N	4,213	4,187	4,212	4,213
R^2	.021	.007	.005	.014

had the highest rate of negative treatment that fell short of overrulings. To some degree these findings may reflect only the number of cases heard within the circuit's jurisdiction. The data do not distinguish between the effects of more citations within and more citations outside the circuit but they do show a cumulative significance in frequency of citation (and negative citations). Some circuits generally produce more total positive and total negative precedents but these circuits have a slightly lower rate of precedent reversal. This finding is evidence of some disparity between circuits in opinion quality, perceived prestige, or both.

Given the disparity in circuit frequency, the circuit effects should be incorporated as a control variable into analyses of precedential impact. I created a new variable (Circuit) that weighted each circuit by the average number of total precedents that its judges produced. This number serves as a proxy for the general influence of particular circuits that may be more persuasive or prestigious. The purpose was to assess the effect of total precedents per circuit, which tends to be correlated with negative precedents. I introduced Circuit as a control variable into the regressions that assessed the impact of reversals, ideology, and mean ABA rating. Results are presented in Table 8.9.

The control for circuit effects was statistically significant and considerably improved the model's predictive capability for total precedents and for yellow flag probability of questioning the precedent. Circuit effects had no association, however, with total negative citations or red flags indicating an overruling of the precedent. The control for circuit effects did not have much consequence on the role of the other variables. Reversal remains a significant determinant of all precedential effects. The circuit effects

TABLE 8.10
Precedential impact of race and gender background

Variable	Total	Negative	Red	Yellow
Reversal	.064 (.000)	.096 (.000)	.084 (.000)	.142 (.000)
TotalIdeology	−.009 (.617)	−.024 (.173)	−.011 (.530)	−.040 (.023)
Constitutional	.068 (.000)	.031 (.068)	.058 (.001)	.083 (.000)
Statutory	.059 (.000)	.073 (.000)	.057 (.001)	.071 (.000)
Minority	.034 (.045)	.005 (.781)	−.007 (.666)	.020 (.234)
Gender	.046 (.008)	.060 (.001)	.013 (.666)	.038 (.025)
Circuit	.153 (.000)	.012 (.004)	−.019 (.269)	.103 (.000)
N	3,364	3,347	3,380	3,381
R^2	.040	.022	.014	.045

control did cause the association of ABAmean and reversals to disappear, though, suggesting that this finding may be an artifact rather than a true determinant.

Other background effects might conceivably have some influence on precedential impact. Decisions rendered by circuit court panels containing women or minorities might have more or fewer precedential effects. One could theorize that such judges are generally of higher or lower quality or work harder or less hard on the bench, although these effects seem unlikely. The precedential variables enable testing for these possibilities. Table 8.10 reports results of the regressions for each of the precedential variables. I added the minority race mean and gender mean as independent variables.

Interestingly, minority racial mean and gender mean are statistically significant for total citations. Opinions that are the product of panels containing a woman or member of a minority tend to be cited more than opinions by panels without such representation. Presumably, the relationship is not direct. The citing panel is generally unlikely to notice the gender or race of the panel deciding the precedential case. Perhaps panels with women and minorities alter the nature of the opinion, making it more likely to be cited. Such panels may write more powerful or "better" opinions. The significant association of gender with negative citations suggests that panels with women may write more-powerful opinions that are susceptible to more subsequent citation, both positive and negative. The association of more positive citations, but not more negative citations, with panels containing a minority is unusual and may suggest that such panels produce better opinions. The absolute effect of these variables is not great but the association is interesting. These findings are based on panel composition and may demonstrate some panel effect, in which more-diverse panels produce better or more-persuasive opinions. Additional consequences of panel effects on precedents are discussed later in this chapter.

Litigants and Precedential Impact

Much of the theory of litigant effect on judicial decision making involves the precedent-setting effects of judicial decisions. A leading theory is that litigants select cases to manipulate the precedents created and the associated path of the law. According to this theory, repeat player litigants are able to choose cases on appeal that offer the best prospects of success and of precedents to benefit them in future litigation. Although the findings of Chapter 5 revealed little effect of litigant type on case outcome, controlling for judicial ideology was difficult and only a few case types could be evaluated. Moreover, those studies tested only for an indirect effect—case outcome—that did not best measure the theory of strategic manipulation of precedent. By using data on precedential effects, I could more directly examine whether the nature of litigants does indeed influence the indirect consequences of judicial outcomes. Table 8.11 reports the basic regressions on precedential effects for the major repeat player parties (the federal government and business) as both appellants and respondents. The studies use the established control variables of reversal, judicial ideology, constitutional or statutory case type, and circuit court effects.

The results show no litigant effect on the total number of citations, which is a proxy for total positive precedential effect. The only regression in which litigant effects appeared was for red flags. There was a statistically significant association of fewer reversals in cases in which the federal government was an appellant and more reversals in cases in which business interests were the appellant. The strategic implications of this are unclear. The results in Chapter 5 found that the federal government was unusually likely to succeed as an appellant, and the results in Table 8.12 show that federal government victories are less likely to be overturned. These findings add some evidence to the claim that the federal government is an especially

TABLE 8.11
Precedential impact of litigant type

Variable	Total	Negative	Red	Yellow
Reversal	.095 (.000)	.098 (.000)	.085 (.000)	.143 (.000)
TotalIdeology	.000 (.986)	−.014 (.419)	.009 (.587)	−.030 (.078)
Constitutional	.094 (.000)	.031 (.075)	.060 (.000)	.081 (.000)
Statutory	.067 (.000)	.075 (.000)	.060 (.001)	.070 (.000)
Circuit	.166 (.000)	.050 (.004)	−.016 (.354)	.102 (.000)
Federal Appellant	−.019 (.256)	−.020 (.261)	−.036 (.037)	−.014 (.423)
Federal Respondent	.018 (.284)	.000 (.994)	.021 (.227)	.005 (.765)
Business Appellant	.000 (.986)	−.002 (.918)	.060 (.001)	−.029 (.090)
Business Respondent	.028 (.101)	.034 (.053)	.027 (.122)	.020 (.248)
N	3,364	3,338	3,363	3,364
R^2	.053	.020	.017	.044

TABLE 8.12
Precedential impact of panel extremity

Variable	Total	Negative	Red	Yellow
Reversal	.094 (.000)	.096 (.000)	.083 (.000)	.140 (.000)
Constitutional	.093 (.000)	.030 (.082)	.059 (.001)	.081 (.000)
Statutory	.068 (.000)	.075 (.000)	.060 (.000)	.071 (.000)
Circuit	.166 (.000)	.049 (.005)	−.018 (.309)	.098 (.000)
TotalIdeologyAbsolute	−.007 (.885)	.006 (.903)	−.110 (.037)	−.020 (.702)
TotalIdeologyAbsolute^2	.010 (.852)	.012 (.824)	.110 (.037)	.024 (.638)
N	3,364	3,338	3,363	3,364
R^2	.051	.019	.015	.042

successful and strategic litigant in the circuit courts. The same cannot be said for business interests, however.

Panel Effects and Precedential Impact

By their nature, panel effects influence decision making within the circuit court panel, and there is no obvious reason why this effect should translate into precedential power. But some possible associations between panel effects and precedential effects are intriguing and worth testing. One implication of panel effects is that diverse panels simply produce better decisions because of better deliberation within the panel. The results on gender and minority effects support this hypothesis. The theory is contradicted, however, by the results on precedential effects on split panels, reported earlier in Table 8.5. Unified panels tend to produce more precedents but are no more likely to produce reversals than do politically split panels. This section explores the issue further.

The theory of group polarization holds that ideologically unified panels are expected to produce more-ideological and less-thoughtful opinions. One might therefore expect such panels to produce opinions with less precedential impact and that are more subject to reversal when compared with the opinions of more moderate panels. Testing this involves the application of two new variables. The first, TotalIdeologyAbsolute, represents the absolute value of the panel's TotalIdeology score. Thus, it measures relative ideological extremity, regardless of whether the panel was liberal or conservative. The second, TotalIdeologyAbsolute^2, is simply the square of the TotalIdeologyAbsolute measure, exaggerating the score for the most extreme panels to test for their relative effect. Table 8.12 reports the results of these analyses on the four precedential impact variables, with the basic control variables used in the earlier regressions.

The results show little impact from the purportedly inferior decisions produced by the group polarization effect. There is no significant association between more extreme panels and positive or negative citation rates but there is some evidence of a group polarization problem in the red flag reversal rate measure. The statistically significant association of TotalIdeologyAbsolute^2 with reversals plus the substantial correlation coefficient for the variable suggest that the most extreme panels produce decisions that are more likely to be overturned.

Dissent is another panel effect that might be expected to influence precedential impact. A dissenting opinion has been characterized as a form of whistle-blowing, a claim that the majority has departed from the law.[14] Whether this whistle-blowing is aimed internally or externally, it clearly could have an external effect. Circuit court panels might be more likely to criticize or reverse decisions that have a dissenting opinion. Panels might also shy away from citing opinions with such dissents, treating them as if they were less-persuasive authority. Table 8.13 reports the effects of the presence of a dissent on the precedential impact variables, using the traditional independent control variables.

As expected, cases with dissents are associated with a higher rate of negative treatment and much higher rate of reversals. This result indicates that

TABLE 8.13
Precedential impact of dissents

Variable	Total	Negative	Red	Yellow
Reversal	.088 (.000)	.087 (.000)	.072 (.000)	.138 (.000)
TotalIdeology	.000 (.986)	−.015 (.378)	.009 (.616)	−.031 (.074)
Constitutional	.090 (.000)	.025 (.149)	.052 (.002)	.079 (.000)
Statutory	.068 (.000)	.075 (.000)	.060 (.000)	.071 (.000)
Circuit	.165 (.000)	.049 (.005)	−.019 (.263)	.103 (.000)
Dissent	.064 (.000)	.104 (.000)	.120 (.000)	.039 (.022)
N	3,364	3,338	3,363	3,364
R^2	.055	.029	.028	.044

opinions with dissents may have less effect. But opinions with dissents also had a significantly higher number of positive citations. This finding suggests that dissents may not consistently weaken precedent. It is consistent with a conclusion that dissents tend to occur in the most salient cases, those that are the most likely to produce future citations, whether positive or negative. The especially high association of cases with dissents and red flag overrulings, though, suggests that the presence of a dissenting opinion increases the likelihood of future reversals.

Procedural Threshold Rules and Precedential Impact

Chapter 7 considered the outcome effects of procedural threshold rules. The results of that chapter identified a clear ideological association with the decision on the threshold issue, beyond judicial ideology. The finding raised the question of why judges would choose to rule using a procedural threshold issue rather than deciding the case on the merits of the law. One might suspect that a decision on the merits would have greater precedential impact and therefore give greater legal power to the judge's preferences. This suspicion calls into question the use of threshold issues but has not been tested. Perhaps a decision on threshold issues could have more-consequential legal effect than one on the merits. Table 8.14 reports on the precedential effects of a decision in which a threshold issue was not met, with circuit effects, reversal, case type, and judicial ideology as control variables.

These results add some understanding to the preceding chapter's consideration of procedural threshold rules. Cases in which judges ruled that

TABLE 8.14
Precedential impact of threshold issue not met

Variable	Total	Negative	Red	Yellow
Reversal	.066 (.000)	.097 (.000)	.084 (.000)	.143 (.000)
TotalIdeology	.005 (.766)	−.014 (.421)	.012 (.490)	−.030 (.083)
Constitutional	.069 (.000)	.030 (.079)	.058 (.001)	.083 (.000)
Statutory	.058 (.001)	.075 (.000)	.058 (.001)	.070 (.000)
Threshold not met	.042 (.013)	−.006 (.720)	−.005 (.772)	−.018 (.298)
Circuit	.150 (.000)	.050 (.004)	−.019 (.285)	.102 (.000)
N	3,365	3,348	3,381	3,382
R²	.038	.019	.013	.044

the threshold rules were not met had higher than average total precedential impact, with statistical significance. Although positive citation impact is generally correlated with more negative citations, this was not so for the decisions in which a procedural threshold issue was not met. Opinions holding that the threshold issue was not met apparently may have more eventual impact than a decision on the merits. There is no assurance that the precedent will be used in a way that is ideologically aligned with the deciding judge. But the general association of threshold issues with conservative results supports the structural ideological theories of these issues discussed in Chapter 7. It appears that judges produce a pattern of conservative results by using threshold procedural effects, even when the cases are heard by relatively liberal circuit court panels.

The strong precedential effect of the threshold issue not being met might be ascribed to case characteristics rather than the threshold issues themselves. The cases with threshold issues might be particularly important and thus produce more citations. To check for this effect I ran the same regressions on precedential effect for the cases in which the precedential issue was met. The results are reported in Table 8.15.

These results demonstrate that decisions on threshold procedural issues have greater positive precedential impact than do decisions on the merits in cases that raised those threshold issues. But decisions on the merits in cases in which the threshold was satisfied *were* more likely to be reversed and distinguished (red and yellow flags). These findings add to our understanding of the use of procedural threshold issues. These issues may be employed by circuit court judges because they offer greater precedential

TABLE 8.15
Precedential impact of threshold issue met

Variable	Total	Negative	Red	Yellow
Reversal	.092 (.000)	.095 (.000)	.134 (.000)	.076 (.000)
TotalIdeology	.000 (.977)	.014 (.425)	−.031 (.074)	.010 (.570)
Constitutional	.093 (.000)	.029 (.087)	.080 (.000)	.057 (.001)
Statutory	.067 (.000)	.074 (.000)	.068 (.000)	.057 (.001)
Threshold met	.013 (.452)	.012 (.489)	.040 (.021)	.042 (.016)
Circuit	.166 (.000)	.050 (.004)	.102 (.000)	−.019 (.280)
N	3,364	3,338	3,364	3,363
R^2	.051	.019	.044	.015

effect than do decisions on the merits and may shelter outcomes for the defendant on procedural issues from reversal or criticism by subsequent courts. The data on precedents do not help us discern why the ideological decision-making effect disappears in cases with threshold issues. I hypothesized in Chapter 7 that the cases that satisfied threshold issues were relatively clear once the judge reached the merits. Yet those cases appear especially prone to being reversed or limited, which seems contrary to my hypothesis. The findings of this chapter continue to add weight to the importance of legal variables, as opposed to political ones, in directing the path of the law.

Opinion Length and Precedential Impact

The studies on opinion length in previous chapters have found various associations but the significance of those associations remained unclear. Under one theory, longer opinions produce more legal conclusions and could therefore be expected to yield greater precedential effects. An alternative theory would yield the opposite hypothesis, however. Longer opinions might be more fact based and contain more language cabining the holding, which would mean these opinions would have weaker precedential effects. In this chapter I test these contrasting hypotheses. Table 8.16 introduces opinion length as a variable for the measure of citations.

These significant results inform our understanding of the meaning of opinion length. Longer opinions do have greater precedential effect, both

TABLE 8.16
Precedential impact of opinion length

Variable	Total	Negative	Red	Yellow
Reversal	.065 (.000)	.082 (.000)	.071 (.000)	.126 (.000)
TotalIdeology	−.010 (.542)	−.019 (.270)	−.005 (.795)	−.034 (.044)
Constitutional	.054 (.001)	.009 (.613)	.041 (.017)	.055 (.001)
Statutory	.028 (.093)	.055 (.001)	.040 (.023)	.049 (.004)
Circuit	.147 (.000)	.041 (.020)	−.026 (.132)	.091 (.000)
Opinion length	.253 (.000)	.133 (.000)	.124 (.000)	.142 (.000)
N	3,324	3,298	3,323	3,324
R^2	.110	.035	.026	.061

positive and negative. As opinions grow longer, the number of total positive citations increases significantly but the odds of negative treatment or full reversal also grow. This finding offers yet another testament to the importance of analyzing opinions and the law in judicial decision making. The legal content of the opinion appears to be much more significant than the ideological outcome when analyzing precedential effect.

Conclusion

The study of precedential impact should be one of the next frontiers of judicial politics research. The true nature of law is expressed in a pattern of decisions and the language of case opinions, not in individual case outcomes. The precedential impact of opinions, though, has been little studied. This chapter provides the beginning outlines of how such research might be conducted, what variables should be assessed, and what future studies might explore. This future research should involve more-detailed studies on smaller samples of cases. As database sample sizes grow, coding for and segregating the effects of some case details becomes impractical. Studies of precedential effect could benefit from the finer-grained analysis possible with smaller samples, so that other variables influencing this effect could be isolated.

The findings of this chapter are necessarily preliminary and tentative but should help lay the groundwork for the future study of judicial precedent. Understanding why some circumstances produce greater precedential impact is critical to the appreciation of the workings of the law. The significance of the law, including procedural legal rules, is again of obvious importance from the chapter's findings. As in previous chapters, the issue of affirmance deference versus reversal is the major determinant of precedential impact and clearly had greater effect than judicial ideology. Procedural threshold rules also had a substantial impact, as did the content of the opinion as captured by opinion length.

Epilogue

The results of the research in this book illuminate circuit court judicial decision making in several important ways. Perhaps the most important theme, which runs throughout the book, is the importance of the law in determining judicial outcomes. Beginning in Chapter 2 and continuing in the ensuing chapters, the research shows that just one legal standard, affirmance deference to the lower court decision, is consistently significant statistically and by far the most important single variable substantively in explaining circuit court outcomes. Chapter 2 also showed that the legal standard of deference applicable to a case was also a factor in judicial decision making. In Chapter 4, the results showed that the preferences of the past Supreme Courts, reflected in their decisions and precedents, were a statistically significant determinant of circuit court decisions. Chapter 7 found that the interposition of a legal threshold requirement obviously had a significant effect on judicial decisions. For every legal variable amenable to quantitative study, there was consistently a statistically significant association that was robust to different samples and control variables.

It is also noteworthy how very limited the explanatory power of the non-legal variables was. Although a number of these had a statistically significant association with decisions, none of them explained more than a small fraction of the variance. This leaves a huge residual that requires an alternative explanation. While specification errors undoubtedly explain part of the limited effect, it seems unlikely that these errors would multiply the effect manifold times. Even with legal variables, the models had limited explanatory power, but the courts of appeals database and limits of quantitative methods meant that most relevant legal variables were not considered. I would speculate that the determinants of the great residual of decisions are unmeasured legal variables combined with the varying facts of the cases.

After the law, the most consistently significant determinant of circuit court outcomes was ideology. Although the effect was small, it persisted throughout nearly all the scores of separate regressions run in this book. By itself, this finding is an unsurprising one because an extensive body of research has demonstrated the ideological effect in judicial decision making. The book adds some understanding to the role of ideology, though, by helping to refine when it matters and to what degree. Also, Chapter 6 on panel effects refutes the commonly accepted thesis that the median ideology on a panel drives decisional outcomes. In fact, even the most ideologically extreme panel members can have a statistically significant effect on outcomes. This implicitly suggests another role for the law—interacting with ideology; this role demands further investigation.

The results on judicial background, although not highly significant, do increase our understanding of judicial decision making. This was an early area of empirical research that has largely fallen by the wayside. Given appointment screening at the federal level, one would not necessarily expect to find such background effects, yet they appear in some circumstances. Gender seems to be a meaningful factor. A heretofore unstudied variable, judicial net wealth, can also be significant, and the topic merits additional exploration.

Another salient aspect of the book involves the variables that are *not* significant determinants of judicial outcomes. The lack of statistical significance is quite meaningful in such a large-N database, in which even small effects can appear as statistically significant. For example, there is considerable theoretical scholarship, and some empirical research, suggesting that judges adapt their decisions strategically to avert the risk of reversal by the Supreme Court or the Congress. Yet Chapter 4 refutes these theories. There is no evidence of such strategic adaptation, beyond the surprising finding that circuit court decisions have a statistically significant negative association with the preferences of the contemporaneous Supreme Court. This counterintuitive finding cries out for additional theoretical and empirical consideration.

Similarly, some economists have theorized that litigants are the true determinants of decisions by their case selection strategies. Certain results are consistent with this theory but its effect does not appear nearly as significant as some have proposed. Particular categories of litigants are more successful in the circuit courts. When these effects, however, can be integrated with legal and ideological measures, the results do not confirm the importance of litigant strategizing. A certain measure of litigant effect likely exists in at least some cases but this does not appear to be a major factor in circuit court decision making overall.

Finally, the book, especially Chapter 8, strives to highlight new fields of judicial research on the content of opinions and their consequential effects. Throughout the book I have examined opinion length, which is a crude measure but offers one quantitative approach to evaluating opinions. The studies of precedential effect in the final chapter are especially tentative but should strike a path for future research at the heart of public law. The outcomes that are the traditional subject of study by themselves control only the parties to the litigation and have little societal public policy effect. The content of the opinions issued by the circuit courts may have a greater precedential impact than do the outcomes. It is vital to direct more research to the nature of this precedential impact and its determinants.

Although this book contains a considerable number of studies, it only begins the evaluation of circuit court decision making. The breadth of the book incidentally limits the depth of treatment that any individual variable can receive. Further empirical analyses should go far beyond those presented here. The most obvious candidate for such analysis is the role of the law. Researchers should attempt to quantify the substantive legal standards, such as the content of precedent and statutory text, for decisions. While large-N studies may be impossible for such fine-grained measures, the study of these measures appears crucial to understanding judicial outcomes. For other variables, including those not found to be significant, researchers might select smaller samples of cases to examine whether these variables may play a material role in some discrete subset of decisions. The use of interaction variables could contribute to an understanding of how the variables operate in different circumstances. The creative scholars in political science and law will doubtless identify numerous other advances beyond the findings I have presented. I simply hope that this book assists them in identifying those advances.

Similarly, the findings in this book require additional theoretical explication. Although each chapter reviews the background research and presents basic theories about the roles of the variables tested, the book provides no rigorous theoretical analyses. My new theories, such as the judicial utility maximization reason for the importance of law, are necessarily tentative. A more rigorous and detailed theoretical analysis will provide the basis for more-particularized future empirical testing.

In sum, I hope this book helps the reader understand decision making at the circuit court level. I also hope it spurs future research, both theoretical and empirical, that expands on the results I have reported. I would like the book to be something of a "moon base" from which others can explore much more broadly. In this regard, perhaps my greatest hope is that I might provoke the collaboration of legal and social science professors in this future research. Existing legal research has too often ignored the results, and the methods, of the very valuable social scientific examination of judicial decision making. Social scientists, though, have too often used a cramped and inaccurate model of how the law is meant to work and consequently demeaned its role. Joint efforts can overcome these shortcomings and provide a much truer picture of judicial decision making.

Notes

1. See Susan Olson, "Studying Federal District Courts Through Published Cases: A Research Note," 15 *Justice System Journal* 782 (1992).

2. See Evan J. Ringquist & Craig E. Emmert, "Judicial Policymaking in Published and Unpublished Decisions: The Case of Environmental Civil Litigation," 52 *Political Research Quarterly* 7 (1999).

3. *N* is the number of cases (usually individual judge votes or panel decisions) that are analyzed in a particular statistical analysis. Statistical significance is measured by p-scores. These measure the probability that an identified effect is not the product of random chance. By convention, an association is usually deemed statistically significant if there is no more than a 5% probability that an association may be random (though 10% and 1% are also sometimes used as measures of significance).

4. R^2 is a statistical measure that estimates the amount of variance in the dependent variable (usually the outcome of the decision) that can be reliably attributed to the independent variables of the particular regression. It basically captures the significance of those independent variables in explaining the dependent variable.

5. D. A. Prentice & D. T. Miller, "When Small Effects Are Impressive," 112 *Psychological Bulletin* 160 (1992).

CHAPTER ONE

1. Howard Gillman, "What's Law Got To Do With It? Judicial Behavioralists Test the 'Legal Model' of Judicial Decisionmaking," 26 *Law & Social Inquiry* 465, 466 (2001).

2. Frank B. Cross, "Political Science and the New Legal Realism: A Case of Unfortunate Interdisciplinary Ignorance," 92 *Northwestern University Law Review* 251 (1997).

3. See Ziva Kunda, "The Case for Motivated Reasoning," 108 *Psychological Bulletin* 480 (1990).

4. Frank M. Coffin, *On Appeal* 255 (1994).

5. Stephen G. Breyer, "The Work of the Supreme Court," *Bulletin of the American Academy of Arts & Sciences*, September–October 1998, at 47, 58.

6. J. Woodford Howard, *Courts of Appeals in the Federal Judicial System* 164 (1981), table 6.2.

7. Silveira v. Lockyer, 328 F.2d 567, 568 (2003) (Kozinski, J., dissenting).

8. Alex Kozinski, "What I Ate for Breakfast and Other Mysteries of Judicial Decisionmaking," in *Judges on Judging* 72 (David O' Brien ed., 1997).

9. See Jeffrey A. Segal & Harold J. Spaeth, *The Supreme Court and the Attitudinal Model* (1993).

10. See Forrest Maltzman, James F. Spriggs II & Paul J. Wahlbeck, *Crafting Law on the Supreme Court* (2000).

11. Richard L. Revesz, "Environmental Regulation, Ideology, and the D.C. Circuit," 83 *Virginia Law Review* 1717 (1997).

12. Frank B. Cross & Emerson H. Tiller, "Judicial Partisanship and Obedience to Legal Doctrine: Whistleblowing on the Federal Courts of Appeals," 107 *Yale Law Journal* 2155 (1998).

13. Frank B. Cross, "Decisionmaking in the U.S. Circuit Courts of Appeals," 91 *California Law Review* 1457 (2003).

14. See Daniel R. Pinello, "Linking Party to Judicial Ideology in American Courts: A Meta-Analysis," 20 *Justice System Journal* 219 (1999).

15. *Id.* at 236.

16. Douglas Laycock, *The Death of the Irreparable Injury Rule* (1991).

17. See Sheldon Goldman, *Picking Federal Judges* (1997).

18. See Micheal Giles, Virginia A. Hettinger & Todd Peppers, "Picking Federal Judges: A Note on Policy and Partisan Selection Agendas," 54 *Political Research Quarterly* 623 (2001).

19. This variable gives us a continuous measure of judicial ideology that is the best available for circuit court judges. Although the original Giles scores have higher numbers for conservatives and lower numbers for liberals, I have reversed this for internal consistency. Thus, throughout this book the highest number indicates the most liberal on each of the ideological scales.

20. The method of logit regression analysis is the default statistical approach for this book, with the dependent variable of judicial vote or decision outcome as a binary variable. For some analyses, in which the dependent variable is continuous, the reported results use OLS regression analysis.

21. See Erin B. Kaneny, "Agenda Change in the U.S. Courts of Appeals, 1925–1988," 20 *The Justice System Journal* 275 (1999).

22. See Lee Epstein & Carol Mershon, "Measuring Political Preferences," 40 *American Journal of Political Science* 261 (1996).

23. See Cass R. Sunstein, David Schkade & Lisa Michelle Ellman, "Ideological Voting on Federal Courts of Appeals: A Preliminary Investigation," *AEI-Brookings Joint Center for Regulatory Studies, Working Paper No. 03-9* (September 2003).

24. See "Judicial Partisanship and Obedience to Legal Doctrine," *supra* note 12.

25. See James M. Enelow & Melvin J. Hinich, *The Spatial Theory of Voting: An Introduction* (1984).

26. "Judicial Partisanship and Obedience to Legal Doctrine," *supra* note 12.

27. Mita Gulati & C. M. A. McCauliff, "On Not Making Law," 61 *Law and Contemporary Problems* 157, 198 (1998).

28. The computation of opinion length was calculated by subtracting the beginning page of the opinion from the final page of the majority opinion. This yielded some cases with negative numbers for opinion length and some with implausibly long lengths (in the thousands of pages), presumably due to coding errors. The analyses excluded all cases for which opinion length was negative or greater than one hundred fifty pages.

CHAPTER TWO

1. Richard A. Posner, "The Jurisprudence of Skepticism," 86 *Michigan Law Review* 827, 865 (1988).

2. Gregory C. Sisk, Michael Heise & Andrew P. Morriss, "Charting the Influences on the Judicial Mind: An Empirical Study of Judicial Reasoning," 73 *New York University Law Review* 1377, 1390 (1998).

3. David L. Shapiro, "In Defense of Judicial Candor," 100 *Harvard Law Review* 731, 737 (1987).

4. Philip Johnson, "Do You Sincerely Want To Be Radical?" 36 *Stanford Law Review* 247, 252 (1984).

5. See Steven J. Burton, *Judging in Good Faith* (1992).

6. Osborn v. Bank of United States, 22 U.S. 738, 866 (1824).

7. Harry T. Edwards, "Public Misperceptions Concerning the 'Politics' of Judging: Dispelling Some Myths About the D.C. Circuit," 56 *University of Colorado Law Review* 619, 620 (1985).

8. J. Woodford Howard, *Courts of Appeals in the Federal Judicial System* 187 (1981).

9. David E. Klein, *Making Law in the United States Courts of Appeals* 21 (2002).

10. Friedrich Nietzsche, *Beyond Good and Evil* sec. 231 (Walter Kaufman trans., 1989).

11. See Frank B. Cross, "Political Science and the New Legal Realism: An Unfortunate Case of Interdisciplinary Ignorance," 92 *Northwestern Law Review* 251 (1997).

12. See James L. Gibson, "Personality and Elite Political Behavior: The Influence of Self Esteem on Judicial Decision Making," 43 *Journal of Politics* 104 (1981).

13. See J. Woodford Howard, "Role Perceptions and Behavior in Three U.S. Courts of Appeals," 39 *Journal of Politics* 916 (1977).

14. Allan C. Hutchinson, *It's All in the Game* 184 (2000).

15. Tracey E. George & Lee Epstein, "On the Nature of Supreme Court Decision Making," 86 *American Political Science Review* 323 (1992).

16. Harold J. Spaeth & Jeffrey A. Segal, *Majority Rule or Minority Will* (1999).

17. See Donald R. Songer, Jeffrey A. Segal & Charles Cameron, "The Hierarchy of Justice: Testing a Principal-Agent Model of Supreme Court-Circuit Court Interactions," 38 *American Journal of Political Science* 673 (1994).

18. See *Making Law in the United States Courts of Appeals, supra* note 9, at 65–76.

19. See Daniel R. Pinello, *Gay Rights and American Law* (2003).

20. Frank M. Coffin, *On Appeal* 260 (1994).

21. Jonathan Matthew Cohen, *Inside Appellate Courts* 47 (2002).

22. Judges were characterized as conservative or liberal based on whether their Ideology score was above or below the median for the full set of judges in the courts of appeals database.

23. See Brian Leiter, "Legal Realism and Legal Positivism Reconsidered," 111 *Ethics* 278, 295 (2001).

24. Karl Llewellyn, "A Realistic Jurisprudence—the Next Step," 30 *Columbia Law Review* 431, 444 (1930).

CHAPTER THREE

1. Patricia M. Wald, "A Response to Tiller and Cross," 99 *Columbia Law Review* 235 (1999).

2. Frank M. Coffin, *On Appeal* 255 (1994).

3. See Carol Gilligan, *In a Different Voice: Psychological Theory and Women's Development* (1982).

4. See Lee Epstein, Jack Knight & Andrew D. Martin, "The Norm of Prior Judicial Experience and Its Consequences for Career Diversity on the U.S. Supreme Court," 91 *California Law Review* 903 (2003).

5. C. Neal Tate, "Personal Attribute Models of the Voting Behavior of U.S. Supreme Court Justices: Liberalism in Civil Liberties and Economics Decisions, 1946–1978," 75 *American Political Science Review* 355 (1981).

6. Jeffrey A. Segal & Harold J. Spaeth, *The Supreme Court and the Attitudinal Model* (1993).

7. J. Woodford Howard, *Courts of Appeals in the Federal Judicial System* 182–183 (1981).

8. Gregory C. Sisk, Michael Heise & Andrew P. Morriss, "Charting the

Influences on the Judicial Mind: An Empirical Study of Judicial Reasoning," 73 *New York University Law Review* 1377 (1998).

9. Jon Gottschall, "Carter's Judicial Appointments: The Influence of Affirmative Action and Merit Selection on Voting on the U.S. Courts of Appeals," 67 *Judicature* 164 (1983).

10. Cassia Spohn, "The Sentencing Decisions of Black and White Judges: Expected and Unexpected Similarities," 24 *Law & Society Review* 1197 (1990).

11. Daniel R. Pinello, *Gay Rights and American Law* (2003).

12. See Sheldon Goldman, "Voting Behavior on the United States Court of Appeals Revisited," 69 *American Political Science Review* 491 (1975).

13. *Id.*

14. Deborah J. Barrow, Gary Zuk & Gerard S. Gryski, *The Federal Judiciary and Institutional Change* 80–81 (1996).

15. Sheldon Goldman, *Picking Federal Judges: Lower Court Selection from Roosevelt Through Reagan* 86–88 (1997).

16. Edith H. Jones, "Observations on the Status and Impact of the Judicial Confirmation Process," 39 *University of Richmond Law Review* 833 (2005).

17. James Lindgren, "Examining the American Bar Association's Ratings of Nominees to the U.S. Courts of Appeals for Political Bias, 1989–2000," 17 *Journal of Law & Politics* 1 (2001).

18. Michael J. Saks & Neil Vidmar, "A Flawed Search for Bias in the American Bar Association's Ratings of Prospective Judicial Nominees: A Critique of the Lindgren Study," 17 *Journal of Law & Politics* 219, 252 (2001).

CHAPTER FOUR

1. Alex Kozinski, "What I Ate for Breakfast and Other Mysteries of Judicial Decisionmaking," in *Judges on Judging* 71, 75 (David M. O' Brien ed., 1997).

2. Lee Epstein & Jack Knight, *The Choices Justices Make* (1998).

3. See McNollgast, "Politics and the Courts: A Positive Theory of Judicial Doctrine and the Rule of Law," 68 *Southern California Law Review* 1631 (1995).

4. Interview with Jeffrey Segal and Harold Spaeth.

5. See Robert S. Thompson, "Comment on Professors Karlan's and Abrams' Structural Threats to Judicial Independence," 72 *Southern California Law Review* 559 (1999).

6. J. Woodford Howard, *Courts of Appeals in the Federal Judicial System* 82 (1981).

7. Kermit Roosevelt III, "Light from Dead Stars: The Procedural Adequate and Independent State Ground Reconsidered," 103 *Columbia Law Review* 1888, 1916 (2003).

8. Joseph L. Smith & Emerson H. Tiller, "The Strategy of Judging: Evidence from Administrative Law," 31 *Journal of Legal Studies* 61 (2002).

9. *Courts of Appeals in the Federal Judicial System, supra* note 6, at 139–140.

10. Alex Kozinski, "The Many Faces of Judicial Independence," 14 *Georgia State University Law Review* 861, 867 (1998).

11. *Courts of Appeals in the Federal Judicial System, supra* note 6, at 163–165.

12. Donald Songer, Jeffrey Segal & Charles Cameron, "The Hierarchy of Justice: Testing a Principal-Agent Model of Supreme Court-Circuit Court Interactions," 38 *American Journal of Political Science* 673, 690 (1994).

13. David E. Klein, *Making Law on the United States Courts of Appeals* (2002).

14. See David E. Klein & Robert J. Hume, "Fear of Reversal as an Explanation of Lower Court Compliance," 37 *Law & Society Review* 579 (2003).

15. See Tracey E. George, "Developing a Positive Theory of Decisionmaking on U.S. Courts of Appeals," 58 *Ohio State Law Journal* 1635 (1998).

16. See Sara C. Benesh, *The U.S. Court of Appeals and the Law of Confessions* (2002).

17. See Malia Reddick & Sara C. Benesh, "Norm Violation by the Lower Courts in the Treatment of Supreme Court Precedent: A Research Framework," 21 *Justice System Journal* 117 (2000).

18. See Donald R. Songer, Martha Humphries Ginn & Tammy A. Sarver, "Do Judges Follow the Law When There Is No Fear of Reversal?" 24 *Justice System Journal* 137 (2003).

19. See Virginia A. Hettinger, Stefanie A. Lindquist & Wendy L. Martinek, "Comparing Attitudinal and Strategic Accounts of Dissenting Behavior on the U.S. Courts of Appeals," 48 *American Journal of Political Science* 123 (2004).

20. See Christopher P. Banks, "The Politics of En Banc Review in the 'Mini-Supreme Court,'" 13 *Journal of Law & Politics* 377, 396 (1997).

21. See "Developing a Positive Theory of Decisionmaking on U.S. Courts of Appeals," *supra* note 15.

22. See Tracey E. George, "The Dynamics and Determinants of the Decision to Grant En Banc Review," 74 *Washington Law Review* 213 (1999).

23. "The Politics of En Banc Review in the 'Mini-Supreme Court,'" *supra* note 20.

24. See William N. Eskridge, "Overriding Supreme Court Statutory Interpretation Decisions," 101 *Yale Law Journal* 331 (1991).

25. See Keith Krehbiel, *Pivotal Politics: A Theory of U.S. Lawmaking* (1998).

26. St. Mary's Honor Center v. Hicks, 509 U.S. 502 (1993).

27. See Roger Handberg & Harold F. Hill, Jr., "Court Curbing, Court Reversals, and Judicial Review: The Supreme Court Versus Congress," 14 *Law & Society Review* 309 (1980).

28. Eugenia F. Toma, "A Contractual Model of the Voting Behavior of the Supreme Court: The Role of the Chief Justice," 16 *International Review of Law & Economics* 433 (1996).

29. See Pablo T. Spiller & Rafael Gely, "Congressional Control or Judicial

Independence: The Determinants of U.S. Supreme Court Labor-Relations Decisions," 23 *Rand Journal of Economics* 463 (1992).

30. See Jeffrey A. Segal, "Separation-of-Powers Games in the Positive Theory of Congress and the Courts," 91 *American Political Science Review* 28 (1997).

31. Mario Bergara, Barak Richman & Pablo T. Spiller, "Modeling Supreme Court Strategic Decision Making: The Congressional Constraint," 28 *Legislative Studies Quarterly* 247 (2003).

32. Frank B. Cross & Blake J. Nelson, "Strategic Institutional Effects on Supreme Court Decisionmaking," 95 *Northwestern Law Review* 1437 (2001).

33. See Richard L. Revesz, "Congressional Influence on Judicial Behavior? An Empirical Examination of Challenges to Agency Action in the D.C. Circuit," 76 *New York University Law Review* 1100 (2001).

34. Barak Richman graciously provided me the data used in "Modeling Supreme Court Strategic Decision Making," *supra* note 31.

35. Peter H. Schuck & E. Donald Elliott, "To the Chevron Station: An Empirical Study of Federal Administrative Law," 1990 *Duke Law Journal* 984 (1990).

CHAPTER FIVE

1. See Charles R. Epp, *The Rights Revolution: Lawyers, Activists, and Supreme Courts in Comparative Perspective* (1998).

2. See George Priest & Benjamin Klein, "The Selection of Disputes for Litigation," 13 *Journal of Legal Studies* 1 (1984).

3. Keith N. Hylton, "Asymmetric Information and the Selection of Disputes for Litigation," 22 *Journal of Legal Studies* 187 (1993).

4. See Peter Siegelman & Joel Waldfogel, "Toward a Taxonomy of Disputes: New Evidence through the Prism of the Priest/Klein Model," 28 *Journal of Legal Studies* 101 (1999).

5. See Bruce L. Hay, "Effort, Information, Settlement, Trial," 24 *Journal of Legal Studies* 29 (1995).

6. See Amos Tversky & Daniel Kahneman, "Judgment Under Uncertainty: Heuristics and Biases," 185 *Science* 1124 (1974).

7. See Frank B. Cross, "In Praise of Irrational Plaintiffs," 86 *Cornell Law Review* 1 (2000).

8. See Scott Barclay, "Posner's Economic Model and the Decision to Appeal," 19 *Justice System Journal* 77 (1997).

9. Paul Rubin, "Why Is the Common Law Efficient?" 6 *Journal of Legal Studies* 51 (1977).

10. Wayne V. McIntosh, "Courts and Socioeconomic Change," in *The American Courts: A Critical Assessment* 286 (John B. Gates & Charles A. Johnson eds., 1991).

11. Martin J. Bailey & Paul H. Rubin, "A Positive Theory of Legal Change," 15 *International Journal of Law & Economics* 467 (1994).

12. Marc Galanter, "Why the 'Haves' Come Out Ahead: Speculations on the Limits of Legal Change," 9 *Law & Society Review* 95 (1974).

13. See Linda Cohen & Matthew Spitzer, "Symposium: The Government Litigant Advantage: Implications for the Law," 28 *Florida State University Law Review* 391 (2000).

14. See Herbert M. Kritzer, "The Government Gorilla: Why Does Government Come Out Ahead in Appellate Courts?" in *In Litigation: Do the 'Haves' Still Come Out Ahead?* 342 (H. Kritzer & S. Silbey eds., 2003).

15. Joseph D. Kearney & Thomas W. Merrill, "The Influence of Amicus Curiae Briefs on the Supreme Court," 148 *University of Pennsylvania Law Review* 743 (2000).

16. 521 U.S. 1117 (1997).

17. Donald R. Songer et al., "Why the Haves Don't Always Come Out Ahead: Repeat Players Meet *Amici Curiae* for the Disadvantaged," 55 *Political Research Quarterly* 537 (2000).

18. Paul J. Wahlbeck, "The Development of a Judicial Rule," 32 *Law & Society Review* 613 (1998).

19. See Kevin Clermont & Theodore Eisenberg, "Trial by Jury or Judge: Transcending Empiricism," 77 *Cornell Law Review* 1124 (1992).

20. See Daniel Kessler, Thomas Meites & Geoffrey Miller, "Explaining Deviations from the Fifty-Percent Rule: A Multimodal Approach to the Selection of Cases for Litigation," 25 *Journal of Legal Studies* 233 (1996).

21. See Terence Dunworth & Joel Rogers, "Corporations in Court: Big Business Litigation in U.S. Federal Courts, 1971–1991," 21 *Law & Social Inquiry* 497 (1996).

22. See Donald R. Songer & Reginald S. Sheehan, "Who Wins on Appeal? Upperdogs and Underdogs in the United States Court of Appeals," 36 *American Journal of Political Science* 235 (1992).

23. Stanton Wheeler et al., "Do the 'Haves' Come Out Ahead? Winning and Losing in State Supreme Courts, 1970–1980," 21 *Law & Society Review* 403 (1987).

24. See Reginald S. Sheehan et al., "Ideology, Status, and the Differential Success of Direct Parties Before the Supreme Court," 86 *American Political Science Review* 464 (1992).

25. "In Praise of Irrational Plaintiffs," *supra* note 7, at 12.

26. See "Corporations in Court," *supra* note 21.

27. Leandra Lederman, "Which Cases Go to Trial? An Empirical Study of Predictors of Failure to Settle," 49 *Case Western Reserve Law Review* 315 (1999).

28. See Richard A. Posner, "A Statistical Study of Antitrust Enforcement," 13 *Journal of Law & Economics* 365 (1970).

29. The federal government sometimes shows multiple parties in litigation because, for example, more than one agency was involved. I assumed, however, that this is largely artificial and that the number of federal parties was not a significant measure for the intensity of federal concern.

CHAPTER SIX

1. See Duncan Black, "On the Rationale of Group Decision-Making," 56 *Journal of Political Economy* 23 (1948).

2. See Randall G. Holcombe, "An Empirical Test of the Median Voter Model," 18 *Economic Inquiry* 260 (1980).

3. See Lynn A. Baker, "Interdisciplinary Due Diligence: The Case for Common Sense in the Search for the Swing Justice," 70 *Southern California Law Review* 187 (1996).

4. See Richard L. Revesz, "Environmental Regulation, Ideology, and the D.C. Circuit," 83 *Virginia Law Review* 1717 (1997).

5. See Frank B. Cross & Emerson H. Tiller, "Judicial Partisanship and Obedience to Legal Doctrine: Whistleblowing on the Federal Courts of Appeals," 107 *Yale Law Journal* 2155 (1998).

6. See Cass R. Sunstein, David Schkade & Lisa Michelle Ellman, "Ideological Voting on Federal Courts of Appeals: A Preliminary Investigation," *AEI-Brookings Joint Center for Regulatory Studies, Working Paper No. 03-9* (September 2003).

7. Serge Moscovici, E. Lage & M. Naffrechoux, "Influence of a Consistent Minority on the Responses of a Majority in a Color Perception Task," 32 *Sociometry* 365 (1969).

8. R. J. MacCoun & N. L. Kerr, "Asymmetric Influence in Mock Jury Deliberation: Jurors' Bias for Leniency," 54 *Journal of Personality and Social Psychology* 21 (1988).

9. Deborah Gruenfeld, "Status, Ideology, and Integrative Complexity on the U.S. Supreme Court: Rethinking the Politics of Political Decision Making," 68 *Journal of Personality and Social Psychology* 5 (1995).

10. Gordon B. Moskowitz & Shelly Chaiken, "Mediators of Minority Social Influence: Cognitive Processing Mechanisms Revealed Through a Persuasion Paradigm," in *Group Consensus and Minority Influence* 60, 63 (Carsten K. W. De Dreu & Nanne K. De Vries eds., 2001).

11. See C. I. Hovland, O. J. Harvey & M. Sherif, "Assimilation and Contrast Effects in Reaction to Communication and Attitude Change," 55 *Journal of Abnormal and Social Psychology* 244 (1957).

12. See Harry T. Edwards, "The Effects of Collegiality on Judicial Decision Making," 151 *University of Pennsylvania Law Review* 1639 (2003).

13. See Evan H. Caminker, "Sincere and Strategic Voting Norms on Multimember Courts," 97 *Michigan Law Review* 2297 (1999).

14. John C. Turner et al., *Rediscovering the Social Group* 142 (1987).

15. See Robert Baron et al., "Social Corroboration and Opinion Extremity," 32 *Journal of Experimental Social Psychology* 537 (1996).

16. "The Effects of Collegiality on Judicial Decision Making," *supra* note 12, at 1648.

17. See Cass R. Sunstein, "Deliberative Trouble? Why Groups Go to Extremes," 110 *Yale Law Journal* 71 (2000).

18. See C. M. Smith, R. Tindale & B. L. Dugoni, "Minority and Majority Influence in Freely Interacting Groups: Qualitative Versus Quantitative Differences," 35 *British Journal of Social Psychology* 137 (1996).

19. See D. M. Schweiger, W. R. Sandberg & J. W. Ragan, "Group Approaches for Improving Strategic Decision Making: A Comparative Analysis of Dialectic Inquiry, Devil's Advocacy, and Consensus," 29 *Academy of Management Journal* 51 (1986).

20. See Virginia A. Hettinger, Stefanie A. Lindquist & Wendy L. Martinek, "Comparing Attitudinal and Strategic Accounts of Dissenting Behavior on the U.S. Courts of Appeals," 48 *American Journal of Political Science* 123 (2004).

21. See Burton M. Atkins & Justin J. Green, "Consensus on the United States Courts of Appeals: Illusion or Reality?" 20 *American Journal of Political Science* 735 (1976).

22. Jonathan Matthew Cohen, *Inside Appellate Courts* 75 (2002).

23. See Emerson H. Tiller & Frank B. Cross, "A Modest Proposal for Improving American Justice," 99 *Columbia Law Review* 215 (1999).

24. "The Effects of Collegiality on Judicial Decision Making," *supra* note 12, at 1645.

25. See Sean Farhang & Gregory Wawro, "The Influence of Women and Racial Minorities under Panel Decision-Making on the U.S. Court of Appeals," *Institute for Social and Economic Research and Policy, Working Paper 02-07* (December 2002).

26. See Serge Moscovici, "Three Concepts: Minority, Conflict, and Behavioral Style," in *Minority Influence* 233 (S. Moscovici, A. Mucchi-Faina & A. Maass eds., 1994).

27. See Alain Van Hiel & Ivan Mervielde, "The Measurement of Cognitive Complexity and Its Relationship with Political Extremism," 24 *Political Psychology* 781 (2003).

CHAPTER SEVEN

1. Cass R. Sunstein, "What's Standing After Lujan? Of Citizen Suits, 'Injuries,' and Article III," 91 *Michigan Law Review* 163, 168 (1992).

2. Moore v. Ogilvie, 394 U.S. 814, 816 (1969).

3. McCarthy v. Madigan, 503 U.S. 140 (1992).

4. J. Harvie Wilkinson III, "The Question of Process," 98 *Michigan Law Review* 1387, 1387 (2000).

5. Eric R. Claeys, "The Article II, Section 2 Games: A Game-Theoretic Account of Standing and Other Justiciability Doctrines," 67 *Southern California Law Review* 1321, 1353 (1994).

6. Kimberle Crenshaw & Gary Peller, "The Contradictions of Mainstream Constitutional Theory," 45 *UCLA Law Review* 1683, 1712 (1998).

7. Joseph L. Smith & Emerson H. Tiller, "The Strategy of Judging: Evidence from Administrative Law," *Journal of Legal Studies* 61 (2002).

8. Richard J. Pierce, Jr., "Is Standing Law or Politics," 77 *North Carolina Law Review* 1741, 1742 (1999).

9. *Id.* at 1760.

10. Christopher P. Banks, "Access Policy-Making at the Circuit Courts: The Doctrine of Standing and the U.S. Court of Appeals for the District of Columbia Circuit, 1970–1993" (1995).

11. Frank B. Cross, "The Odd Law of Standing" (2003).

12. 504 U.S. 555 (1992).

CHAPTER EIGHT

1. Bryan A. Garner, *A Dictionary of Modern Legal Usage* 680 (2nd ed. 1995).

2. Sophie Harnay & Alain Marciano, "Judicial Conformity Versus Dissidence: An Economic Analysis of Judicial Precedent," 23 *International Review of Law & Economics* 405 (2003).

3. See Michael C. Dorf, "Dicta and Article III," 142 *University of Pennsylvania Law Review* 1997 (1994).

4. Bush v. Gore, 531 U.S. 98, 109 (2000).

5. Smith v. Allwright, 321 U.S. 649, 649 (1944).

6. Jerome Frank, *Courts on Trial: Myth and Reality in American Justice* 274 (1949).

7. 401 U.S. 113 (1973).

8. 505 U.S. 833 (1992).

9. Aleksander Peczenik, "The Binding Force of Precedent," in *Interpreting Precedent* 461, 477–478 (D. Neil MacCormick & Robert S. Summers eds., 1997).

10. See Montgomery N. Kosma, "Measuring the Influence of Supreme Court Justices," 27 *Journal of Legal Studies* 33 (1998).

11. See David Klein & Darby Morrisroe, "The Prestige and Influence of Individual Judges on the U.S. Courts of Appeals," 28 *Journal of Legal Studies* 371 (1999).

12. William M. Landes, Lawrence Lessig & Michael E. Solimine, "Judicial Influence: A Citation Analysis of Federal Courts of Appeals Judges," 27 *Journal of Legal Studies* 271 (1998).

13. *Id.*

14. See Frank B. Cross & Emerson H. Tiller, "Judicial Partisanship and Obedience to Legal Doctrine: Whistleblowing on the Federal Courts of Appeals," 107 *Yale Law Journal* 2155 (1998).

Index

Page numbers in italics refer to figures and tables.